VIETNAM

A Reporter's War

VIETNAM
1967

NORTH VIETNAM

DEMILITARIZED ZONE

Gio Linh
Khe Sanh! • Con • Dong Ha
Thien
Hue

Danang
Que Son
Tam Ky

LAOS

• Dak To
• Hill 875
CENTRAL HIGHLANDS
• Pleiku

SOUTH VIETNAM

CAMBODIA

CAM RANH BAY

• Loc Ninh
• An Loc
Phnom Penh •
WAR ZONE C

• Bien Hoa
O Saigon
Phan Thiet

MEKONG RIVER
My Tho
Vung Tau
Can Tho •
MEKONG DELTA
SOUTH CHINA SEA

GULF OF THAILAND

VIETNAM

A Reporter's War

By Hugh Lunn

Cooper Square Press

Published by Cooper Square Press
An Imprint of the Rowman & Littlefield Publishing Group
150 Fifth Avenue, Suite 817
New York, New York 10011

Distributed by National Book Network

Library of Congress Cataloging-in-Publication Data

Lunn, Hugh, 1941–
Vietnam: a reporter's war.

　　　Includes index.
　　　1. Vietnamese Conflict, 1961–1975—Personal narratives, Australian. 2. Lunn, Hugh, 1941–
I. Title.
DS559.5.L86　　　　　1986　　　959.704'332　　　　　85-40967
ISBN: 0-8128-3088-1 (alk. paper)
ISBN: 0-8108-1150-2 (pbk. : alk. paper)

⊗™ The paper used in this publication meets the minimum requirements of American National Standard for Information Sciences—Permanence of Paper for Printed Library Materials, ANSI/NISO Z39.48-1992.
Manufactured in the United States of America.

Contents

Illustrations

Glossary

ARVN	Army of the Republic of South Vietnam
DMZ	Demilitarized Zone
GVN	Government of South Vietnam
H and I	Harrassment and Interdiction
JUSPAO	Joint United States Public Affairs Office
LZ	landing zone (pronounced L Zee)
MACV	Military Assistance Command, Vietnam (pronounced MacVee)
Medivac	medical evacuation helicopter
MP	military police
Psywar	psychological warfare
R and R	rest and recuperation
VC	Viet Cong
WHAMO	"winning the hearts and minds of"

Sunny Saigon

"Welcome to Sunny Saigon," said the large blue Pan American World Airways sign as I was driven in a VW station sedan into the city centre. Saigon was indeed sunny, as it almost always was, and the roads were crowded with small motorbikes and motor scooters. A man, his wife and three small children sailed past, all on the one motor scooter. It was the only way to get around quickly in a city with almost no buses.

I had expected war. I thought armed men with rifles would line the streets — instead the streets were lined with trees. I expected the press conferences to be in tents — instead they were held in an airconditioned auditorium in an American officers' club which sported a swimming pool on the roof. I thought we would live on combat rations — but Saigon was full of bars and restaurants. It was like arriving in Brisbane in summer, with the bright glare, the heat, the heavy humidity and the light clothing indicating that this was no city of four seasons.

The Volkswagen was driven by the Reuter office driver, a tiny old toothless Vietnamese man named Bien who understood no English. This had proved a great disability a few months earlier when another Reuter correspondent had screamed at him in English to stop because they were driving straight into imminent danger. Bien had just smiled and driven on, and the correspondent knocked him out — as the only way to stop the car.

On my trip in from the airport, there was another Vietnamese in the car, along with the red-headed Reuter cor-

1

respondent, Michael Neale, whom I was replacing. This Vietnamese was also very small and thin, weighing barely forty kilos. He seemed to have burn indentation marks on his right temple and left arm. He spoke a strange version of English and seemed altogether a bit superior — treating me as if here was another rookie he'd have to look after.

His name was Pham Ngoc Dinh and he had the title of Reuters officer manager, but he really played the role of a Vietnamese reporter. He was one of a group of educated Vietnamese who were employed by the major American newspapers and magazines, and international newsagencies like Reuters. Except that Dinh, as he was called (the last name being the given name in Vietnam), was different. Unlike the others, Dinh was an uneducated peasant whose English was so poor I couldn't understand him. In fact his English was so distinctively his own that it had for long been christened "Dinglish", and at first I wondered why Reuters employed him at all — especially since there was a well-educated Vietnamese interpreter in the office whose English was word perfect. This was Dang Tran Lan, whose film-star looks contrasted sharply with Dinh who was too thin, too scarred, and too fierce around the eyes. Besides, he needed some dental work.

Dinh had walked into the Reuter office several years earlier and had offered to work for nothing in order to learn how to be a journalist. He'd been taken on and given a paid job as office boy. I didn't like him at first: he had that almost fanatical hard glaze about his looks which I had expected of the Viet Cong. But that was before I recognized the willing laugh that separates the peasant from the pedant, for Dinh was to become inextricably bound up in my view of life and war.

He told me later that when we met he wasn't very impressed with me either. "I believe it myself too young this man," he said in that curious language he had taught himself since beginning at the office. Dinglish was a language all his own, and the more colourful for it. "That

2

time I say, ooh, too young," he recalled, though I was twenty-five and he was only twenty-eight when we met in February 1967.

The Reuter office was right between one end of the main Tu Do Street and the Presidential Palace, and opposite a big park. It was a long, narrow office with the desks necessarily facing each other across a corridor which led to a back room with two telex machines.

Upstairs there was a small flat for the bureau chief so he would always be on hand should a big story break. On the front of the building was a sign reading simply: "Reuter London" and on the door was a small plastic British flag that was to finish the war with a bullet hole in it.

The bureau chief at that time was an Englishman with swept-back hair and the nose of a boxer, Derek Blackman, whose personality suited a newsagency perfectly. He was probably in his early thirties, but he never said: Blackman wasn't into personal details. He liked to be always in the office ready for the next story. He kept staff at a distance working them as hard as himself, and he filed stories as quickly as he could type, which was very quick. He did not, at least to us, question the war, and seemed motivated only by the desire to beat other newsagencies to the teleprinter. This meant perforce that he was not a social man, and he never did show much humour.

But the person in the office I had been most looking forward to meeting was a legendary correspondent called Jim Pringle who was widely regarded in Reuters as their top man. He was certainly the one they sent to all the worst danger spots in the world — Northern Ireland, the Dominican Republic, New York, Cuba, Haiti, Vietnam. They used to say in London that they wouldn't bring Pringle back to head office or war would break out in Fleet Street — he had such a knack of attracting violent news. His reputation was that of a fearless Scot, and during my previous eighteen months in London I had carried an image of him as a slightly larger version of Sean Connery.

3

When I first entered the Saigon office there was a shortish, slightly round-shouldered man of about twenty-eight sitting at a phone. He looked unfit for his age, and his blue eyes were disconcertingly large, distorted by very thick pebble glasses. When he hung up he was introduced as Jim Pringle. Trying not to look surprised I searched his soft smile for some indication that this was really him. I noted, I thought, beneath the fair, wavy hair and pink face, a pugnacious, almost deadly, fix of the eyes. "Is that you Hugh?" he asked pleasantly in a lilting Scottish accent as we shook hands. Perhaps his strength lay in putting people off their guard, I thought.

Life in Saigon centred on Tu Do Street which started at a big, ugly, red brick Catholic cathedral just near our office and ran down to the river. Two blocks down Tu Do was the central square with the old French Opera House nearby, now the seat of unelected government. On opposite sides of the square stood the two best-known hotels. There was the tall, modern, Caravelle, which stood out like an American in Hong Kong, and the other was the four-storey Continental, an old European-style hotel, with spacious rooms, ceiling fans, palms, and a restaurant opening on to the pavement. The big trees out front made it look like a movie set for a Bogart spy thriller in a tropical outpost of empire. In the square a statue of two giant soldiers running into battle took the eye from the surrounding buildings.

A block from our office a new American Embassy was being built. This was so heavily fortified against attack that it had already been christened "Pentagon East". Our office had a screen door made of thick inch-square wire meshing. I said, half jokingly, "God you've got big mosquitoes here," and was told that this was a grenade guard — the idea being that if a Viet Cong threw a grenade at our office, it would hit this door and bounce back well clear and probably kill someone else. But we never kept it shut — just clung on to it with the fingers of one hand while looking out into the park.

For it was boring at times minding the office and waiting for news to happen.

At first I didn't feel worried at all about the war, probably because no one else looked worried. Everyone was driving around on motor scooters, and bikes, and Saigon generally looked like a happy little Asian city. Only the green military vehicles, and the tremors from B-52 bomb attacks at night, indicated that anything was wrong in this tropical capital.

I was pleased when I found out I'd be staying at the old Continental and not the Caravelle, but not so happy when I discovered I was sharing a large room in dormitory-type accommodation with three other journalists. There was a severe shortage of rooms because of the large number of foreign reporters covering the war.

Back at the office, Blackman told me the first thing I would have to do would be to "get accredited". This meant I had to get an accreditation card which would allow me, as a journalist, to go almost anywhere in Vietnam to write about the war. Without it I wouldn't even get on a plane.

Blackman said I would have to get this card from "MacVee", and when I asked who he was I was told Dinh would take me to "Juspao" and I'd find out. What I was about to find out was how much the Americans loved using acronyms — to the extent that they became a jargon language of their own. MACV was Military Assistance Command, Vietnam — the clear inference being that it was only there to assist the GVN (South Vietnamese government). JUSPAO was the Joint United States Public Affairs Office.

Everything was very close together in Saigon, with three and a half million people struggling to get closer to the centre, and further from the fighting. Nothing was ever very far away. Dinh and I walked two streets down a back road to JUSPAO — which was only one block away from the Continental. At JUSPAO all American military announcements were made. I was happy that my office and my bed were so close, because I knew that newsagencies

5

get very upset if they are even five minutes late on a big story. If they are, then the major newspapers and TV and radio stations will use the opposition agency's story — or start buying that other service.

At JUSPAO I handed over some passport pictures and filled in a couple of forms. My signed card was then stamped within a plastic cover to stop forgeries. The card read as if there were no war: I was "accredited to cover the operational, advisory and support activities of the Free World Military Assistance Forces, Vietnam". "Free World" was another phrase the Americans liked to use. On the back the card said: "The bearer of this card should be accorded full cooperation and assistance, within the bounds of operational requirements and military security, to assure successful completion of his mission. Bearer is authorized rations and quarters on a reimbursable basis. Upon presentation of this card, bearer is entitled to air, water and ground transportation under a priority of 3, but only within the bounds of the Republic of Vietnam." The card was numbered and given an expiry date.

It also mentioned that I had signed a "flight release" — their way of saying I wouldn't sue them if a plane crashed. The priority for travel was about equivalent to that given to a colonel, and the card showed that the Americans were serious about allowing reporters access to the war. But you could lose this card if you wrote anything the American command listed as classified information. This was necessary to prevent journalists unwittingly placing American troops in danger, but it equally had the potential to be used for political censorship. I was also required to get a similar card for the GVN, but it was never necessary to show this Vietnamese card in Vietnam. Which indicated clearly enough who was waging war in Vietnam, despite the acronyms and euphemisms.

As well as a card I needed an American military uniform to wear out in "the field", as everyone called the bush. This was recommended because it ensured no Americans would accidentally shoot you as a Viet Cong, and it stopped snipers from shooting you first, because if you were allowed to dress differently from the soldiers you were obviously very important. It also ensured that the soldiers treated you as one of their own because, in the end, you depended upon them for your life. For day to day wear in Saigon there was a special garb many correspondents wore as a uniform: a green safari suit made by the local tailor, with holes for pens and little pockets on the sleeve for the inevitable packet of cigarettes. But I didn't smoke so I just wore blue or green trousers and white or blue shirts.

To get my military uniform, Dinh took me to the Khu Dan Sinh black market — where most of the correspondents got their clothes. We arrived at a large warehouse with rows of people sitting selling every possible type of American military merchandise. It was a huge Asian-style market right in central Saigon — just two blocks from the official market — and well known to everyone. I tried on boots from a large selection of second-hand pairs — realizing only after I left Vietnam that I had almost certainly been donning dead men's boots. Where else would they have come from? There were also webbing belts, green plastic waterbottles in canvas coverings, and packs: all second hand. A UPI (United Press International) photographer I knew claimed to have bought a brand new helicopter, unassembled and still in its box, at the market and shipped it to Singapore where he sold it for a fortune. To believe this you have to appreciate just how many helicopters were entering Vietnam — for example, the United States had lost about 4,500 of them shot down or otherwise destroyed by 1968. The market sold "everything, no exception", Dinh said — even American weapons, though they were not on display.

It was Dinh who advised me to get things like water-bottles and an army helmet, and I was later glad of his advice. Dinh thought it was very funny that I held various pairs of army trousers alongside my legs to test for size (there were no changerooms). Even so, I had to settle for a few pairs that were too big for me, for I was less than seventy kilos and much smaller than the great majority of American troops.

From the black market Dinh took me to the place where all the Reuter people got their names sewn on their military shirts, above the pockets. This was American forces practice, and the correspondents often did it too. It was always stitched in black writing on green so it could only be seen close up. But when I went back to get the shirts the next day they had my name as HUG HLUNN. I didn't bother to get it changed and remained HUG HLUNN for the next year in Vietnam.

On the drive back to the office, Mr Bien, the office driver, asked Dinh in Vietnamese how old I was. (Dinh always called him Mr Bien because of Vietnamese respect for age.) Dinh told Mr Bien he didn't know as yet, but he would tell him the next day because he would be taking me to get my initial three-month visa. These were the sorts of difficult tasks which fell Dinh's way and which we non-Vietnamese would never have managed — at least not without paying large amounts in bribes. Mr Bien told Dinh that this man was too young and they both agreed on this, as I sat there ignorant of all that was happening around me.

That night, to end my first day in Vietnam, I went up on the roof of the Caravelle — the tallest building in Saigon, at almost ten storeys — because I had heard you could see the war from there, though it sounded unlikely. But from the top I could indeed see explosions like lightning flashes on the ground afar off, without hearing or seeing anything clearly. I had been given to believe in London by Reuters that I would be covering the war from this sort of position. But in bed that night I felt the tremor — and thought I heard the rumble — of bombs. And I soon grew to recognize the distinctive reverberating tremor of a far-away B-52 bombing raid.

Now, I went off to sleep with my helmet next to my bed, I didn't mind as much that there were so many others living

8

in my room, and I began to wonder why I'd agreed to come to Saigon.

It had happened the previous November. I was sitting rewriting a story on Reuters' world desk on the fourth floor of their building at 85 Fleet Street, London, when a smiling character suddenly appeared in front of my typewriter. "Why don't you come up and have a cup of tea sometime?" he said. And he left. My immediate boss rushed over and said, "Go, go!" He told me the person was none other than David Chipp, Reuters' manager for Asia. I wondered what I'd done wrong. I had been working in Reuters' head office for just over a year and I knew the only time anyone acknowledged your existence was when you had made an error in a story.

Upstairs, in David Chipp's office, a woman with a trolley made us a cup of tea, in fine china cups — not like the old mugs downstairs. Chipp asked what I was like at jumping in and out of helicopters. I didn't immediately get the significance of the question, but said I didn't think I would be any good.

He then asked if I would be interested in an assignment to cover the Vietnam War — but I said I wasn't really interested. My only military experience had been in the school cadets where I quickly joined the band and played the cornet. I was the only cadet in my year who was never given even one stripe.

Normally a Reuter journalist had to work at head office for three years before becoming a correspondent, and Chipp said he was giving me an opportunity many others wanted. This was true, and I knew at least two writers on the fourth floor who would have given anything to be sent to Vietnam. But I wasn't keen, even though my own country had sent some troops there. I imagined the Americans were winning the war easily and, being a Catholic-educated boy from the conservative Australian state of Queensland, I had never thought to question America's role in this small country in Asia.

9

Chipp asked me to think about it, and when I got back downstairs several colleagues were waiting. They were all surprised I hadn't accepted at once. This made me begin to wonder if I might be missing out on something. After all, I reasoned, Vietnam was on the way home to Brisbane and I was having my fare paid. Chipp had even said I'd get a holiday in Australia at the end. Thoughts such as these, and the fact that in any event it was only for twelve months, swung me around, and I accepted. Had it been the start of summer, however, I don't think there would have been any way I would have gone — not with Wimbledon and the cricket on. Looking back, I'd guess I was chosen because I had never expressed strong views on Vietnam. (Reuters never did send the two blokes who were keenest to go.) As well, I was single and young, I could write a news story, and Chipp liked Australians.

That I might have been heading for danger had never occurred to me because I knew that the Americans would be such a dominating influence that I would be with the safe side. And this was the impression I was given at Reuters before I left. "All that we require you to do is sit up on a hill with the Americans and watch a battle and write what happens and what they say," a senior executive told me at a briefing.

The popular view of America at the time, and mine, was of a country so powerful as to be untouchable in war, particularly in some tiny little place in Asia. In fact, in Peking eighteen months before I had had an argument with some Chinese students who said the Americans should get out of Vietnam because they could never win. I said that was ridiculous, that they could win anytime they wanted: all they had to do was to get serious and start using jet bombers and other big equipment that had not yet been brought into play.

With my air ticket and £10 in travelling expenses in my pocket I went down to the Fleet Street pub next door to say my farewells. There were several famous agency correspondents there and I said I would buy a round of drinks because I was cashed up. When I pulled out the money and with it the air ticket, an old Reuters hand grabbed the ticket. "Hey this young correspondent's been given a one-way ticket to Saigon and ten pounds to get there by Reuters," he said, and an American correspondent remarked that he got £100 just to go to Dublin. So they all insisted that it was I who should be bought drinks. What they were never to know was that the expenses sheet I sent from Saigon claiming the full £10 was rejected in London as excessive. The letter I received said seven pounds was enough and would I please refund the balance.

Reuters sent me via Singapore, where I worked for several weeks. I couldn't get a visa for South Vietnam because I had been to communist countries, so I had to get a new, clean passport from the Australian embassy. The Vietnamese ambassador had suggested this as a way out and the Australian Embassy happily complied. And we all pretended nothing unusual had happened.

I flew out on a Pan Am Boeing to Saigon.

Learning the ropes

Not twenty-four hours after my arrival in Saigon on 12 February 1967 I slept through my first war action. The Viet Cong dropped several mortar bombs on the city in the early morning. Fired through a hole in the roof of a suburban building, one bomb hit a truckload of government troops and another landed in the front yard of a British Embassy home not far from the office. The explosions sent the other reporters scurrying half-dressed out of the Continental.

When in my own good time I did wake up and discovered what action I had been missing I nearly panicked. I needn't have bothered, however, for I was to learn that a few mortar bombs and deaths were barely a story from Saigon. The real news came from events you were unlikely to witness but were informed of in official American announcements to the press: from the major land or air battles or accidents that had occurred the previous day to the latest breakthroughs or setbacks in the way the war was being handled.

The announcements were the source of almost all the news that came out of Vietnam. Only the military command knew today everything that had happened everywhere the previous day or that morning. They also had intelligence reports from around the country and knew of political decisions made from above. But just because they knew didn't mean they were going to tell, of course. And obviously it was in their interest to announce things in the words they wished to see used, before some newspaper or TV station chanced on the event and gave it a different slant. It was

plain to see that for a journalist the Vietnam War was largely a war of announcements, seven days a week.

Every morning at eight o'clock, the American command
put out a three- or four-page press statement, and every
afternoon at five it held a full press conference at JUSPAO.
This event was known among the journalists as the "Five
O'Clock Follies", indicating that, although they reported
what was said, they didn't really believe it. Perhaps this was
because of the way some announcements were contradicted
either under questioning or in the light of later events.

Entry to the Follies was gained by showing the accreditation card. A complex series of hallways led through a maze
of windowless offices to a small theatre. I assume this
design, or lack of it, was intended to confound any attempt
to attack a specific office from the outside. Certainly I never
did get my bearings when inside JUSPAO.

Outside the press conference theatre army, navy, and
marine press releases overflowed from racks — enough
words each day for a novel, I once heard it said. And I didn't
doubt it. The releases were churned out by a huge number
of public relations writers trying to get a good write-up for
their service or particular unit. Nearby there was a small
room with two phones in it for ringing through big stories
that could not survive a dash back to the office. If you expected a big story you brought Dinh to hold a phone for you
while you were inside. He would fight to the death rather
than surrender his phone.

I was amazed how many press attended each day: an
average of one hundred, I suppose, which almost filled the
theatre. Some covered the war exclusively from this
building because here there was access to quick information
and intelligence. A more adventurous journalist might
wander around the countryside for weeks without seeing
anything much happen. One American reporter who was
there during my time had been in Vietnam several years
without once leaving Saigon.

The announcements were made by high-ranking army,

navy, marine and air force officers, usually majors, colonels, or the equivalent. The person in charge of the Follies was a general, which showed how important the service was to the American government. The general made no announcements, but if one of the briefers or a guest officer started getting into difficulties under questioning he would stand up from the front and help out. He usually began with: "Gentlemen, I think what the colonel means is . . ." This became a famous saying of the war.

The announcements were made from a stage, with the briefing officer standing at a lectern and referring to maps and charts when appropriate. In front of the stage, two soldiers operated a large reel-to-reel tape recorder, and pointed a directional microphone towards reporters during question time. Senior American journalists said these tapes were sent back to the United States where they were listened to by the president and his advisers: as probably the best and fastest way to gauge the feeling of the press on an issue.

For the first four days I didn't know what the announcers were talking about. You had to understand the specialist lingo before you could know what was going on. There was a typed press release of about nine pages handed out at the start and the press conference itself was devoted to late announcements and questions arising from the sheets. The information on the sheets included the weekly "kill ratio" — the number of Viet Cong killed per American, usually claimed at about four to one. There were also listed the number of Americans killed each week. At this stage it was one hundred but by the end of my twelve months in Vietnam it would peak at five hundred Americans dead every seven days. Not many, if you say it fast. But a lot if you saw just forty or fifty of them.

Part of the press release might say something like:

Operation Hickory, the last of three actions undertaken in the southern half of the DMZ, ended today. American casualties in the operations . . . were 142 dead and 898 wounded. North

14

Vietnamese losses were 787 dead. American aircraft flew 109 missions against enemy communications, gun sites, storage areas and water traffic in North Vietnam yesterday. Eight rocket positions in the northern half of the DMZ were destroyed.

Much of this information came from the many public relations staff in each American outfit out in the field. For example, I was surprised to find that there were about twenty in the public relations section of the 1st Air Cavalry Division (they were the ones in the film *Apocalypse Now*). "The Big Red One", as the 1st Division called itself, once sent a man to Saigon seeking publicity. He came to our office saying, "You've got to send a man up to see us in action." Other units also tried to get reporters to cover the great things they were doing. By the end of my time there, however, things had changed: the American units were seeking more troops, not more reporters.

I was surprised that the press conference was so organized and formal and most impressed at the standard of questioning. The American journalists were quick to spot any weakness in a story and probe for holes. They certainly knew the techniques of hunting in a pack. The briefers were trained experts at answering questions, but as the war got out of hand those press conferences became a battle of wits. Generally, I found that the Americans were prepared to be questioned very closely.

Although I could see that they were in a position to orchestrate the news and that they were there principally to justify the US position, I was impressed that they at least did provide an opportunity for questioning in a war zone — an opportunity I knew the British or Australians would never have granted. Or anyone else for that matter. But that is not to say the American military was happy about its daily battles with the media. Once I got to know them these military briefers told me that at the start of the war the army was given the option to permit or deny independent press coverage. "Knowing what we know now," one said, "we should have taken no reporters."

Each day, about fifteen minutes before the American press conference there was an ARVN (Army of the Republic of Vietnam) conference in a nearby building run on scaled-down American lines. The setting there was much more spartan, the seating was poor, there were no stages or props. Apart from agency reporters few Western journalists went to this conference — news from the point of view of the Vietnamese troops was almost ignored. The belief was that the Americans were the ones making all the decisions so they had all the stories.

Apart from these two press conferences, Reuters' major source of news in Saigon was Dinh. For me, he was my one close contact with the Vietnamese, and I was fortunate that we eventually became friends. Dinh had achieved so much respect among previous Reuter correspondents that they had christened him Gungadinh — he was a better reporter than any of them, it was said.

I soon learned that what Dinh lacked in education and English he made up for in cunning and personality. And he knew what was important. He could listen to a speech by a Vietnamese leader and, perhaps half way through, he would swing around and say: "Story now. He say, ..." and that would be the best story out of the speech. He understood what the Viet Cong were up to and monitored their clandestine radio, though that was illegal and he risked jail. For a journalist his contacts were enviable — he even got Christmas cards from President Nguyen Van Thieu. When Thieu arrived back in Saigon from the funeral of Australian prime minister Harold Holt in 1967, he watched troops with rifles push myself and the rest of the press back and said merely, "Dinh, come." Dinh was the consummate journalist. Whoever coined the saying "Never underestimate a journalist's love for his story" was talking about Dinh.

His life revolved around his news sources and journalists and, although married and with three children, he spent most of his waking hours in the office. Thus he proved much more of a journalist than the well-educated Dang

Tran Lan who had to carefully translate a speech before you could start looking for the story yourself. Dinh was so much the reporter that many times he had to take great personal risks in an effort to get a story. A person who showed his emotions easily — perhaps in a big laugh or sometimes tears — he was an unusual combination of the hard reporter who was so human.

Like everyone, of course, he had his limitations. With a big Vietnamese–English dictionary on his desk he taught himself English but, although he knew all the words, he never mastered the structure of the language — he evolved his own word order — or its pronounciation (for instance "louser" for "lawyer"). Any extraneous words he left out. If Dinh saw "one man black pyjama AK arm", it was a Viet Cong. If someone was afraid Dinh would say: "He care." And, if Dinh believed a journalist was wrong in his speculation he would argue, very simply: "Never happen."

He gave straight answers which at first gave the impression of being abrupt: "Very quick and easy to be killed in Vietnam," was the first thing he told me about the war. But this terseness was really just the conversation of a man who knew what was going on. If you asked him to organize something for the office that he believed couldn't be done, he would say: "Cannot." If he believed it was someone else's responsibility, he would say: "Not my problem."

Although he worked for the British, loved Reuters, and dealt with many Americans in his job, Dinh had a surprising love of Australians, and didn't particularly like the others. One of the reasons was that the Reuters man who gave him his first job was an Australian. Dinh said he liked the fact that most Australians were "very quickly journalists"; they had the right background to be journalists, as he saw it, being "victims" of English justice (convicts). Dinh himself was a victim of French colonialism: his father was shot by the French in Quang Nam province when Dinh was a boy. But most of all Dinh, being first a Vietnamese, believed he could tell a good man by looking at him — and he liked the

17

look of the Australians who came in and out of that Reuter office over the years. He found them more "open-hearted", he said, which is how I would describe him. And, of course, it was a Vietnamese belief that you would have a good day if the first person you saw was a man with a smile who yelled out hello with gusto and meaning. Australians were more apt to do this than most.

Dinh didn't like to come to work if the first person he saw in the morning when he opened his front door was a pregnant woman, for that was unlucky. On the other hand if he saw a very old man he would immediately tackle all the difficult tasks, like re-leasing the office or re-registering the car — difficult things to do in a corrupt state. As Dinh himself put it, "If you see a person with beaming face that lucky, like Australian people face. You see me, 'Hello', 'Good morning', that lucky. But many men with mean face so cold that unlucky."

As a way of displaying his feelings, Dinh kept pictures under the glass top on his desk of the correspondents he liked over the years — and I knew I had made it when, after several months in Vietnam, my picture suddenly appeared there too. Who could have known that these pictures would one day be used in his interrogation by the Viet Cong.

Dinh soon nicknamed me Gunsmoke — which had me puzzled, I confess. Australian nicknames, emphasizing so often the opposite of some characteristic of physique or name, are easily understood. But in Vietnam things are not so simple. I once asked Dinh to explain exactly why he called me Gunsmoke — I guessed my name had something to do with the character in the American TV series of that name. Incidentally this show and "Combat" were top-rating Saigon TV programmes, relayed by a plane circling overhead. When I asked Dinh to explain the connection, this is what he said: "The American have TV films called 'Gunsmoke' every night. And one movie star in there he have hair look like you, trousers tight like you, he walk very quick, and his activity very quick. And you like him. So one day you coming back to the office and I say, 'This guy look like the Gunsmoke.' " (Dinh pronounced it Gunsmock.) Also, Dinh thought I was big like the American TV character — though the American marines thought I was small enough for some to nickname me Twiggy.

The only non-Australian Dinh really got close to was Jim Pringle. Unlike many of his British colleagues Pringle did not have the impressive formal education which most often ran to a first-class honours degree from Oxford or Cambridge. Rather he was, like Dinh, self-educated and from a poor background. So Scottish was he that even in Vietnamese Dinh distinguished him as Scottish rather than English — he was "the man from To Cach Lan". Pringle, a Scottish Nationalist, explained to Dinh that Scotland had been colonized by the English, so perhaps Dinh saw him as another "victim", like myself.

Only a few years older than I was, Pringle already had led a remarkable life. I knew he had hitchhiked across the Sahara Desert and taught himself Spanish while touring South America as a youth after leaving school at fifteen. He had covered the war in the Dominican Republic for Reuters where he had been pinned down by machinegun fire. He had been into Haiti and had, so it was said, been hailed on the local liberation radio as "the fearless correspondent come to expose our mad dictator".

Fearless he certainly was. On one occasion he wanted to get to the Demilitarized Zone (DMZ), dividing North and South Vietnam, to cover a US marine invasion of the territory. Unable to get a helicopter out of Dong Ha airbase, he decided to walk and try to hitch a lift. This was in an area where there were supposed to be North Vietnamese battalions roaming around, and the road was one normally negotiated only in armed convoy. As well, the road was mined and three-metre high elephant grass came to within a few metres of it on both sides.

When a huge marine convoy rumbled up the road, Pringle held out his thumb. Just about the only field correspondent who did not wear American garb, there he was standing in his usual attire: very, very loose, baggy blue trousers with one of those thin centimetre-wide vinyl belts that tore at the hole that had held the buckle for the last ten years. And, of course, black lace-up shoes. His only concession to the war was that he had picked up a type of very bright Vietnamese camouflage jacket that was a bit too tight. The convoy pulled up and Pringle, his thick glasses gleaming under the tropical sun, brightening and magnifying his big blue eyes, explained in his brogue that he was a Reuter correspondent and wanted a lift to the DMZ. The marines couldn't believe it. "Well, man, we'll take you if you tell us you're a tourist," said a captain.

In his reporting, he was always concerned to convey the difficulties of ordinary people in a war of generals — which was not easy for a newsagency reporter tied to reporting announcements. And it didn't always make him popular with the office. On the occasion when he hitchhiked to the DMZ, Pringle sent back stories on the effect of the marine invasion on the villagers. He reported how they were being herded, in tears, to make the area a clear battlefield, while everyone else was writing about what military officials saw as the significance of the move. As a result he received a dressing down for "chasing by-lines" — that is, trying to get his name on stories. But he merely saw the news his way. And, from what I saw, his approach told more of the whole story.

Dinh liked the way Pringle dourly fought Vietnamese officialdom, Reuter office rebukes, and the American public relations machine — an unlikely Woody Allen anti-hero fighting impossible odds. Yet Pringle's humanitarian style of writing made life hard for Dinh. "Pringle, he's a man makes trouble for me very much in immigration," Dinh said of his battles to renew Pringle's three month visa. "All the while I must answer the question, 'What story he done?' 'Why Viet Cong radio got his name last night in broadcast?' I say 'Viet Cong got his name not because he support

20

Viet Cong but because Viet Cong very clever: any anti-paragraph they never to say [would never report]. But something supporting them they say.' Jim very difficult for me."

The more I found it easier to understand Dinh's English the more I wondered why I could not before. And the more I saw of the war the more I wondered why it had taken me so long to see I was working with the losing side. I was lucky to have Pringle and Dinh to learn from because it was a war that was difficult to comprehend and weighed down by contradictions.

Getting to know the Viet Cong

The American 11th Armoured Cavalry crashed through the jungle, the armoured cars and tanks seemingly eating the trees and undergrowth from in front of them. We were in what the Americans called "War Zone C" and on what they called "Operation Junction City". This was the biggest operation of the entire war, involving forty thousand troops.

We were searching for Viet Cong and their hideouts and, in particular, for the Viet Cong's clandestine Liberation Radio thought to be hidden deep in the jungle. It broadcast propaganda to the people of South Vietnam. Dinh had told me to be very careful this time because this area near the Cambodian (Kampuchean) border was where the Viet Cong political headquarters were thought to be.

We camped with the tanks and guns pointing out into the jungle — the traditional American covered-wagon formation. Inside a mosquito-proof tent we drank coffee and discussed the war. A young officer was teaching me about Vietnam on a wall map, and showed me why the locals called War Zone C "the elephant's ear" — because of its shape. The Viet Cong had all cleared off by now, he said. I was new to Vietnam then, and it showed. "But what about the eight hundred US troops who parachuted in near the border?" I asked. "The briefers at the Five O'clock Follies said they would act as 'a blocking force'." The officer squinted his eyes together as if my head was a bright light and then decided I wasn't kidding. "Well, each square on this map represents one square kilometre. As you can see there are scores of squares. Yet in this dense jungle eight hundred

22

men can effectively cover one-third of one of these squares," he said. In fact Vietnam was so big and so jungled that even five million soldiers could have covered very little territory.

This was the first night that I'd camped out in the jungle with the US army. We all settled down in the small clearing after the troops had emptied their guns into the bushes, presumably to frighten off any guerrillas nearby. Suddenly there was a huge explosion and I jumped about a metre off my air mattress. I was relieved to find it was one of our own mortars firing off into the distance.

"What are we shooting at?" I asked. "Just firing off H and I," was the answer. This stood for "harassment and interdiction" which really meant the Americans fired off artillery and mortar shells into the bush every ten minutes or so to upset any Viet Cong plans to group for an attack. Or so it was said.

The hot morning was made bearable by the shade of the jungle as the troops formed into groups and moved off into the trees. I went with Colonel Arthur Cochran in his bubble-nosed helicopter to check the positions of the various groups of tanks: it was difficult for them to know their exact position in the thick jungle. We darted here and there over the tree tops and around the occasional tall tree which towered oddly above the green carpet. One group had discovered something, so we landed in a nearby clearing. Two well-armed men and the colonel and I set off through the jungle to take a look. It seemed suicidal to me for the four of us to start walking through this area, but all we were doing was what soldiers do for a living. "Don't jump to the ground too quickly," the colonel said, pointing downwards. I looked and, right in front of me, needle-sharp poisoned stakes called punji sticks pointed out from the undergrowth, ready to impale unwary troops throwing themselves to the ground under fire. The poison was said to kill in twenty minutes.

There was a shout. I was signalled to get down. I thought

the soldier in front had called "Idaho". I could hear noises ahead in the jungle. There was a loud explosion. This was trouble. I wasn't even sure where the explosion came from, so had no idea which way to run. Without speaking, the tall, lean colonel and his two men moved on through a thick patch of jungle to where — as unexpected as a shark in the desert — a huge American tank sat, its gun still smoking. The soldier had actually called "Fire in the hole", American jargon meaning that a gun is about to fire, so get down.

Just past the tank was a Viet Cong base camp. We entered cautiously, but not cautiously enough, we soon realized. The next group after us found and disarmed two anti-personnel mines facing the trail entrance, each of them capable of blasting five hundred heavy pellets if the tripwire was touched. We had been lucky. Inside the perimeter of trenches and firing positions were four thatched-roof buildings, including a large kitchen with a cast-iron stove surrounded by an assortment of copper and cast-iron pots and a large wooden box containing rice. The camp had been abandoned so recently that the stove was still hot. A long stovepipe took the smoke down into an underground tunnel leading fifty metres away from the camp. By the time the smoke reached the end of the tunnel it had been filtered out, said Colonel Cochran, commanding officer of the Armoured Cavalry's 3rd Squadron. The dining room, some twenty metres away, contained two large well-made tables and several wooden chairs.

Thick overhead jungle hid the little camp from the air. Thatched roofs covered some bedrooms the floors of which, for protection, were half a metre below ground level. Most of the comforts of home were there: bamboo-strip beds, tables, chairs. It was most likely these were the officers' quarters. The men — probably up to three hundred of them — would have slept in the open, the colonel said.

There were two small clearings, one of which was a volleyball court. Strangely, in the middle of the other, there were four stakes marking the corners of a rectangle. In the

24

kitchen building a young soldier reached into the roof shouting that he'd found a table-tennis ball. "Don't touch that, soldier," said the colonel. "It could be booby-trapped." Then I saw table-tennis bats stuck in the bunkers. Others found the slabs of wood that fitted on the four stakes in the clearing to make, of all unsuspected things, the table-tennis table. "So these men who are battered by our eight-engined bombers from twenty thousand feet play table tennis," said a soldier, in a way that showed an illusion had been shattered.

Cochran's unit had not expected to find the camp in this area. They thought the Viet Cong would build their quarters near streams. "In this hot dusty area you have to stay clean to survive," said Cochran. "The North Vietnamese, who are not used to the area, have to bathe several times a day. This camp is the second in two days that we have found with its own wells," he said, pointing to a bucket and rope above a hole. Generally, the North Vietnamese regulars who came south to fight fought in the cooler northern provinces nearer home. Elsewhere in South Vietnam the Viet Cong provided the major effort.

"Here is a bicycle repair shop," the sergeant called, and, under a small thatched roof on the edge of the camp, were several bicycles and new spare wheels. Small wild pigs were in a pen nearby and there were live fowls in small wicker cages.

"See that," said Colonel Cochran, pointing at a thirty-centimetre square hole in the ground going deep into darkness. "That will survive anything but a direct hit by a thousand-pound bomb." He said it would go down about three metres and then lead off into a tunnel. With escapes like that, no wonder the Viet Cong were surviving America's military power. And I had already learned that bomb craters weren't a problem, because they quickly filled with water and made good ponds for breeding fish.

There were open tunnel holes everywhere and it would have been a brave Viet Cong who went for a walk round the camp after dark. While some men dismantled claymore mines others guarded the tunnels, their guns pointed at the holes in case a guerrilla appeared with a grenade. Even I held a gun on a tunnel when asked to when we ran short of men — there were fewer than twenty of us. As I held it, I wondered what I would do if one of these men-turned-jungle-creatures suddenly appeared.

Nearby we found a meeting room between some huge trees. Here there were school pads containing exquisitely written Vietnamese script — and crude propaganda drawings of US soldiers being stabbed. Colonel Cochran found a drawing of Ho Chi Minh and posed while I took a picture of him looking at it. Which seems pretty stupid now.

It was decided that someone would have to search the tunnels. Grenades were thrown down a couple of holes, resulting in very muffled explosions and much dust. After the dust cleared a slight soldier armed with Cochran's .38 pistol furtively lowered himself into one of them to take a look. He didn't disappear completely from view but returned to announce there were no Viet Cong down there. We were supposed to blow up all these tunnels so they could not be used again. But that was a Saigon decision. For one thing we didn't have nearly enough explosive. For another, the men reasoned that it would just make the holes bigger for the Viet Cong to dig them out; and they would just dig some more anyway, the colonel said.

Trenches from the camp led about two hundred metres along to one of the many naturally occurring clear patches in the jungle. These patches were ideal sites for the favoured US helicopter assault tactic known as the "search-and-destroy mission". The Viet Cong in this camp evidently were aware of this because they were prepared. The metre-deep trench lines seemed to run right around the clearing, which was about the size of three football fields, and back towards the camp. Other trenches led off to two smaller camps. The clearing itself looked harmless but it was in fact covered with the pointed punji sticks. Also, thin grey poles soared into the air almost unnoticed. These were a danger to a helicopter's tail-rotor, which was vital for keeping the aircraft on course. Once the blade hit a pole the helicopter would head to the ground out of control like a balloon losing air. Another tactic of the Viet Cong was to tie hand grenades by the pin between small trees so that the downdraught of a chopper would dislodge the pin. "Any airlift of troops into here would have been swamped," said Colonel Cochran. "I gather they were not expecting armoured vehicles."

Apparently, dealing with the unexpected was part of the secret of Viet Cong survival: no helicopter assault came to this base camp; instead twenty tonne tanks battered their way through. The Viet Cong were not prepared for this so they left quietly, their ovens still warm from the last meal. And nobody knew where they had gone.

It was my suspicion that they heard every word we said, because I couldn't believe that they would just desert their enclave without a fight. But then, I could not understand many of their actions. I started to get an idea of how they thought after meeting a Vietnamese woman who was a Viet Cong before there were any Viet Cong. In fluent English, she told me her story.

It was 1945, and there was excitement in a small Vietnamese hamlet among the trees and rice paddies in the Mekong Delta. Vietnam now belonged to the Vietnamese, the people were told. News had spread of how Ho Chi Minh's guerrillas had pushed the Japanese out of Saigon and Hanoi. The French, who had ruled Vietnam as a colony for over eighty years, had been kicked out by the Japanese early in the war. But, as was to happen so often in Vietnam in the next generation, peace looked near when it was in fact far away.

The Chinese were to accept the Japanese surrender in Hanoi and the British in Saigon, she recalled. "Our guerrillas were waiting to stop the French re-entering Saigon but all we saw were truckloads of men moving into Saigon under the British flag. Those men were, in fact, French soldiers returning with British help, and this was how they were able to regain control of the city," she said, giving the Viet Cong version of what happened.

Ho Chi Minh and the French went to the bargaining table and he was offered two-thirds of Vietnam, with Annam, the southern one-third, including Saigon and the rice-rich Mekong Delta, remaining with the French. But Ho Chi Minh wanted no French at all in Vietnam and he went to war, reorganizing the guerrillas who had fought the Japanese.

The first the woman knew of the new guerrilla activity was when her brother arrived home with some "moon cakes" wrapped in a red flag with a yellow star. The flag for the guerrillas who fought the Japanese had the colours reversed: a yellow flag with a red star. "Someone has made a mistake," she told her brother. "They have the colours the wrong way round." But, her brother said, this was the flag of a new organization to fight the French, called the Vietnam Doc Lap Dong Minh Hoi (Vietnam Independence Allied Committee). This was shortened to the first and second-last words — the Viet Minh — a means by which Ho Chi Minh successfully kept his name at the forefront of the battle in order to create one united front out of the many political parties.

Eventually the Viet Minh infrastructure reached even her remote hamlet. "A guerrilla gathered the people together and asked them to move forward to listen," she recalled. "But they just stood there — too shy to move.

"Although I was only twelve I went around the back and pushed them forward. My family was the hamlet leader and we were told to make a list of names — but nobody even knew their names. That was the type of difficulty we faced in those days." She said the problem was that the hamlet families all used the traditional Vietnamese method of calling the children by numbers in order of their birth — number one, two, three, etc. "They didn't know how to read or write — I thought it was hopeless," she said. But the Viet Minh knew what to do. They taught them to kill.

"We built a big straw French man. Everyone stood several yards away holding a sharpened bamboo pole — they had no other weapons. My job was to train the children, even those of only five and six. We lined up, sharpened pole in hand, and faced the straw man. I had to call 'Tien' [forward] and take one pace forward with the left foot, and have the children do the same. 'Tien', and another step towards the French man. 'Tien', again . . . until we stepped forward and thrust the poles through the straw figure.

"At first everyone was shy and just poked the stick at the dummy. But within a few weeks the children and others were screaming out 'Tien' and thrusting in their sticks vigorously. They were really beginning to enjoy it. After a while all over the countryside you could hear peasants yelling 'Tien', 'Tien'."

By 1967 those five- and six-year-olds were about twenty-seven and twenty-eight, and no doubt carrying AK-47 automatic rifles instead of bamboo poles.

Every evening the new flag was raised in the centre of the hamlet and the people sang songs that emphasized how they must place the fatherland before all else. As one song said: "If once the fatherland is lost, everything is lost."

Soon all the men of the hamlet, except the very old and very young, were called away to the jungle to fight. "It was so sad that day when all the men left, but the hamlet soon cheered up in the knowledge that soon we would defeat the French and there would be peace."

The girl and her sister kept long vigils watching for the approach of French troops. "We would stand at what we called 'the old monkey bridge'. We could always see the French coming from a long way away. When we did, we would beat on the monkey bridge with sticks as a warning to our hamlet and others nearby. Of course the French

29

knew we were probably Viet Minh supporters but they could not be really sure . . . And they needed the support of the people, so they had to be nice to us unless they had definite proof. This was difficult to obtain. Even if they knew some of our young men had gone with the Viet Minh, all we had to do was say they were abducted."

It all sounded so much like the problems the Americans were having in Vietnam.

Two years later, the men of the hamlet returned with other guerrillas. They were to attack a nearby French outpost. The women noted the dramatic change in the men: those who had been shy and giggling now looked tough and grim-faced; this she described as a "pleasant surprise". That night the women sat out the night listening to distant gunfire.

Just before dawn the men returned and asked the villagers to help them bury their dead. "My sister and our two younger brothers were told where there was a dead guerrilla a mile away and we set off across the slippery ground in the rain. I suggested my sister and one brother grab the hands while my other brother and I grabbed the legs — but they suggested we grab the hands. We went through all the possible combinations — because we were all scared that if we held the hand of a dead man he might grab us. Gathering my courage I bent down and grabbed his arm with both hands. 'He's dead. Can't you see!' I said. The others soon helped me. When we threw him in the hole we had dug his arms and legs were everywhere. But we didn't bother to straighten them — we just threw some dirt on him and rushed home."

For three years the Viet Minh built up its infrastructure in the hamlets and villages, and by 1948 they were ready to reinforce their hold in the capital. As a result, the woman and some of her family were moved to Saigon. But they made by no means perfect agents. On Ho Chi Minh's birthday they were given money to buy one hundred birds from the market. Slowly they made tiny red and yellow-star flags from paper and tied them to the legs of the birds. Then they released them as a propaganda exercise to show the Viet Minh were everywhere. But they made the mistake of releasing them outside their home, where they flew into the nearest trees and the strings and flags became caught in the branches. Desperately, before the French arrived, they climbed the trees and cut the birds free.

Occasionally her brothers would come in from the jungle to visit the house for top-level Viet Minh meetings. "We would hold a party and, while the meeting was held at the back of the house, we would pretend to be chased by the boys into the garden at the front — but that was just so we could watch out for the French." She said hundreds of people in the area saw the comings and goings at the house — but only once were they betrayed. "Once an agent named us. He was brought to the house, his head covered by a bag with two eye holes cut in it. We all had to walk past him and if he nodded his head at any of us we were finished. But he didn't: he must have relented. We would have been arrested anyway, except that we were a good Catholic family and the French didn't believe we could be supporting those they called the communists. But behind our beautiful altar of Our Lady were our secret documents."

It took nine years, but the Viet Minh finally defeated the French at the Battle of Dien Bien Phu in 1954. Under the United Nations Geneva Accords, Ho Chi Minh got the northern half of Vietnam. Ironically this was less than he was originally offered before the fighting, but the accords also stated that nationwide elections were to be held within two years — and Ho was confident of victory. In the meantime, those supporting the Ho regime in the south were supposed to move north, and anti-communists there were supposed to move south. But, according to Dinh, the communists deliberately left half of their number behind in anticipation of having to fight another "war of liberation". And they were right.

The south quickly came under American political influence and, with Ho's popularity well known, the 1956 elections were never held.

According to Dinh the new guerrilla war was slow in starting because the Americans advised the South Vietnamese regime that the communists had left many former Viet Minh behind. In an attempt to find them, an American-backed anti-malarial programme was devised which went, as Dinh put it, "house by house throughout the countryside to spray, look in here and look in there". Dinh said a large number of communist guerrillas were found and killed. "Very good tactic," Dinh told me. "Cancel out communist tactic."

By 1960 Ho Chi Minh had set up yet another guerrilla organization, with yet another flag. This time it was the Mat Tran Giai Phong Mien Nam or National Liberation Front. This time the flag was the Viet Minh flag, except half of it was blue — the Vietnamese colour for peace: red and blue with a yellow star. But the same old guerrilla leaders were still there, with their long experience of fighting the Japanese and the French — and the familiar old infrastructure remained, as did the loyalty of the woman who told me her story. In retrospect, at least, they were a formidable target, even for America.

A significant advantage to the communists, or Viet Cong as the Americans made them known, was the use which they were able to make of Vietnamese religion. It was commonly assumed by Westerners that most Vietnamese were Buddhist, whereas in fact most were Confucian. This meant that they worshipped their ancestors — or, as Dinh put it, "their daddy". While the communists respected no religion, not even Confucianism, there was no need for them to openly oppose praying to ancestors in the home. There were no pagodas or churches to close: being a Confucian was like being a Viet Cong — it was all in the mind. Without accepting Confucian ideology, the communists made propaganda out of the importance of the word "father". "Pray to your fatherland. Adore your fatherland" was their effective catchcry.

The war started slowly, but as the Americans began to increase their numbers in South Vietnam, the casualty count for both sides grew. Artillery, jet fighter-bombers, cluster bombs . . . but the communist threat did not diminish. It grew. And grew. Until, by mid 1967, the Viet Cong and their North Vietnamese brothers were fighting one and a half million men at arms — American, Vietnamese, Korean, Filipino, Thai, Australian and New Zealander. What the Americans had not seemed to realize was that they had come in on the end of a very long war.

It was a war made more difficult by the same enormous problem that had beset the French: how could they know if a Vietnamese was a Viet Cong. In other words: Who was the enemy?

Because of such uncertainty all Vietnamese became suspect to the Americans, who referred to them by the derogatory term, gooks. I presume only the Viet Cong were so called at the start but by 1967 a gook was any Vietnamese. Suspicion led Americans to adopt an aggressive, brusque attitude towards them, an attitude not designed to keep most of the country on their side. They showed little of the great discretion needed when you are a guest in someone else's war. US soldiers said openly they would not camp near the ARVN troops because the gooks might do something stupid. I heard soldiers say of the war in front of Vietnamese: "You only need two Americans to fight this war. One with a rifle to shoot them and one with a slate to chalk it up."

Dinh spoke to me once of the resentment the Vietnamese felt about such behaviour. "They act like big boss," he said. "Sometimes they have 'boss' written on their cap. The Vietnamese very angry about that. 'Is the Americans coming to fight in Vietnam or coming to boss in Vietnam?' they ask."

To the Vietnamese being civilized meant you had to respect old people, visit graves, follow fortune tellers, accept a complicated courtship system — which many

33

American soldiers failed to notice. They missed noticing the little things, too; for example, when you beckon a Vietnamese it is rude to do so with the fingers up: the palm of the hand should be turned downwards. And they showed cowboy films on TV when the influential, elderly Vietnamese specifically disliked these, calling them colonialist "Hanh Dong Cao Boi Texas" — the cowboy activity of Texans.

The Vietnamese were thus not impressed with the Americans. They often called them "Khong Goc", which means "people without roots", and implies people without antecedents, without grandparents. Dinh explained it as meaning "people who don't know who they are". "All the Vietnamese people say this. Mouth by mouth they talking it. They say American set up only four hundred year and they come from everywhere," Dinh told me. I once heard a Vietnamese accuse an American of this directly: "You Americans have no grandparents in your own country, yet you come to tell us how we run our country — and we have four thousand years of civilization," he said.

And the American, thinking of how the Vietnamese ate with chopsticks and balanced loads in two buckets at either end of a pole slung over one shoulder, replied quickly: "Yeah, four thousand years to learn how to carry two buckets of shit with one stick and eat one bucket of shit with two sticks."

Under fire

Black jets dived on the machinegun positions. Bursting napalm lit up the countryside as below us it billowed a mass of red which immediately turned black, a black so dense you could still see it in the dark of night. But the Viet Cong machineguns kept firing their red tracer blobs despite the rockets, the bombs and the napalm which seemed to strike home back down the tracer line.

Still the guns fired. Two more passes by fighter-bombers and the red blobs raced swiftly skyward. How did the Viet Cong do it? What bunkers they must have. Then we were hit. The copter lurched. It was the ground. Suddenly everything was much more real — like the moment they finally wheel you into the operating theatre after all the waiting and preparation.

Immediately the rear ramp dropped the marines nearest the door charged out bravely into the night across dried rice paddies in true US marine assault tradition. The ground was dry but ploughed and my ankles felt they would give as I plunged on, my feet feeling their way as you run in a dream. And all the while I kept wondering how these men knew which way to run. After we had sprinted as far as could be expected we threw ourselves on the ground behind a rice-paddy bank, only to hear calls of "back here" from behind. Small pencil-points of light were flickering behind us and we scurried back at the same speed, despite the fact that we had snatched only a breath of rest. Halfway back, and my breathing was making strange noises. I had last known this feeling when playing rugby — the breath of exhaustion. But this had been taken beyond that by fear and necessity. My thigh muscles tightened as they had once done in an an 880 yards race, bringing me to an almost complete stop while leading within twenty strides of the finish. But I wasn't going to stop here now and I plunged my failing legs into the broken earth even harder than before. They did not feel their way across the ground now — they just plunged on to it, and I staggered into the marine lines. I felt like throwing up but there wasn't time in between rasping for gulps of air.

This was my first close look at battle in the rice paddies. It began when a marine major, a pilot called Caldas, hurried out of a white plywood hut in the middle of the press compound in the northern coastal city of Danang. It was very early morning and he was yelling out something about a battle.

From brick and concrete shoebox rooms around a stony triangle that once was a French motel came sleepy representatives of the world's press. "One of our battalions is surrounded thirty miles southwest in the Hiep Duc Valley," we heard. "We are sending in some companies to relieve them. Anyone who wants to go, be in that truck in four minutes," said Caldas.

It was a very unusual opportunity for journalists to get to see a battle in progress. I felt I had to go because it might be a big story but I wasn't keen. Reluctantly, I donned green American uniform and canvas-sided jungle boots, my mind fighting back all the reasons why I needn't go: for a start, it would only make a couple of paragraphs on the bottom of Follies stories in the newspapers. And, it was only about 5 a.m. and my body wanted to go back to bed. However, staying in the same room was an American lawyer, Jim-Guy Tucker, who was in Vietnam writing for his local paper in Arkansas. He lectured me about how Reuters should be there — and what a great opportunity I had working for them. And I believed him.

36

I climbed into the battered green truck. Bob Ohman of the American newsagency Associated Press (AP) was already inside, his horn-rimmed glasses glinting beneath his green jungle hat.

"Are we ready to roll?" called Caldas, as out of another motel room bustled Virgil Kret, of the rival American newsagency United Press International (UPI). Kret was a young reporter newly arrived from Tokyo who spoke perfect Japanese: even when he spoke English he seemed to be saying "Ah so".

The truck swung up the dusty red road to the hilltop American camp near Danang and then down on to a sloping green field. Spread across the slope was a marine company of less than two hundred in full combat regalia, waiting to go into battle. I expected troops in such a situation would sit staring ahead exchanging one-liners the way they do in the movies. Instead, some read comics, mainly about war; some lay by themselves, staring into the sky . . . at God or helicopter; others spoke in long paragraphs to otherwise quiet groups.

Although young myself I felt their youth. One black marine deftly threw a knife, point first, into the grass between his feet, while a fair-haired man sat next to him continually cleaning his black automatic M-16 rifle with a tiny paintbrush.

It was very, very hot. The grass seemed to smoke. Where were the choppers, as the Americans called the helicopters. There were so many of them in Vietnam that they are my memory of the war — their throbbing noise, the chop-chop of their blades, their cyclone down-draught, their soft hover. But now, just when they were needed, the sky for once was bare. Hours passed and, as the afternoon blazed in, cold cans of beer arrived. I expected the soldiers to cheer and shout and make young men's comments, but they just came over, took their can, and returned to exactly the same place on the grass — as if it were home.

The sun lost its strength eventually, having sapped most

of ours, and the television teams gathered their heavy, cumbersome shoulder cameras and sound-recording gear. The light would soon be too bad for pictures. I wished I were a television reporter and could appeal against the light. They were lucky they turned back then, for I doubt if they would have made it through the night that followed with all that equipment.

At dusk, the Chinook helicopters finally arrived, filling the air, as they were wont to do, with noise, dust, and fuel fumes. These very large helicopters the Americans called "hooks"; they had a rotor blade at each end and could carry about twenty people. They landed in a row. We lined up in groups and, on a command, scrambled aboard.

Following each other as if drawn by some magnetic force, the big hooks swung in ever-higher arcs into the sky. At seven hundred metres it was getting cold because the oval windows had been shot and kicked out by gun-firing marines in the assault landing of an earlier convoy at the point where we were now headed. As we whipped along at about 160 kilometres an hour the rotor blades sent lashes of fresh cold air inside.

Soon we began to spiral downwards — this was a tight spiral, corkscrew tight. From my paneless window I could see blobs of red racing up from three separate North Vietnamese fifty-calibre anti-aircraft machineguns in the dark below. I pointed these out to the soldier on my right. He and I had spent some hours talking on the grass and this was a moment in life when one looks around for friends, not that friendship always inspires confidence. He had told me his company had been in Vietnam four months and had had one fight with the Viet Cong. "I guess we will just be getting good and our twelve months will be up," he had said. Looking at him it was hard to believe that he might now be going quickly to his death. The divided strap of his helmet framed his chin, seemingly setting his jaw. His face had been deliberately blackened. I wondered what he was thinking, but felt I couldn't ask. Anyway it was too noisy. I guessed that he was thinking about his mother and his girlfriend. But then I wasn't. I was wondering why they hadn't blackened *my* face since I would be with them? All my thoughts revolved around this group, this helicopter, this battle.

The soldier hadn't taken any notice of me. Everyone's thoughts had turned inward. So many men and no one talking. All staring into the space ahead, looking already like dead men. Even though it was now pitch dark, they could see as they were coming down what a big fight we were heading into. And there was no turning back. I could see now that armies did not go off and fight willingly. They went along with the system until, too suddenly, they ended up in a situation where they had to fight to survive. A situation in which they just had to keep on going.

Besides the absence of black on my face I also had no rifle; instead, there was an Asahi Pentax camera hanging around my neck. Reuters did not have a photographic service but I had carried a camera occasionally, hoping I might accidentally take a good picture I could sell. As it turned out, it was a stupid idea. I was dressed like any other soldier, except that I was not wearing a flak jacket — a heavy green sleeveless jacket with thin hard bits that felt like steel plates sewn inside the strong synthetic material. Inside the back collar, where washing instructions are normally found, was a tag pointing out that about three-quarters of the wounds received in war are to the torso between the waist and neck. But they would not stop a bullet, or even a hard shrapnel hit. In fact, to make things worse, the impact of a bullet could knock pieces of the jacket into your body, so it was said. But no American soldier doing any fighting would have been caught without one. I didn't have one because they weren't issued to reporters. Although I had yet to appreciate their purpose, I had noticed how expensive they were in the black market. They were worth it, apparently — the flak jacket was a confidence booster that made you feel just a little bit safer in a naughty world.

War seems to be a stop–start affair and once we had gathered together on the ground in the Hiep Duc Valley we sat around for thirty minutes before setting out in a single file in the dark. It was a still, clear, moonless night, black and hot, as we walked solemnly towards the flares and tracer bullets lighting up the sky. They looked close, but it was to take hours to get there. Like most of the soldiers I had no idea where we were or what the plan was, and I fell in about the middle of the long line, feeling safer for having survived that accidental storming attack twenty of us had made on landing.

I felt weighed down by the heat and after a while the heavy helmet made my head roll from side to side. Even these young fit grunts — as some called the marine infantrymen — must have felt burdened with the addition of the flak jacket, rifles, cartridge packs, grenades and, in some cases, mortars. They even carried an implement called an entrenching tool which was a small shovel that could be turned into a kind of pick by folding the blade over at right angles.

We were heading into what the Americans called "Indian country" — a sign that they saw this war as similar to the one their ancestors fought against the Red Indians. And, in a way, it was. The Americans had to plough across country until the Viet Cong found them and ambushed them, at which stage they formed a tight circle and fought it out from there. As a lieutenant told me once when I asked if he were not afraid of an ambush: "Hell, the only way we can get contact is to get ambushed." We hadn't gone a hundred metres when we stopped. Then, just as suddenly, we started again. As I picked up my pack to fall into line, a marine said to no one in particular, and without humour: "I hear our company is going in to surround this North Vietnamese division" — there being about two hundred in a company and ten thousand in a division. "Are you shitting me?" said a voice. "Would I shit you?" he said. "I don't know, it sure beats the hell out of me," the voice replied.

We seemed to be on a narrow track and then a dirt road, but it was too dark to see anything much apart from small trees nearby and the back of the man in front. There was much evidence of fighting and every now and then we passed recent shell and bomb craters. There were many long, silent stops. Word that you were going to stop was passed back down the line, quite loudly I thought, from one man to the next. We would crouch down — or sit if it went on too long — until the man in front said: "Pass the word back to move it up." And we would continue. Then it got more complex. Those behind would want to slow down and I would be told from behind: "Pass the word up to slow it down." One time someone forget to tell the man behind him we were continuing after the only really long stop we made and the word to stop had to be passed up through some hundred people, and then back down the word to reverse and pick up our tail. Next, we had to pass the word up to go again. It didn't seem like a good way of creeping up on the enemy. But no one appeared to worry too much about that, even though we stopped so often; I crouched down on my right ankle so many times that for three days afterwards my right thigh would scarcely work.

This went on for so long that time melted into timelessness and I had no idea how long we had been travelling — except that I was starting to get low on water. In this country no equipment was as important as the two canvas-held plastic waterbottles which were worn one on each hip. It was so hot that you needed to drink water every ten or fifteen minutes when on the move, even at night. More than one of my bottles was already gone. I didn't have a watch because a little Vietnamese boy of about seven I had befriended who came into the office in Saigon at night had pinched it off the desk. Dinh grilled him like an angry father and got him to admit that he had sold it for ten cents.

All I knew was that several hours had passed, with a lot of the time spent crouching in silence on the ground. We had not yet come under fire, although the fighting up ahead was much closer now. It appeared we were zigzagging, trying to pick the best point to help the other company. There were supposed to be other companies moving in to help out as well, so we would also have to stay away from them. But every time I questioned the need to get down yet again I checked myself with: "You are in the middle of a valley in the middle of a war in the middle of a battle and you want to stay standing up?" All the time I had the feeling that nothing was more certain than that fighting would start at any moment. And in the dark it seemed that it would have to be almost at nose-to-nose range. I only hoped we saw them first or, better still, that they would have done their disappearing act again. I also wished that I'd left with the TV people at dusk . . . but, then again, with a bit of luck I might get a really good atmosphere story and on-the-spot interviews without a shot being fired. That was always the most likely thing to happen in this war.

Eventually we stopped for a while near a little thatched-roof farm hut, and there were no more planes in the air or machineguns firing. The Hiep Duc Valley was quiet. It was as if we were the only ones there, but for our uneasy minds. Normally in such a place I would have spent a lot of time looking at the sky, as I loved to do at night in Danang. I didn't notice the stars this time, but wondered what the peasants thought about this war, and where the people who lived in this hut were now. And who the hell was ploughing those rice fields we had so much trouble stumbling over. But I didn't talk. I didn't feel like it, and nor did anyone else.

As we walked through this destruction, with more of it now being hurled again from the sky, it was not difficult to understand how the average peasant must have learned to hate the Americans for helping to maintain a war that was producing everything bad — shortages, disfigurement, lost children, lost harvests, and a lost future. Out here any ism seemed better than war. And, in the rice paddies — where destruction was not evident but the lack of crops was — I wondered if anyone now owned this land and, if so, how they felt about not being able to work it.

I was sweating a lot and had been trying to preserve my drinking water when we came to a small stream. It was only knee deep but, as each man waited for the one in front to cross, our tight column started to elongate dramatically. Those who reached the other side, and the wide flat dirt field crisscrossed with rice-paddy banks, strode out, probably feeling more confident now that all evidence of ground fighting had ceased. "Hold it up, hold it up," some marines shouted at the tops of their voices, trying to contain the stretch. I didn't think to fill my bottles as we waded across.

During the stop at the farm hut I had moved much closer to the front of the line in order to get a better idea what was going on: so far I had nothing to write about, except that I had crept for hours across a valley with some marines. About half way across the kilometre-wide field I was feeling a little easier, though still as tense as a person summoned to see the boss. On the horizon was higher tree-covered ground which we were making for. Suddenly, it took long seconds to dawn on me, I was being shot at and there were malignant things buzzing by near my body in tune with loud noises to my left. I couldn't see these things and I couldn't actually feel them, but I knew they were there. It was as if they were vibrating the air around me. Someone was yelling out from in front to get down and I seemed to be the last one suspended up there before jumping forward on the hard ground to complete the long thin green line. Things were hitting the ground just in front of my face. It was then I realized our attackers could see us — although we couldn't see them — for how else would they know to shoot lower? My pen, which was hooked into the inside of my shirt pocket, hurt my breastbone when I hit the ground and, as I clawed the dirt and wriggled to get lower, it seemed to hold me suspended. I ripped it out and threw it away.

Someone yelled out in the night, "I'm hit, I'm hit," and

then a voice from in front told us to jump over the other side of the knee-high main paddy bank right beside us. Had we been ambushed from the other side we would have been safe, but then I suppose we were lucky we were only being fired at from one point. Jumping over the bank under fire did not appeal to me at all but anything was better than staying where I was. The first thing I did was to throw my camera away; then I flicked my legs up in the air and went straight over, hitting the ground like a whip. My heart was racing so fast by now that there was no way I would have known, I believed, if I had actually been hit. Quickly, as in a desperate search, I felt my body with both hands from the feet up to see if everything was intact. It was, though all my clothes were soaking wet with sweat.

I had often wondered what it would be like to be under direct personal rifle-fire but had never imagined it would be so unexpected. There weren't even any of the rifle flashes they tell you about in movies. Although I can't pretend I was looking. The funny thing was that I wasn't so much afraid of being hit now, for then the issue would be decided, as of having dodged so much only to face still more. For, unlike so many things, a battle is something you can't walk out on when you've had enough. And I had. It is said that it takes a thousand bullets in a war to kill just one person; from the amount of fire so far, I felt I was a good chance of reaching my quota if this went on for much longer.

I turned to the man on my left. "Fuck me that was close," I said, feeling better beneath the ointment of the dirty paddy bank. "That! that's just chicken shit," he said and knelt up to empty his rifle in the general direction of the fire as most of the marines were doing. Suddenly he came straight back down without saying a thing, and the marine nearest where he fell, injured, called out for a medic. Meanwhile a small conference had developed near me, at ground level, about what to do and, feeling that I was very, very involved in this, for the first time in the war I dubbed in and suggested that a few men be sent out to get those blokes.

One of them turned around and said, "Well, who's going out there?" Well I didn't even have a gun. An officer called, "Bring up the light organics," and a minute later two men appeared with small sixty millimetre mortars which they fired off in the general direction of the gunfire. It was like throwing stones at a sparrow in a tree in the middle of the night, and we all knew it.

Sporadic firing continued. After about twenty minutes I was feeling quite happy behind that paddy bank. For this way we were getting no closer to a bigger war, and these Viet Cong had no chance of getting any closer, for the marines were ready to empty their guns at anything that moved. My thoughts even started to wander away from preserving my arms and legs. As I watched some marines along the bank, I could see now why on a hospital ship they told me so many of the injuries they treated were smashed teeth and jaws — they had shown colour pictures of faces that looked like butcher shop windows with bits of teeth sprinkled around. It was not a pleasant memory just now but I could see that the only places these marines could be hit, and still live, would be in the jaw. Anything higher would kill them. Anything lower would hit the paddy bank.

They were incredibly brave, these young marines. Almost all were volunteers. And all wished to emulate the US marine tradition of never taking a step back — like a Boxer dog. Hiding behind rice-paddy banks wasn't their style of war: like Napoleon the marines swept armies before them but suffered when the army wasn't there to fight. The US marines were so famous in Australia that before I arrived in Vietnam I thought that their name was the name for the US army. This certainly impressed some of the marines at Danang, who told me they got their name because they were initially a seaborne assault force.

Back to reality. There was a word to pass: we would press on under fire. That didn't sound like a good idea at all. Perhaps they were looking at it differently from me: to the marines, we were pinned down but to me, we were safe, so why move. I really did consider staying where I was and not going with them; in a way I was unlucky in that, not being a soldier, I did not *have* to go on under fire. Being with these marines right now was like volunteering to live in London during the Black Plague. If a marine refused he could be court-martialled or even shot, I thought, but who is to blame Hug Hlunn of Reuters if he decides he has now got enough material for a story.

"I have been missed eighty-eight times already," I thought. "Am I now to give them another go?" The only trouble was that if I stayed I would be on my own in the middle of nowhere dressed up like an American soldier. And, once the marines moved out, I might get wiped out in the air strike which would no doubt be called in. So there was really no choice. I had to stand up and proceed under fire — sweating, scared, rifleless, and without the orders from above which make dying easier. I went to throw my notebook away too but, for some reason, kept it.

As we stood up we started moving quickly without actually running. I tried to make myself as small as possible, breathing in and bending over and keeping my left arm by my side hoping it would absorb enough to save my life. I bent my head further down, until I thought I had better not get it too low or that might be why it would be hit. In the Spanish civil war George Orwell wrote about bullets that might "nip" you, but it seemed to me they did more than that — they seemed to make very big holes in people. I suppose one of the reasons I felt so scared was that, being a writer, I could imagine exactly what would happen and I could picture, as we moved through the toc-toc of the night, a bullet in slow motion ripping through my jaw. I remembered what the Americans said about the modern high velocity bullets which had so much impact they could powder a bone. Some Americans would say of their modern rifles: "When one of these hits you you finish with half of what you started with."

As I moved into the night, stiff and bent like a khaki

wooden puppet, I began to appreciate the tremendous advantage the Viet Cong (in this case backed up by North Vietnamese regulars) had over the Americans just by being so small: they probably took up only about one-third of the volume of a big marine which, it seemed to me, would mean more than just a straight three times less chance of getting hit. For example, a Vietnamese could seek protection in the tiniest indentation in the ground.

Nobody spoke: they just moved ahead. I don't know what the soldiers were thinking, but I had decided that bravery was lack of imagination. I had a different thought for every bullet I heard fired and what it was going to do to me. We got through — amazingly, with only a few wounded. But this attack, I did not know then, was enough to ensure the success of what was about to follow. We had almost made it to a bushy low hilltop when a machine-gunner opened fire from the front. This was disappointing, to say the least, for I had hoped we were out of trouble and was hurrying to get in among those low trees where I would not be so obvious. The marines quickly killed him — I saw his body and his gun the next day. One of the marines commented that he fired over our heads, which, he said, was common for inexperienced machine-gunners.

At last, the bushes. But just as I entered I heard another gun further away in front. The bush was quite thick although it was no more than a metre or so above our heads and I wondered why. It was probably regrowth after defoliation. Word came back to do something or other and the guy behind me tapped me on the left shoulder and said, "Pass the word up there's nobody else here." The executive officer came back, saying something like, "What do you mean there's nobody else here?" By the time he had the sentence out he could see he had reached the end of our tiny line. Somehow, only eight of us were going off in the dark to attack the North Vietnamese, wherever they were. We pushed on following one another through the thinning bush, but after about five minutes I had a feeling that if we

47

weren't actually going around in circles, we weren't moving far from where we started either. But in the dark I wasn't sure and there was no way I was going to take my eyes off the barely distinguishable back of the man in front and end up alone, unarmed, and lost. After a while one of our group yelled out, "What are we doing? Walking around looking for booby traps?" This had the desired effect and we came to an immediate halt. As we stopped I looked around, squinting into the dark, and was surprised to see two or three marines just next to me — obviously not some of our eight. I was about to ask who they were but they saw me first and said, "Which company are you from?" Just then heavy American M-16 ping-ping firing broke out from behind us followed immediately by the shouts of sergeants imploring their men to conserve ammunition. Cries of "Stop firing," "Wait until you get a target," "Don't waste ammunition," came booming through the blackness. Without a word, our small group turned to move back to within our lines, now that we had heard where they were. I stood on something in the dark: it felt like a rifle. I bent over and there was a marine lying sprawled out like a drunk, his head back over the ditch, his arms hanging loosely. One of the marines we had found in the dark was holding him. He said he was dead. "One bullet. Just one goddamn bullet," he said. At the time, I assumed it was an American bullet because of the volume of fire from the marines at that time, but the assumption could easily have been wrong. I had heard though that armies expect that 10 per cent of their men will be killed by what the Americans call "friendly fire" — armies accept many things that shock civilians. We moved through a short clearing and back into more bushes and when we found our company I was surprised to see groups of them lying close together on the ground in among the bushes facing uphill on the gentle slope. I was happy to join them here because it looked so safe, but I did worry that there might be no perimeter and that the North Vietnamese might just walk in and say hello and shoot the lot of us. But I preferred to believe that some of the marines were out guarding the position and I quickly lay down because it was a much less vulnerable position than I had been in, and it was good to have so much company so close. All I had to do now was wait until first light and no doubt our attackers would fade away rather than face the superior firepower of the Americans, which was useless in the dark.

I didn't think that anyone knew exactly where we were or where the North Vietnamese were. But the next morning I was to learn we were only fifty metres from the marine company we went in to help. And our position was located so exactly that shortly afterwards in the pitch blackness on the hillside a helicopter lit up our bushes with a powerful white light from its belly as it hovered overhead and began to descend, inching its way to the ground to pick up the wounded.

Unfortunately, although this enabled the wounded to be evacuated quickly and treated, it also gave away our exact position. Just after the helicopter lifted off, a marine stationed up front heard a familiar pop. All I heard was the shrill cry of "Incoming", as the helicopter turned off its light and disappeared into the night.

I buried my face in the rocky ground and waited and listened and hoped. Two things were on my mind: I would hear a whistle before it landed because that is what the books I had read said, and what if it lands right in the middle of my back. I could actually feel the part of my back it would land on. There was no whistle, no warning, just a tremendous explosion to my right. It shook my body, but, even more so, my mind.

Dirt and bits of rock landed on me. The explosion was as loud as I would have expected from a five-hundred kilogram bomb. The instant the noise died I heard an even more terrifying sound: the screams of agony from the soldiers who had been torn by the ripping, jagged metal. All of these bombs were made of a metal specially designed to fracture into small chunks with dozens of razor-sharp edges —

something science has done for the world. I still have a small piece the size of a cigarette lighter, eighteen years later, the jagged edges of which are still so sharp it has to be handled with care. Virgil Kret was to write the next day: "I wasn't scared until I heard the screams of the wounded marines."

The marines pulled their entrenching tools out of their packs and started to dig in to the hillside, all the while attempting to remain half-lying down. Digging in seemed like a hell of a good idea to me and, trying to sound as if I were borrowing a neighbour's lawnmower, I asked the bloke next to me in the dark if I could use his when he was finished. He didn't even bother to answer. "Incoming," yelled the marine again. By now I was drenched with sweat again and a bit ashamed that I was so scared. I knew though that everyone else lying there in the dark of the hillside could only be thinking of the same thing — the shell climbing slowly to its full height and descending at an ever-increasing speed to land among us. It was a bit like Russian roulette. Who would it hit? Would it whistle this time?

I remembered now I had been told in Saigon that the Viet Cong hold the mortar or rocket tubes between their knees as they follow the flight of a helicopter and wait for it to land to signal the whereabouts of enemy troops. I was wishing not only that I had a flak jacket but also that I had an entrenching tool when experienced American reporter Bob Ohman told me not to move. "There are no big trees so we won't get air bursts. Cover your face with your pack and don't move," he said. What he was saying was that the mortars wouldn't crash into any big trees and explode, spraying the ground with shrapnel. So the lower and flatter we could get, the safer we would be. Boom . . . to my right again, yet screams came from my left as well. I had noticed that a few soldiers kept digging until the last — they must have stayed too long above the ground. "Medic," "Corpsman," people were yelling. "Get spread out. Get spread out, damn you," said a sergeant, kicking some men near me

50

into action, and walking around as if he were immune to wounds.

So I stayed where I was, as advised, and clawed at the ground to get lower. But it was too rocky: not big rocks, just hard rock-like brittle ground. My right ear was pressed hard on to it, my helmet protected the back of my head, and my pack covered my face. I thought this was probably not the best side to lie on and rolled over. Marines were still sitting up between explosions trying to dig in with their spades-cum-picks, but the surface was too hard: it was impossible to dig in properly. The North Vietnamese knew they were on target from the screams that frightened the valley.

The order came for us to withdraw, carrying the wounded who had been gathered at one point, back into the rice paddies we had come from. "I can't breathe, I'm gonna die. I can't breathe . . ." rasped one. "Just take short breaths and you'll be all right," said his mate, staggering under the other's weight and always ready to dive for the ground. "Tell Susan I love her. Write to her. Tell her I love her. You will? You will?" said another wounded marine lying on his back. "Yes, I will," said the medic. As we retreated we passed a bomb hole which was so big that I thought if you fell into it you wouldn't be able to climb back out. The thought was so vivid I now sometimes think I saw soldiers trapped in the bottom.

As I pulled back through the bushes with the marines I felt very alone. They were all looking after each other and talking for the first time since they sat on the grassy slopes all day waiting for the helicopters. They all had weapons, but I was walking around in my own nightmare wondering where to go and what to do next. Once back on the edge of the rice paddy the marines started to dig in to the dirt but I didn't have a shovel. The mortars had stopped now but there was no way that was likely to last for long. I took off my helmet and took the exterior steel pot off the hard-plastic liner. I put the liner back on my head and started digging into the hard fine soil with the steel helmet in a spot beneath two large rocks; they'd give me extra protection.

It was hard work but I refused to let myself stop. Instead of digging deep as the others could with the proper tools, I found I had to go for length because the surface was easier to dig. This was not as good as the small round holes the Americans dug, because the greater the area of ground your hole covered the greater the chance it would take a direct hit. But it would have to do. Digging was slow because I was stopped every now and then by outbreaks of firing, and because I had to keep getting into the hole to measure if I was yet below ground level and if I fitted in. I was exhausted and out of my precious water when I finished. It must have been well after midnight, I imagined. But this was not the place for asking someone for the time. My mouth was dry and my muscles had had it.

Meanwhile marines eyed the black sky which had been unusually quiet since we had arrived, and they kept asking the obvious question: "Where's our air support?" The Americans relied a lot on making contact and then calling in air strikes in front of them. They had often explained this at the Follies. Yet now we had run smack bang into the North Vietnamese attracting gunfire and mortars and, an hour later, there were still no air strikes. "Where are the medivacs?" asked another marine, referring to the medical evacuation helicopters.

After a while I got in to my grave-length hole and it just fitted nicely, but a marine officer checking his men spotted me and asked who I was. He told me to get out of it because if a mortar hit the big rock I would be sprayed with shrapnel and killed.

I was so tired by now that I almost didn't care what happened and I picked up my pack and just walked further back into the dry rice paddy we had come out of hours earlier. There was no way I could face digging another hole with my helmet. I looked for a spot where two big banks joined with a smaller mound inside and I lay down between them and put my pack at the only unprotected end. My thigh muscles were aching from the effort of bobbing up and down hundreds of times that night.

Above, the air support finally arrived to give cover to the medivacs. A long thin line of red tracer bullets squirted from the front of a Dakota aircraft slowly circling high above and then, as the noise arrived, it roared like a continuous foghorn. These puff-the-magic-dragons, as the Americans called them, were capable of pouring out eighteen thousand rounds a minute from three Gatling-type machineguns, each of which had six barrels. Only one bullet in five was tracer but there were enough to make a continuous red line — it was as if the plane pissed red. The noise of this plane, they told us in Saigon, scared the Viet Cong out of their minds, but I doubted that now. For the point on the ground that the plane was shooting at was obvious enough to make those not in the line of fire feel safe.

A plane dived and napalm set the area behind our little hill alight, bubbling up a glowing mass of flame. The concussion of four bombs dropped by a green and grey, camouflage-painted Phantom jet over to the left hurt my ears.

It was the first time I had seen napalm dropped and by now it must have been almost dawn because I could see the tin cans rolling and tumbling down out of the sky. They were like the unpainted, ribbed tin cans of apple my father used to use in his cake shop — that's how close they were. When they hit red billowed way, way up into the sky, rolling, red clouds of fire which would go suddenly, totally, and immediately, black. The bombs were also being dropped very close, some too close, I think, because the bang hurt and marines called out to get them away. They were really shaking us.

Tiredness was now overtaking me like an anaesthetic. Watching all this from the ground was like being at a big movie, and I vaguely remember seeing a line of more marine reinforcements arriving through the rice paddies in the dawn light about a hundred metres to the left. After that I fell asleep.

I awoke with a start. "Who are you?" asked a big black marine on the other side of the paddy bank. I told him, and blearily looked at a line of rifles peering over the bank next to my right shoulder. "Well, you're outside the perimeter," he said. "Is that the perimeter?" I asked, indicating the bank. When he said yes, I turned over and went back to sleep.

As the sun rose to blaze down on the paddy fields, planes were still battering the surrounding countryside, but for us the battle was over. In the far distance sunlight glinted off more shiny tin cans of napalm as they dropped together from the belly of a plane.

I walked across to where marines were gathered cooking breakfast and collecting waterbottles to be filled from a nearby well. I sat down next to a bank and talked about the fight. The company had lost four dead and thirty-three wounded — including a combat photographer. Back in Saigon such small casualties would be described as a "firefight". Kret rushed across and seemed as if he was about to hug me. "We heard a reporter was dead and thought it was you," he said. But I had only been sound asleep.

The colonel in charge of the relief companies told us how the other relief companies had also been pinned down by small groups of guerrillas with machineguns and mortar bombs. As we talked, Vietnamese in black pyjamas raced across a paddy behind us. "Should we fire, sir?" a soldier asked an officer. "Well, er, are they carrying guns?" "I don't think so, sir, but they must be Viet Cong." The officer looked around, "How the hell would I know?" he said. "If only they had square heads." By which time they had gone.

This was an enduring problem. Just who were the Viet Cong? The question must have been asked thousands of times already in this war, and the doubt resulted in many predicaments. Once, for example, a crowded C-130 I was flying in in the dangerous area of Dong Ha was hit by gunfire that seriously wounded one marine. Later on I talked to the pilot, who said with disgust: "We are always taking fire from that village, but we can't shoot back — it's a friendly village."

Nearby a marine and a Vietnamese interpreter went through the clothing of the dead North Vietnamese machine-gunner who had watched and waited as we walked towards him the previous night. He had been killed with a well-placed hand grenade and carried several letters from home, which the interpreter read out.

There were six bodies in the area, but, out there, under the curtain of napalm and bombs, there could have been six thousand. It all depended how many were there to start with. But certainly no one was going to go out to count them.

Colonel Houghton, the marine regimental commander, flew in to congratulate the troops. "Without you we would have lost that battalion," he said.

He offered reporters a lift out in his "chaser" helicopter — the one that follows the VIP's in support in case the first is shot down. The chaser was an old-fashioned CH-34, so slow and sluggish it sounded like a washing machine trying to take off. Bob Ohman elected to stay on but Kret and I flew out to file our stories to a world interested only in the number of dead. I lay, hands under head, across the floor of the helicopter and smiled. I was elated to be getting out intact. Suddenly there was a loud clatt, then a zing, as a bullet ripped through the floor and ricocheted off a fire extinguisher.

At regimental headquarters Colonel Houghton gave us the figures: 76 marines dead, 300 wounded. He told us that 450 North Vietnamese and Viet Cong had died. In Saigon, the official American spokesman was later to say at the Five O'Clock Follies that in a battle in the Hiep Duc Valley 540 North Vietnamese and Viet Cong had been killed.

55

Managing the news

At night I would sit at my desk in the Saigon office getting bitten on the ankles by mosquitoes while writing "third leads" and "nightleads" and "updating" earlier stories. There were four reporters working for Reuters but often one was on leave. And there always had to be two in Saigon to mind the office.

The reason someone had to be there every hour of every day was because Reuters serviced some six thousand papers in more than 120 countries, as well as lots of radio and television stations.

It doesn't sound like much of a life, but, when you had been out in the field, it was a lovely feeling to sit safely inside that brick office in the quiet of the evening with the satisfaction of another day survived. The best way to describe the relief is to say that no one ever gave a thought to things that worry people in a normal society, things like cancer and career — they were too long term.

From the start I knew exactly what head office wanted because of my work rewriting on the world desk in London. There would usually be several things announced each day at the Follies and it would probably take two people to write them up — one leaving the conference immediately and the other staying for question time. We also had to cover all the airport press conferences held by top US defence people, ambassadors and visiting national leaders such as those of Japan and the Philippines. But while I knew how Reuters wanted the story, I hadn't had as much experience identifying the most significant statement in an hour-long press conference. For example, after the Japanese prime minister left, I had to ask the older bloke from the London *Daily Express* for his ideas on the best story.

After perhaps second and third leads the world desk would require a nightlead or a daylead summing up everything in one story. These were put out to the world every twelve hours for afternoon and morning papers with the beginning rewritten, which saved several thousand editors from having to do it to avoid having the same story as their opposition had earlier. For this reason we were often rewriting our own stories, trying to come up with a new angle. Since I already knew the system I soon got involved in the work and quickly came to be accepted.

Derek Blackman was desperate to do well, which meant beating the American agencies, UPI and AP. They had about twenty or thirty people each so we thought we were pretty good to compete and, with the enthusiasm of youth, I set about with the others to knock them off by trying to send out the big stories better and, most of all, faster. Speed was crucial because newspapers about to go to press, or radio and television stations to air, will use the first story that arrives. The future of Reuters depended on being used ahead of the other agencies.

One of the biggest problems for a reporter in Vietnam was getting your story out. Even in Saigon it was difficult because the Post, Telegraph and Telephone Office (PTT) was so slow and expensive; as a result, many newspaper journalists from around the world used the Reuters office for writing and sending their stories. But the greatest difficulty — in a war with no front line — was getting the story back to Saigon from the field. It was impossible, of course, to send a story from a rice paddy or a hilltop so a reporter first had to get to one of the many major US military bases dotted across the country. If you had been at a battle, that would involve getting on a chaser helicopter, if you were lucky, or one that was bringing out the wounded. More often, however, the reporters left a battle area sitting among dead bodies. These were usually in special zip-up plastic body-bags but occasionally they were just heaped on the helicopter floor, blood and all. Sometimes the bodies were days old and, although these ones were always in body-bags, the stench was sickening.

When the journalist got back to the major camp, the next task was to try to telephone Saigon on the American military radiophones and from there get into the old French telephone system. The radiophone was a simple apparatus on which you talked by depressing a button and listened by letting it go. The Americans had a network of them linking various bases and cities: they ran the telephone system in Vietnam.

The set-up, I thought, was fairly insecure. Although reporters would not give exact details over the line about battles that were going to be held, they would get on and say: "Well, I can't say what it is but there's a big operation up here in two days' time. Can you send up six thousand feet of colour film and two cameramen?" And the next guy would get on and say: "There's something going on in the so-and-so valley but I can't say what it is." If the Viet Cong pieced all the conversations together I often felt they would have the whole story.

It was necessary to give your priority on the radiophones because the lines were always busy. A journalist's priority was very high — number three — but even then it was difficult to get through to Saigon. After a while, you learnt that if a direct line was unobtainable there were various routes you could take via little telephone exchanges all over the country. Getting through this way could take at least an hour so, after a lot of shouting and waiting, it was always a great feeling for me to hear Pringle on the other end saying: "Is that you Hugh?"

The phones were difficult enough to hear on without the problems we sometimes had understanding each other's accents. During my time, in Saigon accents heard around the Reuters office were Australian, English, Scottish and

South African. One night after seven or eight tries to get through from Danang I had been unable to get Pringle to understand the phrase "took the bunker". My voice was rapidly disappearing after an hour of shouting so loudly that I was drowning out the movie the marines were watching nearby. In desperation I called, with vowel sounds as in "coo": "tooook the boooonker"' and, back over the airwaves, Pringle's voice crackled "Aye" to signify he had got it, at last.

On another occasion I had been to the scene of a battle near Dak To, a sizeable camp in the middle of the highlands near the Laos–Cambodia–Vietnam border. But it was impossible to talk direct to Saigon from there — I'd have to get to the highlands capital of Pleiku for that. However I was very late getting in to Dak To and there was no way out until morning. I considered I had a top story, better than the other agencies, because I had stayed longer. But they had gone, and with them their stories. In desperation I lifted up the phone and started twirling the handles and pushing the button on the handpiece with my right thumb. In the end it worked out that I was able to talk to the operator in Pleiku on a faint line, he could just talk to MACV in Saigon, and they rang Pringle. In this way my story was relayed three words at a time between the four of us — and then to London — even though Pringle and I could not hear each other, nor me his operator, nor he mine.

That was one good reason for staying in Saigon and just going to the Five O'Clock Follies. The other even better reason was that if you wanted to go out and find out what was really happening you had to be prepared to take substantial risks.

The risks were even worse for the photographers and cameramen who, in those days, had to lug huge cameras around, their curved, padded stomach and shoulder bars adding to the weight, as did the heavy batteries. They were being paid big money, and were being shot for it. Mostly they were non-Americans and the $600 a week they earned, which was four to ten times what they could earn elsewhere, made them all chance their luck with the American TV reporters who did not have to have such a high profile and who, I was told, got a $50 bonus every time their face appeared on the screen. The risk was big, and the money was big — at least for those working for the Americans. As a Reuter correspondent I got the same wage I had been getting in London, not quite US$90 a week, plus a slightly smaller allowance than a correspondent in Singapore — less than US$190 a week total.

Occasionally US demands for live film of the war, the high wages being paid, and the bravery of the unusual characters who arrived voluntarily as workers would combine to make the whole thing seem like a staged farce. One night in the Chinese area of Saigon called Cholon an American billet (a soldiers' dormitory) was mined and came under rifle fire from a Viet Cong attack from buildings across the road. The billet was about five storeys high, at the intersection of several roads. Three people had been killed and thirty-six wounded. When I arrived, the American military police commander and his troops were standing at the corners, their backs pressed against the walls, their flak jackets done up to their necks, their M-16s held vertically, ready to fire. "Will you just look at that, ain't it unbelievable," said the major in charge as we watched two American camera teams racing across the wide road in front of the billet filming all the action — and setting up arc lights on various corners of the intersection. I always think of that intersection as a movie set, except there were real bullets flying around which, seemingly, were not allowed to hit the non-combatants in the middle.

Among them was an English cameraman who always wore one of those flat English first world war helmets; it didn't help him, though, because he was later shot through the stomach while filming another battle — a fate met by many of his kind. Obtaining action film was one reason why more journalists were killed in the war in Vietnam than in the second world war — according to the London *Times*, it was a total of sixty-three. The fact that eighteen of those were listed as missing shows how easy it was to get cut off — or cut up.

The only thing these TV people had going for them was that they never had to go into the field at night, because they couldn't get good film. But often, of course, they were stuck out there for the night either waiting for something to film the next day or unable to get out. Some of the American TV reporters would come for just three months to take the risk and show that they were willing to serve, thus helping to get themselves promoted. Other young reporters and photographers were there avoiding the draft: this way at least they didn't have to come to Vietnam as soldiers.

Newspaper photographers, too, were vulnerable: they also needed to get close to battle to get good pictures and unlike reporters they often had to focus on one tiny section of the battle to the exclusion of whatever else may have been happening. Sometimes the reporter would debrief a photographer team-mate who had been in a dangerous spot while all the action was happening. At the Danang press centre one night Dana Stone — a UPI photographer who was later killed with fellow photographer Sean Flynn (Errol Flynn's son) — had just come back from a small hill called Con Thien overlooking the Demilitarized Zone (DMZ). There Dana was determined he was going to get a *Time* magazine cover picture because the tiny hill was being hit by one thousand rounds of artillery a day. (Although he was young and inexperienced a picture he took on that trip did make *Time*'s cover.) UPI reporters had been to Con Thien, but none had been that day, so they debriefed Dana to get a story on what was going on. I had been invited to have dinner with the UPI crowd but, as I was working in opposition, I waited alone while Dana was debriefed. He didn't come up with anything new, however, so we all sat down to New York sirloin steaks in the press centre.

When the steaks arrived Dana remarked that we were

eating much better than the guys at Con Thien. "Yeah, I hate those bloody combat rations," I said, just to make conversation. "They haven't even got them," Dana replied. "They are not only almost out of artillery shells but today they were going through the rubbish dump looking for unopened ration tins." From the look on the faces of the UPI reporters I could see he hadn't told them this in the debriefing. That was always the risk of interviewing a non-reporter. They all rushed back to their room to re-debrief the photographer. It would have been cheating for me to have written what he had said. All I could do was arrange to leave for Con Thien first thing the next day.

The best pictures, of course, came from the worst places. A French photographer called Henri Huet, a German called Horst Faas, an American who was part Red Indian, all were eventually hit. The part-Indian was shot through the head when he picked up a rifle to shoot back. But most of all I remember little Cathy Leroy who was too tiny for words in her jungle greens among the big soldiers: like a blonde Rumanian gymnast wearing plaits and her father's army outfit for a family photo.

She was eventually hit just about everywhere when she was with the marines while under mortar attack near the DMZ. Her jaw muscles were cut by the mortar shrapnel and when she returned to the field a month later she could only open her mouth a little. That was why she carried baby food instead of combat rations. Several months later, during a marine battle for what seemed to me yet another useless hill, she was the only person from the media to get anywhere near the action. Her series of pictures for *Paris Match* of a marine desperately trying to save a dying comrade — and showing the anguish of his realization that now he was dead — were unforgettable. Not one of the TV crews could get as close as that, and CBS got the following telex message from New York: "If an 84 lb French girl can do this, why can't we?" Of course to see Cathy's injuries was to know the answer. Not that she complained. She recalled how she had wanted to get a picture of a marine losing his rifle as he was actually being hit by shrapnel. "I got it too," she said, enthusiastically, "but my blood got in the camera and ruined the pictures."

While the cameramen and photographers put their lives on the line more often, the writers were under much greater intellectual and moral pressure. For the photographer, the war was a great picture. When Horst Faas, the AP's champion Vietnam photographer, was asked when he was going to leave the country after being there for ten years, he replied, "You show me a better var." Unlike the photographers, being part of the action wasn't essential for reporters: they could base their stories on interviews held after an event, or on the many press conferences. The choice was to accept the official sources of information, and all the news-management techniques of the large American media information machine in Saigon, or to go out into the field and risk being killed only to find nothing much happening in the place visited, and at the same time missing out on all the big announcements back in the capital.

Although there were significant personal advantages in staying where the news was released, there were problems with simply accepting the information supplied at the Follies, or at the ARVN briefing. Lies were all too easy to come by. Because AP, UPI and Reuters were in heavy competition to sell their services around the world any significant announcement was reported immediately, and almost without question. It went out to the world, by and large, in the way it was released — and the questions were left until later.

At Reuters the announcements were always written with the addition, "an American military spokesman said", in the first sentence, although the American newsagencies did not always feel it necessary to advise the source of the announcement in the first paragraph. And newspapers, liking clear, simple opening sentences that can be easily read and understood, did not always feel the need to carry the attribution at all — particularly if their editorials supported America's role in Vietnam.

I wrote hundreds of stories based on the official announcements and rarely got a chance to check the facts for myself. When I did, however, I sometimes discovered new angles on what had really happened. For instance, we had been told at the Follies that the Viet Cong had "abducted" eighty villagers from a village near the province capital of Hoi An. This was not far from Danang and Bob Ohman and I decided to visit the place where it had happened. There, US troops at the small military outpost laughed when we mentioned the incident. What had happened was all very normal, they said. "The VC were pulling back through here with a lot of casualties and some of the people in the village obviously went off to carry the wounded . . . some men may have joined up," a soldier told me. "But when we ask where the people have gone they tell us the VC took them. They don't want to be labelled a VC village. They think if we think they are VC we won't be so careful bringing in artillery next time." I knew what he meant. I had flown over villages in the Viet Cong stronghold of the Que Son valley and saw the artillery and bomb craters in and around villages. "But they'll drift back again," the soldiers said. "They already are."

So much for abductions, I thought, but I was soon to find that the same unreliability attached to "defections". I had wanted to meet a guerrilla face to face (a captured one), because I thought an interview with a Viet Cong would make a great story. I didn't expect it to be difficult because I could interview one of the eight hundred or so who defected every week. I knew the figure because it was announced regularly at the Follies. It was all part of the "Chieu Hoi" (Open Arms) programme to accept defectors and train them to rejoin society. The only difficulty was that there were no Chieu Hoi camps near Saigon.

However, in Phan Thiet, a province capital 160 kilometres to the northeast, there was a big camp holding six hundred Viet Cong and it was there I decided to go. "I would like to interview a guerrilla who has actually fought against the Americans," I asked the Vietnamese government interpreter–organizer. "Oh, there's no one like that here, sir," he replied. As it happened, the only people they got were peasants and their families who came in from Viet Cong areas, sick of war. They never got any Viet Cong soldiers, and he seemed disconcerted that I should think they did. Yet each week at the Follies these people were counted as "Viet Cong defectors" implying, to me at least, that they were hardcore troops, not villagers forced away from home by war.

A better term would have been refugees — except that it had a special meaning too. "Refugees" was the word used in cases where people had been forcibly evacuated by American and South Vietnamese troops. I thought a more correct word for such people would have been evacuees. The main problem with writing about something you had seen, as opposed to heard about at the Follies, was getting your story believed. A single story dissenting from the official announcement in Saigon merely made the story seem wrong. After reporting on a trip to the battle-plagued Que Son Valley in September 1967, I wondered why some of the looks I was getting from the marines in Danang were so unfriendly.

One morning a marine lieutenant friend in the Danang press centre shook me awake at 5 a.m. and whispered that I should get to the Que Son Valley, southwest of Danang. With Tom Corpora from UPI I hitched a ride on a big new CH-53 helicopter which had wheels just like an aeroplane. It could carry up to eighty people and travel at nearly 300 kilometres an hour. The Americans called them Jolly Green Giants. But near Hoi An we were hit by bullets and the helicopter lost height. The hydraulic system of the US$5 million aircraft had been hit, so the pilot switched to the emergency system and headed for the nearest landing pad or "L Zee" — landing zone — as the Americans called them.

65

As the pilot was to tell us later, there was a hand system if this emergency system also failed. "But you need two elephants and a ninety foot pole to use it," he had said.

Luckily the nearest landing pad also had an airstrip — a beach next to some high hills near Danang called Marble Mountain. As we arrived the second hydraulic system did fail, but luckily the half dozen of us standing in the back of the almost empty helicopter didn't know. The pilot said he just pointed the helicopter at the landing strip and hoped for the best. But I did wonder why he lowered the rear door as we came in. At about 150 kilometres an hour, we bounced, tipped, tipped again, each time the long rotor blades hitting the airstrip and giving us balance like a man on a tightrope with a pole. Then we straightened up and raced down the strip — with no brakes.

When I looked out the lowered rear ramp when we were more than halfway down the long airstrip, I was aware for the first time how fast we were moving: the fire engines desperately chasing us up the strip seemed to be moving rapidly backwards. Right at the end we rolled into the sandhills and stopped. This had probably been the first helicopter to use up an entire airstrip for a landing. The pilot seemed upset as we made our way back to the central tower. And it was only when he started muttering over and over, "That was close," that we realized just how close it had been.

In a fit of relief, Corpora and I decided we had done our bit for the day. We had lost all enthusiasm for trying to tell the world what was happening in the Que Son Valley and decided instead to spend the day relaxing at China Beach. When we got back to the press centre, however, we were unexpectedly offered marine commander General Cushman's personal helicopter to reach the fighting: "You will be going right into the battle," we were told, which was very unusual and immediately I thought the Americans must be winning. An AP reporter joined us and it was no longer an exclusive chance between the two of us.

As we hit the ground on our arrival, I jumped straight to the dirt, lay flat, looked around, and sprinted towards a bunker with Corpora and we leapt in. The American soldiers sunning themselves with their shirts off looked on in disbelief. We were not at the battlefield at all. Actually we had landed in the rearmost camp in the valley, Hill 63, and for the next eight hours we waited there to get in to interview the troops. That they wouldn't take us in suggested how bad it was in there. All day helicopters shuttled back and forth bringing out 201 wounded. It was only at nightfall that they would start bringing out the dead, although the battle had ended at dawn.

It was dusty, there was very little greenery, and there were lots of trench holes. Just a hot, dusty, bloody camp like all the others in the north of South Vietnam, a cleared camp cut out of the bush and the rice paddies. The area was large, so we sat and waited on a little hill almost by ourselves. A couple of scrawny trees gave scanty shade.

Nearby they were bringing people out. They kept promising we would be able to go in — at any moment, they gave us to believe — but the impression I got was that no one was inviting the press along on this one. I must admit that from the high piles of helmets I could see growing in front of me, I was hoping we wouldn't get there, although I knew Corpora was hoping we would. But as the day wore on it became less likely: they were giving priority to the battle, an officer said. We never did get in, and it seemed as though we'd only be left with a Follies type of story: sixty marines dead, so-many-hundred Viet Cong killed, etc.

Earlier I had told some marines who had only a few days to go in Vietnam and who were therefore not involved in this battle, that I hoped to get in to interview Delta Company (which had been ambushed): "Don't go to dangerous Delta," the marines said. "They have been on four operations and ambushed four times." "Perhaps I will go to India Company," I said, quickly changing my mind. "Not ignorant India," said another marine. Morale was not high.

Wounded men said that Delta Company was down to sixty-nine men from about two hundred and that the two battles in the four days began with ambushes as the marines moved through hostile villages in the valley. In this latest ambush the marines had been completely surrounded. "I had one man left in my squad of fifteen," one wounded sergeant said. Medics spoke of more than ninety dead — but the official figure was to be sixty. Maybe sixty was right. Maybe it wasn't.

At dark, Corpora and I climbed into a big helicopter with eleven dead marines and flew back to Danang. I didn't smoke but Corpora offered me a Philip Morris and I smoked it. It helped drown out the smell of death and calmed my sagging, unhappy mind. I had seen a lot of missing pieces of head but still didn't know what had happened in the Que Son Valley. As soon as we hit the ground at Danang concerned medics almost had us on stretchers before we could explain that the wounded were finished and now the dead, and the journalists, were coming out.

I didn't have much of the story but I described as best I could what was happening at Hill 63. The North Vietnamese newsagency was quick to pick this up and use the story, quoting me. This is what it said:

Hanoi, V.H.A., September 11   . . . the fierce attack by the liberation armed forces in Quang Nam province on two battalions of the U.S. marine First Division in the Que Son area on September 6th. Reuter correspondent, Hugh Lunn, published a report revealing the heavy losses sustained by American troops in that battle. Following excerpts [sic] from his report.

". . . helicopters shuttled back and forth to bring out 60 marines killed and 201 wounded in the overnight battle . . . it was the second major battle in four days in this valley floored with rice paddies and straggling lines of trees. A 20-hour battle ended early Tuesday with 138 marines killed or wounded. . . . Throughout the day yesterday medical orderlies worked here with the wounded in small, open-sided brown tents, before they were transferred to hospitals in the marine garrison city of Danang. Black American M-16 automatic rifles, no longer

68

needed, overflowed from two large wooden boxes. Outside the tents, helmets and boots were piled like small haystacks."

Sometimes the North Vietnamese newsagency changed the emphasis of our stories to make it look worse. But this time they didn't. Perhaps they felt they didn't need to.

Both battles occurred as the marines moved west into the valley stronghold in a brave attempt to force the North Vietnamese to stop and fight. But, according to the marines who had just come out, there were tunnels in the Que Son Valley that could hold eight hundred men and ambushes were easy. To the west lay more tunnels, more hostile villages, more traps. The marines were no longer in a position to continue into the valley any further: they would have to regroup and be reinforced. Also, the North Vietnamese were not stupid enough to come out in the open to fight a nation seeking quick victory: they had plenty of time. Let the marines walk bravely up to them if they wanted, at such enormous disadvantage.

At the Follies the next day the briefer announced: "The enemy is moving east towards the coast and the marines are pursuing the remnants." At least two reporters knew that this meant the marines were pulling back. The trouble was that the other hundred or so didn't.

A few days later at the press centre in Danang I noticed I was getting some unfriendly looks from some of the marines at the centre. I asked one I knew well and he told me to look at the noticeboard outside the restaurant. There the North Vietnamese story quoting me was pinned up and it differed significantly from the one the marines had read in their newspaper *Stars and Stripes*. I went to see the colonel in charge of the press centre and he was obviously angered by my report. I said something like: "Are you going to accept communist propaganda?" This swung him and he walked across the compound and took it off the board.

The North Vietnamese had quoted the story correctly, if only in part, but I felt that in a job where everybody else had a gun it was in my own interests not to be seen as an enemy in the camp.

I could see it would have been easy for troops reading the story to think I was making it up. *Stars and Stripes* was their main source of news and it didn't have articles like mine. Not that the troops were alone in this — because there was no certainty that the version of the reporter on the scene would reach readers. Even if you got the real story and what you wrote made it through the head office editing system to newspapers around the world, it was on the cards that papers would use another agency's version. Large western organizations were under intense pressure to be very careful what they put out about this politically sensitive war.

If a general told a press conference: "The light is at the end of the tunnel, we can start withdrawing our troops by the end of 1966," then that was what the reporter wrote. The reporter cannot normally add, except if he has established a reputation as an expert on the subject: "But I think that is all bull. We need three million men here and then we couldn't stop them." The sort of story that was most likely to get through the intricate system was the very straight story on a bodycount claim, with no comment on implications — a story that stressed merely what the Americans had announced. And, naturally, the US military media machine wasn't there to announce defeats.

Of course, this problem did not apply to the by-line writers on great and powerful newspapers — people like Johnny Apple Jnr. and Tom Buckley of the *New York Times*, Bill Tuohy of the *Los Angeles Times*, Lee Lescaze of the *Washington Post*, and Pat Burgess from the *Sydney Morning Herald*. But it did apply to the journalists reporting the war for the great majority of people in the world.

What was needed as a reporter in an unpopular political war, of course, was confidence: confidence that you knew what to ask and how to ask it. And this only came with experience. I was struck by the age of most American reporters when I first arrived in Vietnam. They were usually experienced, very well educated career journalists and I soon learnt the value of older heads when it came to asking questions of the military officers, and to writing with impact and style.

Tall, silver-haired, respectable-looking Bill Tuohy worked from our office for the *Los Angeles Times*. His copy went out over our radio telex to Tokyo and then to London and on to New York and Los Angeles. I would often read it and was surprised he wrote in such a balanced fashion: some say this, but others say that.

For months and months I wondered what he really thought of the war.

After he had been three years in Vietnam, in the second half of 1967, Tuohy wrote a story about the press there. Only in his last paragaph did he finally show his feelings. As I remember it, he wrote:

> The press say it is on the spot and the government is not. Government officials say the press feels the war is being lost because they see only small pinpricks of the war while the government has the overall situation at its fingertips and can see the big picture.
>
> But there are many who are starting to believe the big picture is dangerously out of focus.

American public opinion had just started to turn against the war at this time, and the United States went to elaborate lengths to let it be seen by the press that they had a mandate from South Vietnam to manage their side of the war for them. A good example of this was when — in the midst of fighting — they decided to hold an election, but only in the part of Vietnam they largely dominated by force of arms, South Vietnam. It was September 1967.

As a public relations exercise, however, the election was not an outstanding event. And, as an exercise in democracy, it was badly flawed.

Ho Chi Minh, of course, was not invited to stand. Neither was the popular General Duong Van Minh — "Big Minh", as he was known — who previously had won military leadership in a coup, then been overthrown himself, jailed, and exiled to Bangkok. The South Vietnamese authorities would not allow him to return for the contest.

That left two military candidates Nguyen Cao Ky and Nguyen Van Thieu, already premier and chief of state, respectively, and ten civilian candidates. For a while it looked as if Ky and Thieu would run on separate tickets. However, this would have split the military vote and possibly have paved the way for a non-military or even "peace" candidate win. So the Americans started the election run-up by forcing an obviously reluctant, poker-faced, Catholic Thieu and "the Young Cowboy" Ky, as he was known to many Vietnamese because of his youth and flamboyance, to stand on a joint ticket. Surprisingly, they did not have to resign their posts in order to stand.

They started with a great advantage: their 650,000 subordinates in the armed services who, it could be assumed, would support a military ticket. The civilian candidates had no such advantage, and in fact, could not reach some provinces on the hustings because they needed armed escorts.

The election was observed by twenty political leaders sent by President Johnson, including the Pittsburg mayor, Mayor Barr. In the middle of the Danang tarmac Major Barr, confronted by representatives of the world's press, said, "There are some of our young Pittsburg boys up here and I want to see them. They are doing a marvellous job."

But all was not marvellous. Journalists under pressure for headlines in a predictable election came up with the failsafe "Viet Cong mount massive anti-election campaign". In fact, the number of "terrorist incidents" was not much higher than usual; the Viet Cong were all but ignoring the election.

The villagers, however, could not ignore it. Some Vietnamese told me that village headmen would make the people vote, "otherwise the village will be considered Viet Cong". And, they added: "You know what happens to VC villages." They were right. In Saigon a little over half the people voted — a percentage akin to the turn out for a British election. But in the countryside the voluntary village vote was around 87 per cent. From many villages the votes could only be securely brought out by Thieu and Ky's armed soldiers.

The American military hailed the election as a "major step forward" and proof of strong Vietnamese approval for the war. But to me nothing had really changed. Ky and Thieu kept office, and the Americans were still running South Vietnam.

Playing the game

Many newspapers and TV and radio stations around the world only buy one newsagency, but most probably get two, and the big ones buy all four — Reuters, AP, UPI and the French agency Agence France Press (AFP). They do this not only to make sure they get everything, but also so they can compare the various stories and try to reach a better judgment about what happened. The BBC, for example, would not report a major world happening until it had the news from two newsagencies, just to make sure there was no mistake. For mistakes do happen and even Reuters had a standard procedure for stopping a story. The message went out everywhere with bells on — ringing bells on telex machines — beginning "kill . . . kill . . . kill" and giving instructions to "kill" a previously telexed story. If there was a doubt about accuracy the first instruction was "hold . . . hold . . . hold".

The importance of being first when writing for a newsagency — as well as being right, of course — explains why Reuters held a month-long inquiry once to find out why a story was held up for two minutes en route to Tokyo. Admittedly it was Senator Robert Kennedy's assassination. But the bigger the story the more important it is to be first or at least equal. And Vietnam at this time, 1967, was big news. The Japanese press voted the Vietnam War the biggest world story of that year.

In Reuter language, AP and UPI were our "primary and secondary opposition" and they were aided in the battle to get the news first by the fact that they were Americans. I always felt there was a second reason for the US briefing machine to stay close to their newsagencies, and I have no doubt the British government would do the same with Reuters if Britain were involved in a war. The closer any one newsagency stayed to the Follies announcements, the closer the others had to stay so as not to appear behind the news. Or wrong. Certainly the wire services (newsagencies) — including Reuters — stayed close to the official announcements and certainly the American briefers went out of their way to help AP, or "the AP", as they preferred to call themselves.

When President Lyndon Johnson came to Vietnam on his way back to the United States from Australian prime minister Harold Holt's funeral, it was a huge story because an American president had never before been to a war zone outside the United States. He was putting himself in apparent danger and newsagency offices were frantic to have men on the spot when he arrived. But security was such that no one in Vietnam could even tell us if he was coming or not. The worst thing for me was that Pringle, who had just replaced Blackman as bureau chief, was on leave and I was in charge of the office. If we missed the president I would suffer the same fate as a later Saigon bureau chief — the sack. But at midnight that night a phonecall from Dinh told me that Johnson was going to Cam Ranh Bay — the safest place in Vietnam, at the end of a long peninsula. Such was the security in that war that the American journalists didn't even know if he was coming, yet a Vietnamese reporter knew where he was landing.

Shortly afterwards the American command telephoned. Would Reuters like to send a man on a trip tomorrow? No, they could not say what for. No, they could not comment on their president's movements. Just come if you wish and if so be at JUSPAO at 5 a.m. "This had better not be a new helicopter demonstration," muttered Bill Tuohy as we waited outside JUSPAO before dawn next morning, about fifty of us. It was not until the plane was airborne that we were told we were on our way to see Johnson, and we were not told our destination until we landed, at Cam Ranh Bay.

Johnson flew in with an escort of fighter-bombers under his Air Force One jet, and they pulled out just before he landed. He had the White House press corps following him in a similar plane. After making a speech on the importance of the war and his friendship with the late Harold ("all the way with LBJ") Holt to a satisfactory number of American troops standing in rows at attention — but really to the press — he got into his plane and took off, escorted by more fighter-bombers.

We thought that, like any other news event, we would be able to file our stories immediately we found a phone, but all sorts of obstacles were put in our path; for example, we were put on a bus that didn't go anywhere. As I found out later the White House press corps were being given time to land in Bangkok and file their stories before ours. It was an example of what all presidents, prime ministers, and premiers know: that if they are nice to the people who report on them day after day and let them get, exclusively, the biggest, most interesting stories, then they will get a better press.

Because I knew that the American military command and AP saw each other as one another's "most important", I decided my only hope was to watch the AP man very closely. After about half an hour — with the presidential party almost in Bangkok — I saw an officer come up to him and say something, after which they walked away together around a large tin shed. I followed them, which made the AP bloke turn around and give me an ugly look. When I walked into the office where he had been taken he was on a phone trying to get Saigon, and I was reminded of the agency reporter who had pulled out the phone cord in the press car after he had phoned through that John F. Kennedy had been shot in Dallas. "How come Reuters isn't given the same treatment as AP?" I asked angrily, and was given the only other phone by an embarrassed officer. By the time I got through to Saigon the AP man had filed a couple of paragraphs — "paras" as the British call them and "graphs" as the Americans say. "Come on, we are running neck and neck with Reuters," he urged his copytaker, though I was still trying to get through. I then had a stroke of luck because we were both cut off at once, which was nothing unusual in Vietnam, but, because he spent his time in Saigon and I spent half of mine 700 kilometres away in Danang, he didn't know all the various telephone detours that I was familiar with. I was able to get straight back on again and had almost finished my forty paras when he at last got through. This was vital because it was around midnight New York time and the big papers were going to get the Reuter story first. It was one time AP didn't get the news break.

Newsagencies make the most of their scoop stories in selling their service. In 1968, for example, when I was working for Reuters in Singapore the company spent hundreds of thousands of dollars in the United States advertising the fact that on a major story they beat the other agencies by just twenty-one minutes. In May that year a Vietnamese friend of the then Asian manager for Reuters, Jimmy Hahn, knocked on the Singapore office window in the dark and said she had been listening to North Vietnamese radio and had heard Ho Chi Minh say he was willing to talk peace. She was a most intelligent person and Jimmy said there was no doubt she could be trusted to be correct. The office sent off a "flash" story (a "flash" rings ten bells, a "snap" seven, and "urgent" only three) that Ho Chi Minh was ready to talk peace.

After ten minutes of self congratulation on a scoop Reuters started to panic. They telexed our office "both primary and secondary opposition still without your story" (suddenly it was "ours"). This was most unusual as all wire services are tipped off as soon as a big opposition story breaks and they immediately follow it up and confirm or deny it on the wire within minutes. Had it been, say, AP's

story we would have received a message immediately saying something like: "Primary opposition reporting Ho Chi
Minh wishes to talk peace. Need matcher urgentest."

After fifteen minutes we received a message saying even
the White House was bemused by our story and that it had
caused so much activity on the New York stock exchange
that trading had to be suspended for an hour. "You had
better be right," the message warned, or something similar.

Then, at last, after twenty-one minutes, in came the opposition. What had happened was that Ho Chi Minh spoke
first in Vietnamese, then in French, and then in English.
And it was not until he started speaking in French that
other agencies monitored him. (Normally the wire services
would have monitored the Vietnamese speech in Saigon but
it was illegal to listen to North Vietnamese radio there.)

Reuters was so happy they spent a small fortune in the
United States — where it was aiming to expand its service
to papers, radio and TV stations, and stockbrokers —
advertising the "beat". "You waited 21 minutes to hear
that Ho Chi Minh wanted to talk peace in Vietnam . . .
unless you bought the Reuter service," the advertisements
said.

A couple of weeks later, Ho Chi Minh announced he
would be making a major statement about the peace talks
later that night and we received a message: "Know you will
use usual arrangement to ensure we first with story." But,
of course, there was no "usual arrangement", unless it was
a woman knocking on a window in the dark. The difference
was that since the boastful Reuter ads both AP and UPI had
been instructed to employ a staff of Vietnamese outside
Vietnam to monitor the broadcasts around the clock.

But, even so, Jimmy and I were reasonably confident. We
knew from monitoring Indonesian radio in Singapore that
the translators — with no journalistic training and little
knowledge of world affairs — would laboriously translate
the broadcast before the reporters could get the story.
Whereas, like Dinh, our woman would know the important
part the instant Ho Chi Minh uttered it.

The trouble was that when we got to her house there was nobody home. Jimmy and I walked around the flat yelling into windows, hoping that she would pop out of the dark rooms. We had half an hour, at most, to find her. After ten minutes a woman arriving home at a neighbouring flat said she thought our Vietnamese expert had gone to a piano concert in the Wisma Indonesia.

When we arrived, there were several hundred people sitting in the dark listening to the performance. Each of us took one side of the hall and, bent over, we crept past each row whispering loudly the woman's name. After many irate looks and some calls for quiet we found her at the front and rushed back to the office just in time for the speech.

She gave us the lead even before it was finished: "Ho says the peace talks will be held in Paris," and I sent it off. This time, despite the newly installed Vietnamese monitors at the other agencies, we were still seventeen minutes in front — because this time our informant didn't have to drive around to the office and tap on the window.

These beats were worth much to Reuters, as a circular we received later showed. It was from a major New York stockbroking firm to its clients which said: "And we get the Reuter service which seems to have an edge on all other news sources out of Vietnam."

It was the same in Saigon during the war: we had to make sure we were never behind in the announcements from the Follies. Sometimes we managed beats, and on one occasion Derek Blackman engineered a beauty. All the reporters knew the marines had entered the DMZ — a major world story because the Americans (like the North Vietnamese before them) had entered a United Nations no-go zone. But the story was embargoed by the Follies briefers "for callout"; in other words, you could not send it until an American JUSPAO official rang and said: "OK, go." That was a part of what the Americans called "the ground rules".

There was always a danger here that they might ring the

American agencies first and us last so Blackman kept on to his American officer contact in JUSPAO throughout the day. He explained that he wasn't urging that he be given the story first — far from it — but merely asking that he be told the callout time as soon as it was decided. He would not break it, he promised. Finally he was told, at about noon, that the callout would be at 3 p.m. — a vital time because it would just make the last editions of the east coast American morning papers. Blackman knew that it would thus be first-in, first-used when such a story hit New York after the morning papers had been put to bed (prematurely, as it was to turn out). So before 3 p.m. he wrote the story, got it punched up by the telex operator, put it in the autohead and rolled it at exactly the prescribed time — while an American officer began calling all the news organizations with the word to go. It only gave us a few minutes jump but the message came back that night from London: "Congratulations. All east coast American newspapers replate front page splash Reuter story: Marines enter DMZ".

Blackman's American army contact had known that Blackman would never break the callout because reporters who failed to comply with the ground rules could lose their accreditation. The threat was enough to make reporters careful about what they wrote. There was no vetting of copy before it went out, but in a way you vetted your own in order to keep accreditation. Moreover, reporters had a responsibility not to endanger the troops. It wasn't much use having soldiers in a battle if a reporter sent off a story saying: "And tomorrow the Americans are going to push six miles further to the east with no air cover or reinforcements for two days."

The US military had an advantage in that by far the great majority of stories that went out to the world were written from the Follies conference or the morning press release — and the authorities had all the information for these and could think carefully about how to announce any event. For example, defeats could be glossed over or attempts made to make them sound like victories.

Even if a reporter in the field saw the story as an eye-witness it could be officially denied to the other hundred reporters. What was just one small report stacked up against a pile of official announcements and denials? Like the battle of Loc Ninh.

With David Greenway of *Time* magazine and Bernie Weinraub of the *New York Times* I walked slowly, almost leisurely, down the winding track into the district capital of Loc Ninh near the Cambodian border. We could hear the occasional distant rifle shot — but that was not unusual in Vietnam.

"Hey. Are you guys armed?" called an American special forces man from behind his automatic rifle and a wall. We were not. "There are Viet Cong in there," he said, sounding worried. We had come to Loc Ninh to see an American victory. It was late in October, 1967. The American briefers in Saigon had announced that the Viet Cong had twice assaulted Loc Ninh, but had been driven off, leaving nine hundred guerrillas dead. One American writer immediately hailed this battle as a turning point in the war.

When we got there we found that the government camp and the US special forces position had indeed successfully, and intrepidly, held off assaults from large Viet Cong forces. But these positions were not even in the town of Loc Ninh: they were a kilometre away at the airstrip. The rubber plantation trees that lined the airstrip were broken and shattered — the result of fire from one US artillery piece that had been levelled — that's when you know you are in trouble; it was levelled so as to bounce no less than five hundred shells off the strip, spraying the attacking Viet Cong with shrapnel.

The special forces men said the Viet Cong were "all drugged up". They said they had to be because "you shoot them four times and they just keep coming." I felt this was better explained by the motivation of fighting foreign forces on home soil. An army doctor had found some white powder after a fight north of Saigon and said he thought it was heroin: "Drug-crazed reds hit US base" made headlines around the world. But one reporter took the powder and had it analysed: it was washing powder. Also I had heard *New York Times* reporter Tom Buckley suggest that since drugs like heroin are designed to put the user on cloud nine so everyone is a friend, "anyone taking drugs won't want to attack: he'll want to fall asleep."

In the course of the interview on the Americans' heroic stand, the special forces soldiers chanced to mention that the Viet Cong had held Loc Ninh for three days and nights — the town that was supposed, in Saigon, to have so gloriously defended itself against the Viet Cong. "It's a ghost town now. We led two attempts to fight our way back into the town and both failed. They've still got the town and all the people have left," a soldier said.

Greenway, Weinraub, and I ventured slowly to the central market. The town was empty except for ARVN soldiers drinking beer in the market or guarding the streets. The few of the population of seven thousand still around were preparing to leave. Market buildings had been burnt to the ground. Clay bottles lay piled in the burnt rubbish. Government buildings, police posts, and a dispensary had all been blown up and were smouldering ruins. Almost the entire population of the town had fled south down the highway.

Vietnamese soldiers carried ducks and other goods, the spoils of war, and Greenway borrowed a duck to have his picture taken while sporadic rifle fire echoed through the streets. He explained that his daughter in Hong Kong was crazy about ducks and, to keep her happy, he had told her not to worry about him in Vietnam because he had a pet duck. Here was living proof.

Back at the airstrip a big silver C-130 was broken down in the middle of the bumpy runway that had been shot up by the bouncing artillery. Everyone stood to watch as a second C-130 came in to land. It pulled up short of the broken-down plane with only metres to spare, and a big, happy pilot climbed out. Weinraub and I asked for a lift back to Saigon. "Sure, hop in," he said.

We sat behind him and his co-pilot and navigator in the cockpit of the huge empty plane. He looked down the runway which disappeared over a slight rise to the special forces camp with its big gun, still levelled, at the other end. "We should just about do it," he said after doing a U-turn, and pulled the accelerator handle back with the brakes fully on until the plane strained to go like a dog on a leash.

Suddenly he let go and we roared along, bouncing through partially repaired artillery holes, past the wrecked rubber trees shattered by the shells. We began to lift and I could feel the unfamiliar weightlessness of the plane. Somehow we cleared the artillery piece at the end of the runway. "We don't want to take dings," yelled the pilot, almost brushing the rubber trees as we circled low and close to the camp — for at tree-top level a plane moves too fast to be shot at: the great danger time is climbing the first thousand metres.

Now we were up a bit we could see American jets dive-bombing presumed Viet Cong positions disconcertingly close to where we had been walking. Then, directly over the camp, the pilot pointed the aircraft skywards and we roared straight up — at least it seemed straight up. And up. Like a moon rocket. The pressure pushed me down in my seat. I looked at Weinraub and he gave me a look which said: "Don't ask me." I tried to lift my left arm against the thrust but it was pushed back down by the pressure of acceleration. The pilot was going to Bien Hoa but said he would divert the plane and drop us in Saigon. This was typical of the Americans' friendliness.

That night I filed my story from Saigon that the Viet Cong had held Loc Ninh for three days while American military personnel were claiming it held out in a significant victory; that Loc Ninh was deserted; that there were five thousand or more refugees. I quoted one Vietnamese official as saying: "From now on anywhere within fifty miles of Loc Ninh if the Vietcong say jump, the people will jump."

At 4 o'clock the next morning the phone in the Reuter office awoke Pringle. It was an American colonel. He wanted it known that the American command was not happy with the story. "What is the specific complaint?" asked Pringle. "You are not reporting this as a victory and it is one of our most telling victories," was the reply. That afternoon a friendly American spokesman dropped into the office: "Why did you have to write it that way? Why couldn't you have written about the staunch defence of the lone artillery piece . . . the large numbers of Viet Cong dead?" he asked sincerely, mystified that I saw it differently from him. I told him my office had already written all that from the US briefings, including statements that the Viet Cong had attacked "behind walls of civilians". But not one had told us that Loc Ninh had been lost: that five thousand people or more had been forced to evacuate.

That day at the first press conference of the new Vietnamese prime minister Nguyen Van Loc a Vietnamese reporter asked him if he was going to do anything about a "false report from a foreign newsagency that Loc Ninh was captured". He said "appropriate measures" would be taken after he had met with his cabinet. To an American reporter's follow-up question: "Is censorship to be imposed on this foreign press?" the prime minister said no, but action would be taken in this case.

At the afternoon Follies, I saw my closest friend among the American announcers, or he saw me. "They are very angry," he said. He then showed me a message from Washington that he said he would never have shown to anyone else: "Reuters correspondent Hugh Lunn erroneously reporting that Loc Ninh held by the Viet Cong for three days and nights. He says it is the district capital (it is not, An Loc is). He says it has a population of 7,000. It is a village of a few hundred. He does not report the military successes as a victory."

My friend told me a team of three had been assigned to investigate. But they already knew that Loc Ninh *was* the district capital, and that An Loc *was* the smaller province capital. Also that Loc Ninh *did* have a population of seven thousand. If I had been wrong I stood to lose my accreditation card. But three days later my friend phoned. "Don't worry," he said. "They know what the score is now. You won't hear any more about it." And, of course, nor would the world. To them, no doubt, the battle at Loc Ninh was successfully portrayed as a victory, since 99 per cent of the stories were reports of the official announcements.

But to me, although Loc Ninh, militarily, was lost for only three days, the people living in that area knew that they could not be provided with security: that if the Viet Cong wanted to they could take the entire town.

In that sense Loc Ninh was lost, forever.

There were various techniques that could be applied to unfavourable news at the Follies that either dampened its impact or killed its story value altogether. The best example of this concerned the A Shau Valley in South Vietnam. It is hard for people who weren't there to believe this: the A Shau Valley was about 80 kilometres long and it was such a North Vietnamese stronghold that they had a four-lane road running through bearing trucks, and with bulldozers to fill the bomb holes.

Reporters who wanted to have a go at the marines used to say: "When are you going into the A Shau Valley?" and the usual reply was "Well, are you comin' in with us?" Towards the end of 1967 the 1st Air Cavalry Division, which had four hundred helicopters, finally went in instead of the marines who were bearing the brunt of the fighting below the DMZ.

Bruce Pigott, a Reuters reporter who had recently arrived in Vietnam, went in with them and somehow or other got out. He filed a story I will always remember:

"A Shau Valley, South Vietnam, Reuter — American helicopters were shot out of the sky like gas-filled balloons

85

here today . . ." and he reported that forty-five helicopters had been shot down in the assault. We got the story in Saigon and, at the same time, a phone call from MACV saying that this operation was embargoed and that they were only releasing, officially, fifteen of the downed helicopters. This was accepted as an accreditation instruction by everyone and the world was told that the 1st Air Cavalry lost fifteen helicopters on its assault. Although it was a lie, the American military would have argued, with some merit, that they could not encourage the enemy, in the middle of the battle, to think the Americans were vulnerable to attack.

Obviously the Americans knew they couldn't get away with that completely, because once the danger was past someone would write the true story, making it bigger by calling it a cover-up. So, after about twelve hours, they released the second lot of fifteen helicopters — and so all the agencies said: "Another fifteen helicopters have been shot down in the A Shau Valley." And, the next day, the third fifteen were released and that story went out too — but I never heard of it appearing anywhere or causing any trouble and I am sure it had the desired effect on editors around the world, who would have said: "Shit, we've got this bloody fifteen helicopters from the A Shau Valley again. We've had it three times this week." It was really a brilliant means of making the whole story disappear into the voluminous bins newspaper offices keep for the huge number of stories they don't have space to run. And it prevented Reuters from using Pigott's brilliant "gas-filled balloons" introduction because, with fifteen helicopters, it sounded a bit distasteful, an exaggeration.

Another effective way to make a story disappear was to bury it in a terminological gloss of euphemisms, acronyms and trite analogies. For example, at the Follies the briefer would use words such as Free World forces, negative, I Corp, free fire zone, dust-off, Chicom rockets and WHAMO to ensure reporters like me were continually kept off balance.

A typical announcement might begin: "There was a major battle 80 klicks [kilometres] northwest of Saigon and there were 45 enemy KIA, 16 enemy WIA, 17 enemy KBA, and 22 enemy WBLCs were sunk." I remember the reporter from the *Times*, Fred Emery, asking the following questions of a Follies announcer when he first arrived.

Emery: "Could you tell us what that all means?"

ANNOUNCER: "If you don't know the rules sir you can't play the game."

Emery: "I assume KIA is killed in action, WIA wounded in action, KBA presumably killed by air, but what is WBLC?"

ANNOUNCER: "That's a waterborne logistics craft, sir."

Emery: "Is that a sampan?"

ANNOUNCER: "That's correct."

Playing the game was all too easy: the system got inside your mind. A spokesman might use the word "enemy" four times in one sentence. Although I knew I was supposed to be an independent journalist writing an independent coverage I sat there one night after a few months in Vietnam and found myself writing about "the enemy" because it had been drummed into me at these press conferences. It was the same with the phrase "Viet Cong-infested-jungle" which put the Viet Cong, subconsciously at least, on a par with cockroaches.

At the Follies and in press releases and callouts the DMZ was always described as "the six-mile strip of land which divides North Vietnam from South Vietnam". And, in every story I wrote, I typed as my thoughts raced ahead: "the Demilitarized Zone which divides North Vietnam from South Vietnam" . . . until one day I was writing this and Dinh lent over my typewriter and said, "That wrong." Upset, I said, "Listen, how come you are telling me how to write?" to which he replied, "The demilitarized zone not divide North Vietnam from South Vietnam — it divide Vietnam." And, when I thought about it, I agreed there was a big difference.

"The improvement of jungle visibility using weedkillers"

also sounded fair enough to me at the time. But it really meant that millions of litres of untried chemicals were being sprayed over large areas of one country — over people and food. CBUs didn't sound too bad either, but these were cluster bomb units: round, silver, anti-personnel bombs which unleashed thousands of slithers of steel on explosion.

The "free fire zone" was an area that the American military declared was Viet Cong held, and thus anything in that area was enemy and could be killed. Or any plane with some bombs left after a mission could just drop them in a free fire zone before returning to land. In other words, it was a perennial target. To use an acronym for "Free World forces" would have been to lose the propaganda value of the euphemism. For Follies commanders never talked about the role of the Americans when they talked about the war as a whole: they talked about "the Free World forces", hoping to get as many journalists as possible to use the phrase, to help make the war more acceptable. Often it worked, but there were failures. In late 1967 they dropped three million leaflets over North Vietnam saying that anyone who helped an American pilot (who had been bombing North Vietnam) escape would get fifteen grams of gold. An American reporter asked at the press conference how this would be paid, which seemed a logical question, and the PR man up on the stage was in no doubt at all. He looked down at the questioning reporter and said, "It says on the leaflet sir. I'll read it out. It says: 'The money will be paid in any Free World bank.' " "Maybe they have a different version of the Free World," retorted one reporter, and others made similar comments.

When one of the American reporters asked how much the fifteen grams of gold was worth, the briefer said he had anticipated the question and they had worked it out at about US$1,600. The reporter then asked if this had ever been done before. "Yes, we believe this was done at the end of World War Two over Germany," the briefer replied. And Tom Buckley of the *New York Times* — never one to dissemble — stood up and said, "Can you tell us what the going price for a US pilot was then?"

There were many other ways of playing the game. Instead of announcing they were bombing elephants a spokesman would say: "A large elephant was observed sixty klicks [kilometres] west of Pleiku in the Central Highlands. An air strike was called in, and a large secondary explosion was observed." Which made everyone laugh. I found it an amusing, if awesome, image: an elephant exploding. But what they really meant, as we worked out later, was that the elephant had been carrying ammunition — which caused the second explosion following the first explosion of their bomb. So they bombed elephants because they believed they were carrying arms. I don't know if elephants were used for this purpose, but I imagine the Viet Cong were using everything available to move rockets and bullets to battle zones. An American colonel had told me when I first arrived: "They use bicycles as utilities and elephants as five-ton trucks."

Not that the Americans wanted to be cruel to elephants. That was the enigma of the war: they would drop napalm and then carefully tend the wounded; they would bomb elephants and then try to organize replacements for villages by buying others from the Montagnard tribes.

Often the American briefers would take a journalist to task for being anti the war, or against them and their announcements, and the usual urge was to "get on the team". Normally this did not happen to newsagency reporters because we were supposed to stick to reporting announcements, and leave the denials to Hanoi. But Jim Pringle, to his credit, saw his job as more than that.

Reuters was not particularly popular though it was treated with respect on account of its network of world purchasers and its reputation for accuracy. The American briefers never did seem to know how to handle non-American writers; and Pringle encouraged their xenophobia with questions such as: "Why is it that you can tell us

89

how many Viet Cong you killed this morning, but the announcement that you accidentally shot up a South Vietnamese village was delayed two full days?"

One frustrated colonel was moved one day to ask him, "How are your friends in Peking?" Pringle replied that neither he nor Reuters had any friends in Peking and that Reuters correspondent, Anthony Gray, was under arrest there. He asked for, and received, a formal apology. The American colonel marched into the office in full dress, saluted Pringle, apologized, and marched out again — to Dinh's astonishment, and everlasting admiration.

Another way the American military had of dealing with difficult questions when the press were unkind enough to suggest that they might not be winning the war was to say: "The light is at the end of the tunnel," or, "We're over the hump" or "rounding the corner". Lee Lescaze of the *Washington Post* killed the tunnel one when he wrote a story that began:

> "A year ago none of us could see victory. There wasn't a prayer. Now we can see it clearly, like light at the end of a tunnel." An American official told *Time* magazine this in September 1953, eight months before the light went out for the French at Dien Bien Phu.

It became such a standing joke among reporters that for a New Year's Eve party they threw in 1967 the invitation said: "Come and see the light at the end of the tunnel".

Actually one American official tried to blind everyone with the light at the end of the tunnel towards the end of 1967 by using computer-analysed figures to *prove* that the Americans were winning. He was in charge of what they called "pacification", which really meant getting everybody under control.

His analysis took about six months of pouring figures into a computer about who was on whose side in Vietnam. He divided the 12,600 hamlets in the South Vietnamese countryside into six classifications ranging from complete government control to complete Viet Cong control. From there he worked out how many people in the villages of South Vietnam were under American-backed government control. The following were his figures.

A	Complete government control	660,000
B	Almost secure	3,460,000
C	Government clearly dominant, but perhaps half of guerrilla forces still on duty. Viet Cong still collect taxes	4,117,000
D	VC terrorism, night activities. Guerrilla forces two-thirds intact	2,103,000
E	Minimal government presence	331,000
V	VC Supremacy	3,989,000

It soon became clear why what should have been item F had been labelled V: the official saw items A to E as under government control, and the last item as under Viet Cong control. To make the distinction in the press release a horizontal line was drawn between items E and V.

It was claimed that the figures showed that two-thirds of the villagers in South Vietnam were under government control. But journalists covering the war were puzzled and then shocked by the figures. Instead of placing the line between E and V they drew it under A and concluded that less than one in twenty Vietnamese villagers were in wholly secure areas: a frightening figure after years of war and with more than half a million US troops (and 100,000 allies) in the country.

It was about this time that many journalists in Saigon were starting to change their minds about the war and were beginning to think that maybe American military might was not prevailing. These figures only confirmed their worst suspicions. They compared figures A and V and noted that 30 per cent of villagers were listed as under total Viet Cong control but only 5 per cent under total government control. And they noted a single attack could turn C hamlets into D hamlets at any time. As one reporter said as he whistled at the figures, "A C hamlet remains a C at the discretion of the Viet Cong."

That was one attempt to build up a facade that went wrong: when the system backfired the disasters were obvious. But nobody knows how often the system worked to perfection. I imagine it was almost every time.

Sometimes the military PR machine appeared to allow journalists behind the carefully tended facade by holding "background" or "off-the-record" or "deep background" briefings. This is a common method all over the world of passing on views to reporters (ever eager for a story) about something you want published but aren't prepared to put your name to. It was particularly effective when you were trying to control a huge press corps you knew were in heavy competition on the biggest news in the world: most reporters would happily grab any extra information and write it. If you were in a position to call a press conference and say something on background you could be certain that they would all have to write it because they knew everyone else would. Even if the story could be proved to be untrue, which was rarely possible, no military official could be left looking like a liar since no attribution was permitted to either a name or specific title.

The off-the-record or background ploy was particularly effective if the military wanted everybody to stop writing about a certain embarrassing battle or event that had made them look bad — and if they didn't want to get caught out telling lies. Some of the more cynical journalists felt the best thing the Americans could do at that stage in Vietnam was to announce at a massive "deep background" Follies that they had won the war. This would have immediately been reported by all the newsagencies and, once published, editors around the world would have demanded more on the end of the war from their men on the spot.

To understand how effective this sort of announcement is it is necessary to realize that it doesn't matter if the journalist on the spot doesn't believe it: the agencies merely quote the spokesperson. Even the big-name journalists in Vietnam, most of whom filed through our office, would get long memos from New York or London saying something like: "Everyone here is wondering this and this and this. Send 1,500 words explaining why." It wasn't a matter of the journalist just sitting down and bashing out the story he believed the readers were interested in. So if the editor or news editor or features editor saw stories pouring over the wire from newsagencies saying that it had been announced that a certain battle or event was over, then it was over. News media don't want stories about old events. As an editor once warned me, "We don't run serials."

The most important person was often not the correspondent taking risks on the scene in Vietnam, but a journalist sitting in an office in some far-off country. For example, one morning I picked up the American press release at JUSPAO and was amazed to see that they announced three destroyers had been despatched to bombard North Vietnam from the coast, which had never been done before. I ran the two streets back to the office because there was no one back there for me to phone and wrote a story, labelled "urgent" saying something like: "The United States has escalated the Vietnam War by sending three destroyers off the coast of North Vietnam to bombard coastal targets." Often I had written stories warily but this one seemed clear cut and I never gave it a thought that I might have transgressed the rules of writing. But within several minutes I received a blast from the boss of the world desk in London. The rebuke was that it was not my job to decide whether or not this move constituted an escalation of the war: my job was merely to report that three destroyers had attacked. I was more worried than amazed, and then watched the story come back with the reference to escalation deleted.

This was one end of the problem — the rewriting that went on in the London head office by those who wanted to make our stories "clearer". (I had been guilty of this myself on the world desk.) At the other end, when the story reached newspaper offices it would again be edited by a subeditor whose job it was to put a heading on the story, place it in the paper, cut it to fit — and make it read so he or she, too, knew what it meant. With an agency story parts of it would probably be married with other agency stories or with their own correspondent's story — or else it would be rewritten to avoid any chance of having the same story as the opposition papers or the radio or TV. Often papers seemed to find it unnecessary to include "an American spokesman said". Which left it as us or, more significantly, Reuters saying it, not the US military announcer.

Even in between the two ends there might be other editorial interference, which was the case in Australia. There the system was that instead of all the papers having stories pouring into their offices from all four newsagencies a newspaper-owned consortium called Australian Associated Press (AAP) bought them all and tailored them to a single service; almost every newspaper, radio and TV station in the country received the news in this form. Consequently papers wouldn't see the Reuter version of a battle, even if they wanted to. A journalist sitting at a desk in AAP's Sydney office would look at all four wire services and either discard three in favour of the fourth or else blend a few of them. The people who did this were, in my experience, as young as Reuter correspondents in Vietnam — often in their early twenties. Yet it was their decision what news virtually one whole nation would hear.

Sometimes Reuters' name would appear in Australian newspapers on stories sent by the American agencies. I presume this happened because of the haste with which everything is done in newspaper offices, and the fact that many subeditors seemed to assume then that almost anything from AAP was a Reuter story — which, in fact, was far from true. Anyway, to subeditors sitting in Brisbane or Sydney what did it really matter?

As an Australian I was unhappy that AAP seemed to favour the American agencies ahead of Reuters at that time. When I returned to Australia in March 1968 I agreed to do a week with AAP in Sydney so I could complain about this. Naturally, in a busy newsagency, no one was very interested in such an esoteric problem, though one desk subeditor did say that the Americans were faster into Sydney than Reuters. Also, he said, the leads to the American stories were more exciting and suited radio and TV, which AAP had to think of as well as the papers. While I was there he was putting out an AP story instead of the Reuter one which looked better to me. The AP one was the usual cliched lead written from Saigon, something like: "Fierce jungle fighting has broken out in . . ." And he commented, "If it hasn't got 'fierce' in the first paragraph then I don't put it out."

The best example of AAP's penchant for stories in radio–TV style was when Jim Pringle went to the Mekong Delta in a press party flown down to see a Viet Cong defeat. The American wire services sent out their story like this: "One hundred and eighty-nine Viet Cong guerrillas have been killed in one of the biggest battles ever in the Mekong Delta. The battle erupted at dusk yesterday and American gunships firing gatling guns at 6,000 rounds per minute were called in during fierce fighting."

Jim Pringle didn't write that. Such stories were hard to avoid if a reporter had merely covered a press conference but, if you were actually there, surely a reporter could do better than make the results of a battle sound like an announcement. Pringle wrote: "Viet Cong child soldiers lay like broken dolls along the banks of this canal today and an American sergeant said: 'If they're old enough to pull a trigger they're old enough to die.' "

The London *Sunday Times* ran Pringle's story on the front page with his by-line. But AAP preferred the American version. I asked a subeditor at AAP who remembered the story why, and he replied, "Pringle's story was more of a feature. You couldn't have read it over the radio."

The worst example I saw of a breakdown in understanding along the long line from Vietnam to the public, came out of a Viet Cong mortar attack on Can Tho, the biggest city in the Mekong Delta.

With AP and UPI reporters I flew to Can Tho by helicopter from Saigon after it was announced a Viet Cong mortar attack had killed 30 and wounded about 150. The wind whipped about that morning making it difficult for the helicopter pilot to take off. At the American military head-quarters for the Delta in Can Tho, some officers showed us what had happened: the Viet Cong had set up mortars five kilómetres away and apparently zeroed them in on the US military headquarters, and the government Delta head-quarters two kilometres away.

But the strong crosswind that day carried the bombs into a government military hospital next to the American head-quarters, and into a thickly populated area next to the government headquarters. We visited the province hospital where the wounded were being treated. A mother fainted as she saw her young son with a big, bloody hole in his back; bandaged babies and mothers were in the same beds; a small Vietnamese man sat on his wife's bed fanning her head which had been wounded beyond recognition. There were two patients to a bed, and American male nurses in blue uniforms raced around treating them, carefully stepping between male patients lying untreated on the floor. A doctor showed me those they were not trying to save at one end of the hospital. Relatives stood outside crying, watching patients on stretchers being raced out by concerned US soldiers to be flown to nearby hospitals for urgent treatment. As usual, the Americans worked slavishly to save lives in a war where hundreds of thousands were dying.

A month later, in an old American newspaper, I read a UPI story on what happened that day. It began: "Viet Cong guerrillas crept up out of the rice paddies and with bombs and guns killed the people in their hospital beds."

I guessed it had come out of the Five O'Clock Follies — or had been rewritten in New York.

Big monkeys

While the Americans happily called the Vietnamese "gooks", most did not know that the Vietnamese called them "Khi Dot", or big monkeys. According to Dinh the clandestine Viet Cong radio always used "Khi Dot" when speaking of the Americans. This was presumably about as often as Americans talked about the "gooks", or "slopes", or "dinks" — but almost always "gooks". Why the Vietnamese thought the Americans looked any more like monkeys than anyone else, I couldn't imagine. However, as it turned out, it was not so much a reference to American looks, as a comment on their habits.

Girlie bars were a favourite terrorist focal point from the outset of the war, presumably because there were always lots of Americans there and less stigma attached to blowing them up in such a place. For safety, wire grenade guards were fitted over the doors and windows. As the Americans sat talking loudly in the steamy bars, their shirts unbuttoned far enough to reveal chests that to the Vietnamese were strangely hairy, they looked for all the world from the outside like people in a cage. Yabbering, hairy, and very big: the big monkeys.

It was the clash between two vastly different races which made the American effort in Vietnam so difficult — and who better to bring this home to me than a friendly CIA pilot. I was in Hue, seven hundred kilometres north of Saigon, waiting for a lift back to Danang. After four hours a small twin-engined Beechcraft landed on the tiny strip inside the walled citadel. It was an Air America plane, which I later found out was the CIA airline in Vietnam. Several Americans climbed out accompanied by an important-looking Vietnamese man dressed in a Western-style blue suit. They appeared to be embassy personnel and visitors. The younger Americans could have come straight out of a Graham Greene novel — one of them even carried a small book called something like "Communist Subversion in South-East Asia".

The pilot, tall and lean, had been a fighter-pilot against the Japanese in the second world war. He had had plenty of Aussie mates then, he told me, and said he would be glad if I jumped aboard. Back on the plane the American civilians invited their Vietnamese guest to sit up in the spare co-pilot's seat in the cockpit. I was in a back seat. "Get out of here," said the pilot to the Vietnamese. "It's all right," called an American civilian. "We told him to sit up there." "Then you just get him out of here," demanded the pilot.

The dejected Vietnamese dignitary, insulted, returned to his seat and the embarrassed embassy man reassured him, saying that no doubt the pilot liked to fly alone. But soon there was a call from the front: "That correspondent down the back, come up here with me." I obeyed. "Don't want any gooks in here," the pilot said loudly as I climbed in. "You never know what they might grab if we have any trouble on take off."

It reminded me of an American I'd seen who was sitting on the edge of a bomb crater and talking about the difficulties of fighting the war. At least it was good to be in War Zone C because here there were no villages and everyone was enemy, he said. Then he told of the best way to end the war, an idea I was often to hear repeated. "We should build a huge ship at least two miles long and go around this goddamn country and collect all the Vietnamese we know for sure are definitely on our side and put them on that ship. Then we should sail that ship out fifty miles to sea. Then we should go through this country and kill every gook we see until there are absolutely none left."

He paused.

". . . and then we should sink that goddamn ship."

It was attitudes such as this that lost the Americans a lot of their credibility with the South Vietnamese. Dinh knew that they weren't going about winning over his people in the right way, and this worried him because he did not want to live what he saw as a drab life under communism. "The Viet Cong have more spirit to fight", he said, "because they see Americans occupy their country."

And he was right, as an incident at Tam Ky prison showed. Sometimes I couldn't work out if the things the Viet Cong did were very stupid or very brave, but Dinh consoled me. "We have old saying: It take a lifetime for a Vietnamese to understand the Vietnamese. What hope you, Gunsmoke?"

In successive raids the Viet Cong had released prisoners — most of them Viet Cong — from three of the five northern province capital prisons. It was a safe bet that the province capital Tam Ky was probably next on the list, so its prison holding eight hundred had been turned into a fortress. The Viet Cong surely knew this: they were local guerrillas with relatives and friends in town. But still they attacked.

For the Viet Cong to take Tam Ky prison they had to assault thick, three-metre high, bunkered, hard-mud walls mounted with troops and mutually supporting machinegun posts on the corners. An adjacent ammunition depot and combat-police school were also heavily defended. Between the Viet Cong and the walls were eight rows of barbed wire, ten metres apart, across a green, open, paddy field. To send a thousand men across that field would have been suicide. The Viet Cong sent fifty. They were in black or khaki shorts and shirts, or bare chested. They were very young. Some carried modern automatic Chinese weapons, others old carbines. One Viet Cong had a black American M-16.

The bodies of these guerrillas in shorts were draped over the barbed wire in a trail where they had cut their way through to the walls. Somehow, I can't imagine how, they

99

took a whole corner of the wall — but they now lay dead in a trail through the streets of Tam Ky. All who attacked had died. They had no shoes and no ammunition. Only rifles. One entire leg lay ownerless at the corner of a wall. In the bunker, still clinging to the machinegun, were two young boys. They were about thirteen years old. A government officer swallowed and, with surprising reverence, almost whispered, "Brothers". And they were his enemy.

Some ARVN soldiers arranged the dead guerrillas — in one-man bunker holes like flowers in flower pots. I watched as tiny-tots unwrapped green sweets and put them in the open mouth of one grotesquely twisted Viet Cong. (I wrote this in my story, but by the time it left London it read "Children, used to war, stuck twigs in the mouth of a dead guerrilla.")

The local Americans were so chuffed with this undeniable victory over their famed enemy that the bodies were left there all day for the visiting local population to see and realize that the Viet Cong could be defeated. But, as I watched elderly Vietnamese women in conical straw hats slowly walking past the bodies, perhaps looking for that familiar face, I wondered if it might not have the reverse effect. And why had the children tried to feed a dead guerrilla their lollies?

But the most surprising thing was that it was not the fortifications which had saved the prison, nor the state of readiness of the defenders: the Viet Cong had been out-generalled. A troop of a dozen US armoured cars had been hidden in the scrub nearby for several days waiting for the moon to wane and the Viet Cong to attack. The Americans came down the dirt street with blazing machineguns shooting the guerrillas into drains in an unexpected and swift attack from behind: just as the Viet Cong were capturing the defences.

The American troops said that if it hadn't been for the armoured cars the attack would almost certainly have succeeded; it had been so ferocious.

To try to overcome the difficulty of fighting among another race the Americans devised many techniques designed to convince the majority of Vietnamese that they were on their side — and that they were the winning side. One of these techniques they called "psywar" or psychological warfare. It came in many forms: and leaving the dead guerrillas' bodies on display at Tam Ky was one of them.

Once near the Cambodian border I caught a lift on a helicopter which started emitting a terrible whining noise as we cruised just above the jungle. Sitting on the floor was a Vietnamese soldier speaking into a microphone in Vietnamese. An American was telling him in English what to say. The loudspeaker was strapped beneath the chopper. "Tell 'em that what they have seen so far is nothin' compared with what is coming." "Tell them to surrender." The only problem I could see was that we didn't really know what the Vietnamese soldier was saying in his own language. For all we knew he could have been giving them intelligence information — blaring it to the jungles — if he wished. But I guess that is a risk of fighting a war in a country where you don't understand the language.

Inside the helicopter the psywar operations were directed by a young Chicago lawyer, Captain Greg Bembinster, aged twenty-six. We were about twelve kilometres from the border and Captain Bembinster was saying: "Tell them we have them surrounded, to come out of their bunkers and they will not be harmed. But if they stay and fight they will be destroyed. Tell them they will be well treated . . . and to bring their weapons." I was surprised we were not being shot at because we were moving so slowly, but Bembinster said this was not an indication that the Viet Cong were happy to let us fly around. Psywar choppers were a prime target, he said. "Normally they are instructed not to shoot at a lone copter except if it's a psywar aircraft."

Sometimes we used tapes and blared announcements from previous defectors. For thirty minutes we psywarred around ten square kilometres. There were seven teams doing this twice a day in this border area: a lot of money for a total of three defections in the entire operation. In any case, it seemed to me, one could never be sure if a defector was a real Viet Cong, or, if he were, was he a real defector?

The helicopter was also dropping leaflets saying: "You will be well treated," which seemed pretty pointless to me. I could imagine the reaction of Australians if Vietnamese flew over them in the bush and said: "Surrender and you will be well treated." It would arouse enough suspicion to keep up a fighting edge for days. In any case, with the noise of the helicopter and of surrounding guns and artillery, it probably would have been impossible to understand the loudspeaker from down on the ground. Not only did the exercise seem a waste of time, but it seemed a very dangerous waste of time flying so low and so slowly. I suggested we go a bit higher, but the pilot — who kept turning around and shouting comments — said that with the big operation going on around us we risked getting hit by American artillery if we got up much higher. Which didn't leave much room for manoeuvre.

The Americans often had the idea in Vietnam that various tactics were going to scare the Viet Cong into sudden surrender, things that I would never have imagined would scare a group that had been almost constantly at war for more than a generation. For example, they painted sharks' teeth on the nose of their planes to give a monstrous living face to the machines of destruction. They favoured B-52 bombing raids because this way the bombs dropped from out of sight and sound — they appeared as if from nowhere. The leaflets they floated into the jungles showed tanks as semi-human machines with eyes and long claws, and breathing fire, but whom did they expect to believe that? One marine told me how he had been in Vietnam once before, in the early sixties, when the United States shipped out six thousand marines and marched them shoulder-to-shoulder in full battle-pack up the main street of Danang;

then they shipped them down to Saigon for the same display — and sent them back to America. They had given the Vietnamese guerrillas a dire warning of the might that awaited them if they didn't give in.

This psywar was all part of a programme given various jargon titles such as "revolutionary development", "pacification", or "WHAMO", which stood for "Winning the hearts and minds of". Overall this was called "the other war". It also involved sending young civilian American officials to small towns to live and work with nearby villagers with sufficient funds to employ locals to build bridges and roads, and generally help make life easier for the people. This was where the term "pacification" came from: constructing a bridge across a stream that had separated people for years would help pacify them — make them less hostile towards the Americans.

I went to meet one of these "revolutionary development workers" because he had quite a reputation, even with the military, as a successful pacifist. His name was Jim Pratt, a thirty-four-year-old former marine turned volunteer from Salt Lake City, who had just been put into an area of thirty hamlets which until a few months before had been controlled by the Viet Cong. Pratt, and a few more like him, were working to win these people to the government's side. Each had the backing of fifty-nine Vietnamese government "cadres" who worked as a team. Pratt had just volunteered to stay on for another twelve months.

The hamlets were in the province of Binh Thuan, about 160 kilometres northeast of Saigon; the province was said to be a "testing ground" for the whole country because all of the physical characteristics of South Vietnam were there. There was a long coastline for infiltration; the borders were lined with rugged mountains where guerrillas could seek refuge; the huge Le Hong Phong forest was an ideal Viet Cong hideout; and, in the south, a fertile rice basin supplied everyone — including the Viet Cong — with food.

Pratt was squatting in the dust of Dai-Hoa, one of the

villages, when I arrived. He was joking in Vietnamese with the laughing villagers — or at least the women, old men, and very young boys among them. Outside there were two dead Viet Cong in the sun, like rotting shot animals in clothes, left as reminders by American troops in the area. More psywar. Pratt was talking to the hamlet elders and instructing the members of his team. They had stopped work on the crudely made school building and a new concrete well. He explained to me that we were next door to a Viet Cong-controlled village, but these people were now sending their children across to the government school, which he felt showed the Americans were achieving pacification.

The peasants proudly showed me their children and their government family-book, which was a record of all the people in the family so the government could find out if anyone was missing. Pratt said the missing men were either in the South Vietnamese army or had been recruited by the Viet Cong, depending on who got to them first. Clearly, the villagers liked Pratt. He told me proudly that at all the villages they called him "the man who smiles".

A short distance outside the village Pratt stopped the car to ask some small boys if any Viet Cong were around. He smiled. The children laughed. He ruffled their hair. This was how he had managed to stay alive so long — the kids knew what was going on and would tell him if the Viet Cong were in the area. A big man with a lot of ideals about working with the people, Pratt was still a realist and carried an M-16 rifle in his left hand, though his build made the rifle look like a toy. He was a very unusual, rugged, happy type — and if anyone could make a success of this job he could. Even his outfit showed that in him the two sides in the war had attained some sort of harmony: he wore Viet Cong-style black pyjamas and cowboy boots. As he sat sipping sweet, sickly-smelling Vietnamese tea from a handle-less cup, children played barefoot in the dust, and bearded old men and young peasant women did all the work. They probably didn't care that until six weeks ago they had been doing what the Viet Cong wanted, and now they obeyed government officials. The old men watched with that knowing unfocused look, no doubt remembering that the Viet Cong took over two years previously and bearing in mind that they might well do so again.

Pratt's boss, Chet Richardson, a fifty-one-year-old former marine major, had been directing these "other war" operations in this province for three years. He didn't seem to have the optimistic outlook of the Follies briefers in Saigon. We drank orange juice in a small shop made out of old wood and sheets of galvanized iron. He had seen the Viet Cong take over most of the surrounding hamlets in those three years — and then saw the government and American forces move them out again. Now they were back about where they started. Richardson refused to use the impressive Follies word "cadres" for the members of the government teams working in these hamlets. "Cadre is the wrong name. They are just ordinary Joes, some draft dodgers, some dedicated. Mostly they are just the men left after the army and militia have finished picking." As his mood became more sombre the high hopes held out for WHAMO in Saigon disappeared faster than the orange juice in the hot tin shed. "And mostly it depends on these team members. *They* have to do it. Not Jim Pratt. If Jim Pratt did it, who would do it after Jim Pratt goes home — or after Jim Pratt's successor goes?" Thus it was back to the old problem for the Americans — in the war, or in the "other war" — just about everyone was there for a year, but the Vietnamese were there forever.

When I got back to Saigon I couldn't sleep in my safe room at the Continental for wondering why the Viet Cong didn't knock off a dangerous man like Jim Pratt in case he did win too many hearts, even if not minds. But Dinh said that while Pratt was fixing taps and digging wells and building bridges the Viet Cong would leave him alone because, in a way, he was helping them as well. And it would be "bad propagandants to stop him to do that". Also the Jim Pratts were probably no real threat because there were so many places that were so insecure they couldn't go there. Thus the work of these civilians was limited to militarily safe areas. The "other war" was really only being fought in areas of peace.

The American marine brass in the five northern provinces, where fighting was heaviest, were quick to realize this limitation, and came up with what seemed a good idea at the time. Because it was unsafe to send an individual into an area where the Viet Cong were active, they formed teams of twelve tough, hand-picked, marines to live and work together there. The idea was that these CAP (Combined Action Program) teams, as they were called, would help the villagers by day, and sleep in a tough fortified bunker at night that they would build on the outskirts of the village — shades of a fort in the old west. They were supposed to be supported by local villagers-cum-soldiers — but you can imagine those who remained for this task after the ARVN and the Viet Cong had had their go. This backup was seen as next to useless by the marines — yet another "good Saigon idea".

The presence of the CAP teams didn't stop the Viet Cong from entering the village at night, of course, while the team defended its bunker. But that wasn't supposed to matter. The idea was that the good works done by the marines during the day would make the Viet Cong unwelcome in the village where the hearts and minds were becoming pro-American. To work, the marine force had to be able to hold off any attacks by the Viet Cong angry at their success and, it was estimated, it would take a force of more than two hundred guerrillas to overcome an entrenched CAP bunker at night. Though each morning the twelve marines had to check for mines before starting work.

I went to look at one of the teams and there was no doubt the marines had gone out into the scrub to live with the people.

Along red dirt roads four marines escorted David

Greenway of *Time* magazine and me to the village. Under the tough war conditions in the northern provinces, helping Vietnamese in their villages and giving them security if they promised to be on your side was a huge problem.

The village was nestled in a stand of trees surrounded by patterned rice paddies. We meandered along a small track off the road in single file, keeping ten metres apart in case of a landmine. The shade of the village was like a long, cool drink. In between clusters of trees and bushes were small, leaf-roofed houses with thatched walls. Thick bushes marked them off from the rice paddies — like a wall of security keeping out the heat.

Reluctantly we left the trees to go out into the boiling sunlight for a long walk across paddy banks to a small concrete dam. It was a big day for the local Vietnamese, who had turned out in their best clothes to see a small, shiny WHAMO water pump — courtesy of the CAP team — being tugged to a start. Behind the people an old man sat dejectedly. A marine said he was unhappy because, before the new pump, the village people had had to pay him 20 per cent of their crop to get him to do the pumping on his big pump. With a 30 per cent crop-tax to the Catholic Church for use of their dam, and another 30 per cent to the government it made a lot of tax. So the marines put him out of business, thereby effectively doubling the amount of rice the villagers could keep. "They would still be better off under the Viet Cong with a straight 50 per cent tax, though," a marine said, accepting a fact he obviously did not like.

The locals cheered as the motor turned over and exhaust fumes rose. They cheered again as the precious liquid appeared out of a hose running into the paddy channels to flood the fields. The marine CAP team began celebrating the successful installation of the pump, which had been obtained by what they called "cumshaw", meaning, I gathered, "unofficially somehow or other". It was steaming hot standing out there and, when the first water had been

pumped through, the marines stripped off to their under-
pants and jumped into the cold, green dam. On the other
side was an area the US military had designated as a zone
not to be entered by forces under battalion strength — that
is, at least six hundred. Going for a swim normally would
have seemed like a crazy thing to do in the middle of the
Vietnam rice paddies in "Indian country" especially if you
didn't even leave a guard. But in that sort of heat it was the
only thing to do, and I ripped off my thick green uniform
and jumped in to splash around and be ducked by laughing
marines. It was the coldest, most delightful swim I had ever
had. But each time I came up from under the cool water I
gave the other side of the stream a quick glance. A marine
noticed how wary I was and yelled out, "If a battalion of
Charlies turn up now they'll just have to pinch our clothes
and we're done for."

These CAP operations were staffed by marine volunteers
from farm backgrounds who had been screened for any
anti-Vietnamese prejudices. It made me think that a similar
programme for the entire US force in Vietnam would have
done much more for the war effort. A fast-talking, fast-
thinking marine colonel who spoke Chinese came up with
the CAP idea. He reckoned that if the Americans put one of
these teams into every village in the northern provinces the
war would be over in a year. He openly scoffed at the idea of
the fifty-nine-strong Vietnamese teams in the rest of
Vietnam. "They can't provide the security. But this way —
with a strengthening of marines — you get a backbone for
security and a rapport between the two races," he said.

But to me the CAP teams still appeared too vulnerable to
large-scale assaults. It reminded me of the father who
showed his son seven sticks being broken one at a time and
then the impossibility of breaking the seven together. Even
allowing that in their dug-in positions the units could
withstand an attack from 200 Viet Cong . . . what about
210?

Strangely, the Viet Cong didn't seem to worry about

these teams too much, just as they seemed to ignore the good work of the Jim Pratts. Perhaps they felt that they had the people's minds and hearts anyway. Also, no doubt, the Viet Cong felt they could do more damage to the Americans by shelling their bases, or storming a prison with a thousand men in it, or ambushing a marine battalion that was out in the open looking for a fight, rather than attack heavily entrenched groups such as the CAP teams. With an attack there would also be every chance that a lot of villagers would be killed: which was not what winning hearts and minds was all about for either side.

Every administrator who had anything to do with the Vietnam War had a brilliant plan such as this to make the war work by doing something completely different. It was an obvious sign of the frustration at the administrative level that a war that, from an office window, seemed so winnable was not being won. Many of these plans seemed impractical: such as the one to win over the peasants by giving them a pig. This scheme unfortunately, turned into an allegory of the whole American war effort in Vietnam.

Food wasn't easy to come by because, with all the men and a lot of women away fighting, there wasn't much farming being done. To help overcome this shortfall the Americans sent in tens of thousands of tonnes of rice in bags emblazoned with the symbol of a brown hand shaking hands with a white hand and, of course, the stars and stripes as well so the people would know whom to thank. These bags were in both the Viet Cong base camps I saw, and I'm sure the Viet Cong were grateful. But there is nothing like pork to win over a hungry Asian soul. In the cause of better food for the Vietnamese, some Americans brought out a 150 kilogram pig called George all the way from the United States to help breed bigger, fatter little pigs for Vietnamese tables. The marine CAP squad in the village of Tuilong, just south of Danang, considered George the pride of their outfit. Fat and white, he ate everything that came his way from the Vietnamese, and demanded his way with the local female pigs. But the trouble with George was that he couldn't keep up with the local, skinny, black-and-white Vietnamese pigs who were as fast across the ground as a hungry dog. The big white American pig proved a failure. The villagers in Tuilong didn't really want him because he ate too much but they kept him, presumably because he was delivered by twelve men with automatic rifles. The story was the same for the hundreds of other big hogs brought out by the United States Agency for International Development (USAID) — the organization in charge of pacification.

On one occasion the Americans accidentally killed two elephants in a mountain village in an air strike. Because the elephants were used for important local tasks, the Americans had to replace them if they were going to win back local hearts and minds. It seemed an impossible task, in the midst of war, to herd two elephants up through the mountain jungle. But, believe it or not, they decided to load two three-ton bull elephants on to a C-130 and parachute them into the isolated village of Tra Bon. The elephants were to be drugged and tied to inflated rubber life rafts and the operation was codenamed "Baroom". This announced plan may never have come to pass (I don't know) but it certainly illustrated that the Americans, almost automatically, could find big solutions to small Vietnamese problems.

They also tried to help the Vietnamese plant better strains of rice and increase productivity with the aid of water pumps and chemical fertilizers. However, at the same time the military were using planes to drop chemical defoliants over large tracts of land to destroy all vegetation. The C-130s would load up and fly low over the jungle spraying out the defoliants like a farmer driving his tractor over every inch of a huge field. At that time there was no controversy over the use of the chemicals and no attempt by the Americans to cover up what, in retrospect, was an horrific operation.

The only thing that upset anyone in the Saigon military

about this gruesome operation was that it was yet another brilliant theoretical idea that didn't work. In tropical jungle no sooner did the vegetation die than the sun hit the ground for the first time in centuries and, within months, the regrowth was higher than head height again. And now it was denser at ground level than before, when the canopy of the higher trees had restricted the undergrowth. The guerrillas became harder to find. Such a decision could only have been made by a well-meaning administrator sitting in an office far away. To anyone who had seen all the jungle in Vietnam, for hour after hour beneath a plane or helicopter, the idea of trying to keep it defoliated would have been similar to giving a few people cans of paint and four narrow paintbrushes and telling them to go and paint the bitumen roads in Australia white. Except that the painting job would have been easier.

Even more disastrous for the WHAMO programme were the military decisions to create free fire zones and thus to move all villagers out of their traditional thatched houses in groves of trees "for their own protection". Especially when they were moved to acres of dusty, bulldozed, treeless land behind the protection of rolls of barbed wire on the edge of secure cities and allocated ten sheets of roofing iron and ten bags of cement to build a house.

This is what happened to the sixteen thousand Vietnamese moved out of the Demilitarized Zone in May 1967 in order that the Viet Cong could not — to use Chairman Mao's words — move like fish in the sea of people. Officially listed as "refugees" the people were actually removed by armed soldiers. When, months later, I visited this camp of crowded, shining, tin-roofed huts set on a dirt and dusty treeless plain far from water with Vice-President Nguyen Cao Ky, a dozen people stood dutifully in line to receive gifts from the moustached, purple-scarfed leader. As he moved along the second line, Ky came to an old woman, and spoke to her. Her brow furrowed, her jaw trembled and she broke down and cried uncontrollably. Ky put a hand on her shoulder to comfort her. Slowly she told him she wanted to return to the graves of her people in the Demilitarized Zone. Ky promised her that one day she would return. But the woman could not be consoled.

Nowhere was the failure of the WHAMO programme more apparent than in the so-called Chieu Hoi programme in which deserting Viet Cong were forgiven and then turned over to be re-educated for a time. As I had found out for myself, there were very few genuine Viet Cong defectors. The single major defection of the war was that of a North Vietnamese colonel. He had a wife and several children in the north, yet defected with a young Viet Cong woman he had been fighting with. A journalist friend of mine got the only interview with him and he showed me the article when he finished it. Being a brash twenty-five, I said something like, "Gee, the only reason he deserted was because of the girl", but when I saw the article years later in an American magazine, the reference to her had been removed.

The thing that all these WHAMO programmes had in common was that none of them worked. And the reason they didn't work was because of the war. In peacetime they would have been admired and hailed as innovative and philanthropic. But it isn't the same when you are shooting, napalming, and defoliating at the same time. With more than half a million troops so engaged, you cannot win hearts and minds with a couple of hundred social workers, however dedicated.

This was not the only propaganda failure in Vietnam. The big monkeys also turned their psychological weapons on their own troops. To try to keep them on the straight and narrow, for their own good and the good of WHAMO, the armed forces issued comic-style pamphlets on how to behave. One of these showed pencil sketches of two young American soldiers in Vietnam called John and Droopy — in case the troops didn't get the idea from the story who was the good bloke and who the bad.

Droopy covered his scruffy hair and huge nose with an ill-fitting cap, while John had the good all-American crew-cut and clothes neatly pressed. And, while John was pictured in the library — studying Plato of all things — our friend Droopy was heading down to the girlie bars aboard a cyclo, laden with all sorts of junk he had been buying. In the background a sign read: "Sexy Oriental Bar".

Wanting a break from Plato, John adjourned from the library to the sportsroom for table tennis . . . by which time the naughty Droopy was now in the bar. Above him the signs showed the quick inflation of the high-priced drinks for bar girls with 100 piasters crossed out, 150 crossed out and the going price now 180 — almost US$2. A long-haired, big-lipped ("never happen") Vietnamese girl tickled Droopy's chin telling him: "I luv you too much." Droopy, obviously impressed, had pulled out a wad of notes: "It's soldiers like Droopy who cause inflation in Vietnam," the leaflet warned.

The last we saw of poor Droopy he was hanging out of a bar window blind drunk with an empty bottle of beer in his hand, while John was shown finishing his year "in country", as the Americans would say, with a bankbook full of money entries. "Which one would you like to be, soldier?" the pamphlet asked. Most American troops I saw had come up with the wrong answer.

For a bit more moral uplift there seemed to be a disproportionately high number of chaplains. I was surprised when half an hour after I arrived at Gio Linh on the DMZ the colonel invited me to Mass. Whereas only about one-fifth of Americans are Catholics, here, with shells coming in every now and then, they were all prepared to pray to God through any medium. Most of the base stood in flak jackets and helmets, heads bowed, while the priest officiated. But I think everyone strained with one ear for the first telltale whistle of an artillery shell.

Besides chaplains, other influences were the armed-forces radio which played mainly country and western music and Frank Sinatra, and told the troops to write home often and not to forget to take their malaria pill once a week and sleep under a mosquito net and not stand in crowded groups at bus stops. This last piece of advice, which referred especially to "Downtown Saigon", as they called the city centre, was not in order to keep the footpaths clear for the Vietnamese but to make the soldiers less of a target for the Viet Cong. The troops' newspaper, *Stars and Stripes*, carried stories on how well the American forces were doing. Everyone read it because it was the only newspaper the armed forces had regular access to. To keep morale up, lots of entertainers, film stars, and movies were flown in.

The Americans ran large, military supermarkets in Vietnam at which troops could do all kinds of shopping at bargain prices. Such a store was called a PX, though I never did work out that piece of shorthand, and soldiers could always be seen staggering out under the weight of big tape decks and record players. They were the privilege of American troops and their allies and, despite all my privileges as a correspondent, the one thing my press pass did not authorize me to do was shop at one. (Not surprisingly, all the Asian troops thought all their Lunar New Years had come at once when they found they could buy scarce luxury goods cheaply in these shops and sell them for much more on the extensive black market.)

While this was all very well for the American troops in their base camps, no matter how well they were catered for, sooner or later somebody had to go out in the bush and fight (even though it was estimated that only about one fifth of the troops actually did). There aren't too many ways to lift the spirits of soldiers who are going out to get blown up or shot at when they least expect it — except perhaps to promise them the best medical attention in the world soon after they are hit. It gave hope, and the American psywar machine emphasized that an American wounded at the front, even up near the DMZ, could be on a hospital ship sailing just off the coast being operated on by specialists in twenty minutes. Although it was sometimes impossible for a helicopter to get in to a battle, the American pilots were prepared to take almost any risk in a desperate race to ensure the wounded were evacuated. This was why, by the end of 1967, the Americans had admitted losing more than four thousand helicopters in Vietnam.

Something else the combat troops could look forward to were the traditional tools of military psywar: medals. For combat troops are a bit like sportspeople: many are athletic, young, and fighting for recognition, and the coveted reward for endeavour is often a medal or cup that can be seen by all. An American soldier who was wounded automatically qualified for a purple heart medal. According to the troops, if you were wounded on three occasions you not only got three purple hearts but you never had to fight for your country again: and you could go home. I spoke to a soldier leaving Con Thien and heading home with his third wound. It was to his arm, and what he said showed he had read the look that crossed my face: "It isn't the size of the wounds you get, it's what you go through getting them." And, of course, the soldier was right. Even not getting wounded was a terrible experience.

Overall, finding effective propaganda was difficult for the American command because one of the unusual things about the composition of the American troops was the high proportion of those who were well educated. Many saw holes in some of the psywar arguments. The increase in higher education levels among troops in Vietnam was exaggerated by the drafting of large numbers of university graduates in 1967 who until then had managed to escape the draft. They already knew that the reason the Viet Cong were fighting so well was because of the motivation that fighting at home gave them. Unlike the young committed soldier, and the Saigon command, these reluctant draftees did not talk about the Viet Cong by the impersonal pronoun "he" but rather by the personal name "Charlie": in fact, I found it was almost possible to determine an American soldier's view of the war by seeing which of those two words he used. The word Charlie came from "Victor Charlie" for the initials VC, Viet Cong. When the hawks spoke of the Viet Cong they would say, with a hint of satisfaction: "He's hurting," while the doves among the troops would say: "Charlie's out there someplace."

At the scene of a battle at a place called Landing Zone Gold — just a jungle clearing that the Americans had temporarily occupied — there was one young, university-educated lieutenant who, like many of his kind, never really learned to hate his enemy. The base had come under direct ground assault and they had only just held off the Viet Cong by levelling the guns and firing beehive rounds — artillery shells filled with thousands of little nails shaped like arrows. (These had nailed rifles and arms to the chests of the dead guerrillas.) It was so hot in the jungle that I could not stop drinking cans of the ice-cold chocolate milk that had been specially flown in for the troops . . . and the lieutenant was having an ice cream — that was the sort of war it was. "You know," he said waving his ice cream at the treetops, "poor old Charlie's out in one of those trees someplace and he's looking at you and me and he's just cursing his head off. He's saying to himself: 'Boy we can outshoot 'em, we can out-manoeuvre 'em, we can outfight 'em . . . but hell can they outsupply us.' "

Some of these draftees could even tell stories about the war with undertones of sympathy for their opponents. One told me the story of why one Viet Cong defected: "For months Charlie carried two big mortars down the Ho Chi Minh trail over mountains in Laos, through swamps in Cambodia, hacked his way through the jungle into South Vietnam, and survived a couple of B-52 bombing raids before he made it to his destination. Carefully he placed his precious cargo on the ground and two fellow Viet Cong picked them up, fired them, and turned to him and said: 'Well hurry up, go back and get some more.' "

But these were not the ordinary soldiers — the ones whose only thought on the war was that they wanted to

Hugh Lunn and Dinh. The inscription on the back of this photograph reads: "Dear Gunsmoke, Sent you all my love, Gungadinh".

The author's MACV accreditation card, which gave him American authorization to cover the war. All journalists were required to "get accredited".

Aboard a C–123 aircraft, journalists sit cramped in makeshift seats of harness webbing on a typical press flight lasting many hours. Hugh Lunn is pictured third from the right.

Hugh Lunn wears the American military uniform in the field, a practice adopted by all journalists. It was important to resemble an American soldier so you could be sure the Americans wouldn't shoot you.

Hugh Lunn (centre) and Tom Corpora of UPI interview Captain Frank Southard who had just returned from a disastrous attempt to enter the Demilitarized Zone. He was explaining why the marines' elaborate pincer move into the region had failed.

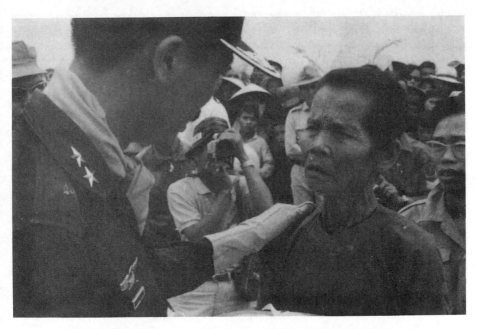

A Vietnamese woman complains to Premier Ky about her forced evacuation from her home in the Demilitarized Zone.

The legendary Jim Pringle in a Saigon market, the man of whom it was said that wars seemed to follow him wherever he went.

Pictured at a Reuter office dinner in Saigon are, from left to right, Richard Beckett, known to many Australians as Sam Orr. Saigon office bureau chief Derek Blackman, Barbara Beck, and Hugh Lunn.

Hugh Lunn at work in Saigon, in the long, narrow Reuter office.

This young girl who lived next door to the Reuter office in Saigon would sometimes drop by to visit her neighbours. Pictured here with Hugh Lunn, she became friends with the reporters, although she could speak no English.

Pham Ngoc Dinh, known always simply as Dinh, poses with his son Trung outside the Reuter office in Saigon. Before long the Reuter sign behind him would end up with a bullet hole in it.

The view from the Reuter reporters' room in the Continental Hotel, Saigon.

Australian reporter Bruce Pigott fell in love with Vietnam and its people the day he stepped off the plane.

Jim Pringle and Hugh Lunn at a party in Saigon.

Hugh Lunn interviews Buddhist monks engaged in an anti-government demonstration in Danang while armed government troops keep a close watch behind barbed-wire barricades.

Colonel Cochrane (left) outside the sleeping quarters of a Viet Cong hide-out discovered in the jungle on a search and destroy mission codenamed "Operation Junction City".

In Phan Thiet province the director of America's pacification programmes
Chet Richardson takes a break with Hugh Lunn in a roadside snack bar
made of corrugated iron walls and roof enclosing a dirt floor.

A technique of American military psywar (psychological warfare) was to
leave the bodies of dead Viet Cong on display as a warning to villagers
that the same fate might be theirs if they joined the guerrillas.

U.S SERVICEMEN!

During the first half of 1966, the US Exp. Corps suffered over 45.000 of casualties.

In the days to come, the number of American casualties will increase manifold.

The more Johnson escalates the war, the greater the danger you are facing.

The war becomes fiercer and fiercer!

If you yourselves don't look for a way out, nobody could help you!

Oppose to your being sent to the battlefront, as the men of the 3rd Brig, 1st US Inf. Div. at Lai Khê did, on last April 66.

If forced to join the battle:
— CROSS OVER TO THE FRONT'S SIDE!
— LET YOURSELVES BE CAPTURED BY THE LIBERATION ARMED FORCES!
— DON'T RESIST, THROW YOUR WEAPONS 5m FAR AWAY AND LIE STILL!
— HAND YOUR WEAPONS OVER TO THE LIBERATION COMBATANTS, QUICKLY FOLLOW THEM OUT TO SAFER AREAS!

That's how to save yourselves from a senseless and useless death! Through the Front's lenient policy, you will be treated with humanity, and the Front will arrange your repatriation as it did with 2 US prisoners George C Smith R.A. 1352278C and Claude Mc Clure R.A. 14703075 on last Nov. 27th 1965.

THINK IT OVER AND ACT QUICKLY!
THIS IS FIRST OF ALL FOR YOUR OWN BENEFIT!

U.S SERVICEMEN!

THE SVN PEOPLE ARE NOT ENEMIES OF THE AMERICAN PEOPLE.

AN INDEPENDENT AND FREE VIETNAM CANNOT BE A THREAT FOR THE U.S.A!

WHY YOU, SONS OF THE AMERICAN PEOPLE ARE YOU MURDERING THE SVN PEOPLE, DESTROYING THEIR HOUSES, VILLAGES AND PROPERTY, TO DIE A SENSELESS AND USELESS DEATH FOR DEFENCE OF THE U.S MONOPOLIST CAPITALISTS' INTERESTS?

★ DON'T MASSACRE CIVILIANS!
★ DON'T DESTROY THEIR HOUSES, VILLAGES AND PROPERTY!
★ DON'T DESTROY THEIR CROPS!

PEACE FOR VIETNAM!

Colored American servicemen!

20 million fellow - countrymen of yours in the U.S.A. are being abused, oppressed, exploited, manhandled, murdered by Racist authorities. You don't forgot the bloody Alabama cases, don't you?

Now, they are misleading you, driving you to S.VN and using your hands to slaughter the South Viêtnamese people who are struggling for PEACE - INDEPENDENCE - FREEDOM-DEMOCRATY - NATIONAL - REUNIFICATION, for EQUALITY and FRIENDSHIP between the peoples all over the world!

Is it conceivable that you resign yourselves to help the US aggressors, the common enemies of Colored Americans and Viêtnamese people, in murdering your Viêtnamese brothers for US monopolist capitalists' sake?

Resolutely oppose to your being sent to the battlefront as the men of the 3rd Brig. 1st US Inf. div. at Lai khê did on April 66.

If forced to join the battle:
— CROSS OVER TO THE FRONT'S SIDE!
— LET YOURSELVES BE CAPTURED BY THE LIBERATION ARMED FORCES!
— DON'T RESIST, THROW YOUR WEAPONS 5m FAR AWAY AND LIE STILL!
— HAND YOUR WEAPONS OVER TO THE LIBERATION COMBATANTS, QUICKLY FOLLOW THEM OUT TO SAFER AREAS!

Though the Front's lenient policy, you will be well treated and the SVNNFL will arrange your repatriation as it did with Claude Mc Clure RA. 14703075, a colored American ... on last Nov. 27, 1955.
prisons

PEACE FOR VIETNAM!

A sample of North Vietnamese propaganda leaflets denouncing the Americans that were distributed in South Vietnam. On the back of each the message appeared in Vietnamese. The Americans used the same technique over North Vietnam, scattering plane-loads of propaganda leaflets from the air.

ARVN (South Vietnamese Army) soldiers wear numerous military decorations — it was one way of keeping morale high.

An aerial view of the flooded Mekong Delta. It was an area the size of Denmark — almost all under water — and a formidable Viet Cong stronghold.

The night after the picture was taken in this street of flowers in central Saigon, the Viet Cong attacked the city in what became known as the Tet Offensive. Hugh Lunn stands beside the white Mini Minor that was to play a crucial role in his life within twenty-four hours.

THE SUNDAY

Viet Cong could do it again, say US leaders in Saigon

By Hugh Lunn, Robert Kaylor and Tom Buckley

Saigon, Saturday

IN A SERIES of bitterly contested battles American and South Vietnamese troops today began to regain control of the country after the Viet Cong's massive offensive against 35 cities and towns in South Vietnam. In the capital of Saigon, the Viet Cong appeared to be withdrawing, though their forces still held strong points near the airbase and in the Chinese district of Cholon.

Despite this, and despite President Johnson's claim that the Viet Cong had failed to attain their objectives, a high-ranking Embassy official in Saigon said that the Communist forces still had the power to launch a second wave of attacks, especially in Saigon. "They have shown they are still capable of presenting a real military challenge," he added. "They certainly gave dramatic evidence of this ability to terrorise and disrupt."

The enemy threw 36,000 troops into the offensive, and these included North Vietnamese regulars as well as Viet Cong guerrillas. About a third of these are reported to have been killed.

"I don't mean to imply that the Viet Cong are on the verge of collapse because of their losses," the official said. "But even though the challenge is considerable and the fighting will be severe and bitter, I think we will be able to handle it."

The United States Command's Director of Combat Operations, Brigadier General John Chasson, confirmed the Embassy's assessment of the continuing Viet Cong threat. "I must confess the V C surprised us with their attack," he said. "It was surprisingly well co-ordinated, surprisingly impressive and launched with a surprising amount of audacity."

Asked if the U S had enough forces, General Chasson said: "From the operations side I would take all I can get. I don't have a surplus. But around the major populated areas we have enough forces."

He described the enemy offensive as very successful. When asked if the U S might have to abandon the countryside to protect the cities and towns, he said the Americans might have to "redisposition" their forces.

The first detailed picture of the Viet Cong's handling of the assault in Saigon was given by American U S military spokesman.

He said reports from prisoners and other sources showed that the Viet Cong's command post for their Saigon task force had been set up in a Buddhist pagoda. A brigadier-general conducted the operations from the pagoda through a command structure known as the 214th Hanoi unit. When Vietnamese Marines stormed into the pagoda they seized enough military equipment to run a major command.

At the Saigon race track on the Western outskirts of the city guerrillas put up a stiff fight for the grandstand, the spokesman said. "We found out why when we took it. They had set up an aid station there with medical supplies and were determined to hold it."

The Viet Cong succeeded in infiltrating 12 to 15 battalions—some 4,500 men—into Saigon for the offensive. As the attack broke, the Government rushed in 7,000 Marines, paratroopers and Rangers, and about 4,000 infantrymen from divisions in the field.

Prisoners said they had walked about 30 miles to get to Saigon, then began moving into the city on Monday night and were led to various points where they were issued with weapons, ammunition and food for one and a half days. The spokesman added: "They were told to hold out for 48 hours and then they would be relieved."

In Saigon today, the centre of the city was relatively calm as the 24-hour curfew was lifted for six hours and the distribution of essential food supplies—rice, salt, bread, pork and chickens—began.

No reliable accounting of civilian casualties is yet available, but the reports of the street-to-street and house-to-house fighting suggest that civilian deaths may well exceed the total of military deaths on both sides.

The fighting in Saigon today was still concentrated in densely populated areas. Circling helicopters rocketed and machine-gunned closely packed rows of houses. According to intelligence estimates there are still 1,000 Viet Cong troops in reserve in the Saigon area.

Tonight, the American command announced that 13,195 Communist troops had been killed and 3,576 suspects detained. A total of 1,814 individual weapons and 545 crew-served weapons, such as machine guns, were said to have been captured. The casualty count, compiled mainly by South Vietnamese sources, was thought to be considerably inflated.

Allied casualties throughout the country were put at 1,213 killed, 3,987 wounded and 53 missing. Of these, 318 of the dead and 1,639 of the wounded were American troops.

Elsewhere in the country, this was the situation:

In the Allied First Corps area (the five Northernmost Provinces) the city of Hué is still largely in the hands of five battalions of Viet Cong and North Vietnamese. But the guerrillas are reported to have been cleared from Da Nang and other major cities though the big Da Nang air base was attacked with rockets again this morning.

In the Second Corps area, the mountain resort city of Dalat, home of the Vietnamese Military Academy, is still in enemy hands.

No recent reports were available for the Third Corps area, the 12 provinces just to the north of Saigon. Early yesterday at least eight towns were said to be under attack.

In the Fourth Corps area (the Mekong Delta and the peninsula), sections of the major cities of My Tho and Can Tho were still in enemy hands early today.

Near the demilitarised zone in the north, the U S Marine fortress at Khe Sanh was reported to be quiet. In the American view, the central anchor on the D M Z line is Cam Lo, where heavy Communist attacks took place on Friday. Since then there have been no fresh reports of fighting.

Moscow took a hand in the South Vietnam struggle today with a report that a "union for the struggle for independence, freedom and peace" had been set up in Hué to run Viet Cong-occupied territory. The chairman of the union was named as Dr Le Van Hao, a professor of Hué and Saigon universities.

In Korea, four new gun battles were reported along the truce line. A further secret session of the Panmunjon military armistice committee has been held in an attempt to free the Pueblo and its crew, seized by the North Koreans.

New York Times, Reuter and United Press International.

The I who on H quays

This boy's fath the St. Romanus trawler presum sea while anoth missing. Every the boy is down fish dock with h see if his father in. While the men's wives ha demonstrating anger to the t cameras, this b waits.

Three trawl refuse to sa

Two of eight Hull due to sail yesterd fishing grounds stay The crew of a thi Keverne, refused t Humber without a tor after a demo fishermen's wives who tried to jum St. Keverne shout without a radio One of the St. Andronicus, in dock, said: " jackets are no Sunday morni refuse to s trawler in d

Lead story on the Tet Offensive in the London *Sunday Times* of 4 February 1968.

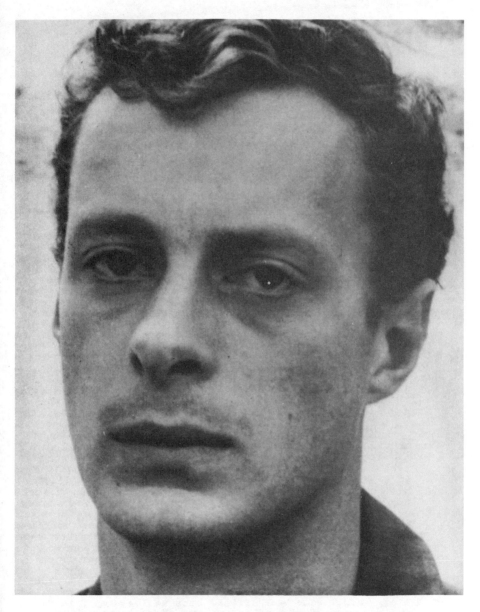

Bruce Pigott, about whom Dinh once confided his fear to Hugh Lunn that his melancholy expression meant "Bruce not long live man".

Saigon , july 10 . 1968.

Reuters Limited P.O. Box P. 9 15 Han Thuyen Saigon Telephone 91429 Cables Reuter Saigon

Dear Gunsmoke.

   Private Dinh say helo gunga gunsmoke, ₤ l hope you
are ok. After you left saigon office one month, l has draft
military service by our government. Three months in traning
near saigon l work secretary for battalion headquarter. every
weekend returning saigon with rx 24 hour holiday. Mr. Pringle
and Bruce Pigott worry when l left office. James go to defense
ministry with mmx his application spy war. propaganda for l
and he very to rasomdmix request l get job defense ministry
  You know what my job. Defense minstry reporter political
and war stories. l would like sent letter to say thanks James
but l mmx d'ont know where he adress now, If you know, please
write to me ixxx letter.
  You know, v.c. general offense second mmyxx time,
very lacky to me. because if mr Beker not stop l go with Bruce
to cholon, l think no more dinh today? eturning from training
saturday afternoon, may 4, at 3a.m. may 5, l hear gxx big gun
fire, l checked police chief my firend (No more head killed
by accident rocket) he confirmed that .v.c. opened second attac
ed, l called mr. Beker and gtbmx give him story, after that
from 3 a.m. to 7 a.m. l has work with my telephon. 7 a.m. mr.
Beker pick me up to office, Beker and l went to cholon area
v.c. fighting with policemen. After that we returned office l
so mr Pigott, he very happy see me. Because one month l did
not to see him, Pigott invited mmx l go to lunch with him.
l accepted. After that he went to cholon on jeep, Bruce ask
me go with him, but mr. Beker stop becuase Beker want E gmt
go with him to bien hoa haiway. Onehour later come back from
haiway l hear rumour say that hmmmx no more burce and laramy
l ask mr. Baker go to cholon. you know fighting every where
  in Cholon l ask mr. Beker stay near police station, only me
voluntees went to bruce car about two kms but very quiet area
  about 50 m from Bruce's car l soo four bodies, l let go
one bmx black uniforme ask me with sk arm, that your friend
l denided, no, not my friend, why you come here, l say l
would like to look imparaiaaixbmdima bodies. he v.c. t ll me
this area no security, goaway quick₤. after l runing away.
  l cry when l come back office, because lose my friend.
l hope you understand any happnyd whm chanded only three
months you left saigon.
 Now l still work with reuters. only office mamanger

Part of a letter from Dinh to Hugh Lunn explaining the events leading to
the tragic death of Dinh's friend and fellow reporter at Cholon in Saigon.

return "to the land of big PX", and who said "Sorry about that" to most things and "Mother-fucker" to the rest, and drank only beer, Coke or a soft drink called Dr Pepper. It was easy for the real-life Droopys among them to believe the evolving American slogan: We've never lost a war and we're sure as hell not gonna lose this one.

However, every now and then one wondered if the ordinary soldier did not have a more practical grasp of what was going on in Vietnam than his superiors. Certainly the troops saw the joke when Washington announced plans to build a barrier across the northernmost tip of South Vietnam to stop the North Vietnamese infiltration of men and supplies.

Although the then American defence secretary, Robert McNamara, did not announce the proposed construction of this barrier until September 1967, reporters first heard of it a few months before when Premier Nguyen Cao Ky said in a speech that a barrier was being constructed across South Vietnam below the DMZ. Until then the construction had been unannounced but, within hours, Dong Ha had been invaded by a dozen Danang-based reporters demanding to be shown what was being built. At first the military denied anything was happening, but — after it had been confirmed that Premier Ky had revealed the plan — reporters were loaded into two amphibious vehicles and driven up to near Gio Linh just below the DMZ.

There, stretching away to the west down and up a long valley was a cleared ribbon of land looking like a giant firebreak. In the distance, we saw bulldozers pushing on up the far rise towards Con Thien eleven kilometres away. High wooden watchtowers were under construction in Dong Ha, but no one would say how the strip would be used. No one in Dong Ha that day — marine or reporter — imagined Washington hoped it would stop infiltration from North Vietnam: they thought there must be a different reason.

The story failed to stir any interest outside the Danang

press centre and was overlooked until McNamara announced in September 1967 that an electronic barrier would be
constructed below the DMZ with sensitive devices capable
of picking up North Vietnamese troop movements. With
the involvement of the US Defence Secretary the strip
suddenly became big news and editors around the world
who had ignored the previous stories were now vitally
interested: something had been announced, not just described, and stories were demanded. The strip was still the
same. It was slightly wider now, and it had been extended
about three kilometres west of Con Thien — now covering
just twenty of the sixty-nine kilometre width of South
Vietnam at this narrow point. It still stopped well short of
the huge mountains rolling west into Laos and, everyone at
Dong Ha agreed, could never be built across them.

None the less, it was argued in Saigon now that the strip
could turn south about twenty kilometres and run across
South Vietnam through Cam Lo, Camp Carroll and on to
Khe Sanh and the Laotian border. It seemed to me,
however, that that would be no good either. The North
Vietnamese could just continue on down through Laos and
enter South Vietnam further south, even as far down as the
Central Highlands — or anywhere along the hundreds and
hundreds of kilometres of jungle border with Laos and
Cambodia that, seen from a helicopter, stretched into
infinity.

I decided to do a troop reaction story and asked a veteran
marine "Gunney" (sergeant) what he thought. "Sure," he
said, "build a barrier to stop these mothers [mother-
fuckers], only don't forget to build it right across Laos and
on to India, and five hundred miles out across the South
China Sea and five thousand feet down — or those mothers
will just tunnel under it."

No one would say what type of electronic devices would
be used, but they were expected to include those that
picked up body heat and small seed-sized devices capable of
detecting movement. The marine commander in the

Pacific, General Victor Krulak, a small impressive man with a wide vocabulary, often visited his troops in Vietnam and came to the Danang press centre several times for press conferences. The general always handled reporters better than the Follies briefers in Saigon. But there were fewer reporters in Danang. This time the correspondents were angry at his hopeful outlook on what appeared to them a dismal situation, and they handed out some tough cross-examination. The correspondents wanted to know why the marines didn't have enough helicopters. "Gentlemen, I find that for things like R and R and helicopters there is an endless demand," he replied. General Krulak spoke freely on everything except the proposed barrier. In mysterious tones he said, "It looks like a giant golf fairway, doesn't it? But you wouldn't want me to tell the enemy something that would help him. He's out there now looking at that barrier wondering what it is or what it will be. He is worried, really worried."

One famous American commentator hailed the barrier as the answer to the war. Infiltration would be reduced to a trickle, the Viet Cong would lack ammunition and surely the United States, with its mighty industrialized economy, had the technology to build a barrier forty-three miles across, or further into Laos, he argued. Others with their feet closer to the Dong Ha dust said a barrier could not be defended in such rugged terrain. The timber watchtowers were duly erected and, of course, duly shot down with anti-tank guns or burnt down by the North Vietnamese, as predicted by local marines.

Despite all the fuss over the barrier, by 1968 it was a forgotten story. Only the reporters remembered McNamara's strip as they spotted the wide fairway of new green undergrowth from helicopter windows as they headed for the isolated US base of Khe Sanh which was, by January 1968, surrounded by large numbers of North Vietnamese troops. Ironically Khe Sanh was to have been the western extremity fortress of McNamara's strip, but the barrier never got to within forty kilometres (twenty-five miles) of it — as anyone who had spent time in and around Dong Ha, Gio Linh, or Con Thien would have known at the outset.

Such plans showed how out of touch the American administration in Washington had become ... fooled, perhaps, by their own statistics. Statistics were not only the bodycounts and kill ratios but things like the large number of US soldiers who elected to stay longer than twelve months. We were told that this showed that morale was high. But out in the field many soldiers who were extending saw it a different way, though it is true that some found a mateship in war they hadn't known back home. Some told me they had, say, sixteen months to go in the army when their term was up. If they returned "stateside" they could find themselves back in Vietnam four months later for another year's tour of duty. But an extension of six months meant they could not be sent back. Others I met extended their tour of duty so that their young brothers could stay home — according to soldiers if a family had only two sons and one was in Vietnam, the other didn't have to go. As one marine told me one day, "I would just hate my young brother to have to go through this, even to see it. I'm staying here as long as I have to to stop him from coming."

For most soldiers one of the main topics of conversation centred on being "short" or "shorter". It had nothing to do with height, but was an indication of how soon a person would be out of the place. After six months a soldier became "short" because he had a shorter time to go than he had already been through — and he would go around yelling out "Short!" when his six months were up ... until someone called out, perhaps: "Shorter! Twenty-two days and a wake up to go." "Are you shitting me?" the newly short guy would ask with mock incredulity.

These troops started counting the days to go when they were down to 100. Some would mark 100 spaces on a *Playboy* centrefold — the last space invariably ending in the same spot — and obliterate each space as the day dawned, not as it ended. They always said they had so-many days "and a wake up" to go — for the last day wasn't worth counting because by then it wouldn't matter anyway.

By this method eighty-seven days could become eighty-five, which made a very big difference in the Vietnam War.

Taking a breather

When fellow-Australian Bruce Pigott arrived in Saigon from the London office in mid 1967 he was shocked to find that, apart from the bureau chief (who slept in the office), the other three correspondents shared the same room-and-a-half suite in the old Continental Hotel. For such a private person this arrangement was most displeasing.

Before I moved in to the suite with Jim Pringle and Pigott I had had no television, radio or record player in the old room I shared, so I immediately took heart when Pringle told me he had a record player. It was a small portable one and Diana Ross and the Supremes was his only record. He had carried "Baby love, oh baby love" around the world with him and we played it so many times in the next year that I'm surprised the needle didn't wear through. Often I sat there in the hotel room playing the record by myself, when the other two were out working. There was no question of going to a movie — there were no English language movies in Saigon, except on one or two occasions at the British Embassy.

This dormitory existence in a third-floor apartment, its narrow balcony overlooking the city centre, made things pretty awkward, especially if you had a girlfriend. I was lucky to get the bed in the suite's enclosed verandah cum lounge, which afforded a little privacy, but the other two took it in turns month by month to sleep in the double bed and the stretcher in the bedroom.

One of the first things that struck me about Bruce Pigott when he arrived was that he appeared to miss none of the things I did: sport, movies, TV, radio (there was only one station), and female company. The tall, thin twenty-three year old was extremely quiet and reserved, one from whom a smile was a laugh, a thinker who kept his thoughts and feelings to himself. Dinh, as usual, quickly summed up the new man: "He keep quiet all time, nod head something like that. He funny man, stay quiet. Exactly like that. He look sad . . . like Buddhist monk."

Almost from stepping off the plane in that whimsical city of Saigon, he had found a cause. It was as if he'd been destined for the place — although he'd never mentioned anything about it in the queue for the tea trolley at Reuters in London. He had started as a journalist on the Melbourne *Herald* and, like me, had gone to London looking for experience. In Saigon Bruce seemed to be bursting to write everything he felt about the country, although that was next to impossible writing for a newsagency. In that way, he was like Jim Pringle, except that Pringle saw himself more as a guardian of the rights of the Vietnamese people (or anyone else for that matter) and Bruce saw himself as one of them. So it did not seem at all strange when this pale-faced Australian, who looked even too young to be a soldier, fell in love with a Vietnamese girl soon after his arrival.

All his waking hours with us seemed to be spent either writing stories or critically looking at others' stories on the war. The little bit of talking he did do was on stories and papers, and the relative abilities of writers. He always left me wondering if he considered I was a bit of a bash-em-out artist because my priority was trying to beat the other agencies to the story. He never gave me any indication that he either liked or disliked anything I wrote — which was most unusual for a fellow journalist working in the same office. Normally it would be taken as tacit criticism, but with Bruce it just seemed normal.

Bruce probably went to more of the most dangerous places in Vietnam at the most dangerous time of the war than any other reporter. I am sure no other surpassed him for bravery. One reason for this was that his arrival coincided with the arrival of the war in the towns and the cities, and with the last throes of the Americans, who were then lashing out into impossible and improbable places. Also, he was unlucky in the way assignments fell — though he didn't see it like that. Bruce was in Saigon when someone had to go to Hill 875; he was in Danang when Khe Sanh was falling; and he was there when the Americans disastrously entered the A Shau Valley. Because he was so conscious of the historical significance of the war, he was willing to go anywhere at any time, even if it were not his turn or if everyone else thought it not worth the effort.

His account of the bombing of the ancient imperial capital city of Hue by the Americans inside its huge castled walls was one of the best stories I read in Vietnam. He described what the bombs had done to the emperor's ancient statues, how there had been a direct hit on the eunuchs' quarters — the detail that made such a story live. Later I asked him how he got such information in the midst of war. "I found an old tourist brochure in some wreckage," he said. He was at that time a man searching for the real story, but, as so often happened in Vietnam, the real story was to get him.

Perhaps the nicest thing about Bruce was that he wasn't phoney-tough like some reporters: he said little about where he had been — he just went there and phoned in his story. But despite this nonchalant exterior Bruce was, I felt, quietly proud of being such a young war correspondent. When I looked back years later at the few photographs I had from Vietnam I found most of them were of Bruce, or included him, though we were never close.

Bruce's arrival enabled me to take my "R and R". The only way to really relax in Vietnam was to leave, which was why correspondents and troops took whatever holidays they got outside the country. This "rest and recuperation", or R and R as it was known, was the one thing everyone looked forward to almost as much as their last day in the war. Troops and reporters could go just about wherever they pleased in Southeast Asia and the Pacific for the ten-day break; some Americans even flew to Hawaii to meet their wives. By 1967, the American troops were even allowed to go as far as Australia. This made many of them very happy because, after months and months chatting to Vietnamese girls in broken English in bars, they could try their luck with some "round-eyes who speak our language". But UPI correspondent Tom Corpora was shocked by this news. He was concerned about America's increasing isolation in the world on account of Vietnam. "Goddamn it, you Australians are the only round-eye friends we've got and we're gonna send our troops there on holidays to stuff up the entire relationship," he told me.

Getting away from Vietnam was a great idea because there was very little for troops to do in a war in their time off — especially if they were in the middle of the jungle. It was the same for reporters, with the added incentive that you were always tense if you stayed there not working in case you might be missing the biggest story of the war. Each three months we at Reuters had a week's holiday wherever we wanted in Southeast Asia to make up for the tough working conditions and no weekends. I always went to Singapore.

But in Saigon there was little to do except work. The alternatives were to go to a bar and talk to prostitutes in their twenty-word vocabulary; to drink with other reporters and talk about the war; to eat with other reporters and talk about the war; or to stay in the hotel room where whoever was there talked about the war.

If there wasn't much to do in Saigon, at least getting about was easy enough: you could walk to most places. Unlike normal cities, which sprawl out into the countryside, Saigon was as if someone had put a belt around it and every month had pulled it in another notch until it could hardly breathe. No one wanted to live in the last house before the rice paddies.

If it was too far or too hot for walking you could jump on a cyclo (a bicycle with a seat in front) or on the back of Dinh's motor scooter. Catching a taxi was like taking a step backwards in time: they were all rear-engined Renaults which had long since vanished elsewhere in the world but had been kept going in Vietnam by the people's resourcefulness and frugality. The streets were crowded with these antiques, as well as swarms of little motor scooters and new 50 CC Japanese motorbikes.

One night I got hold of the office VW and went for a drive with a Vietnamese girl. Everything had looked promising for a serious romance, but because she did not wish to be seen as a bar girl she would not come to our flat, nor walk down the street with me. Setting off in the car together I realized there were very few places we could go and it was even difficult to find a satisfactory place to park in that crowded city. Very soon we found ourselves on the outer edge of Saigon on the road to Bien Hoa. About a kilometre further on I found a peaceful spot off the edge of the road and we pulled over. After a few minutes close together I thought I saw something through the windscreen. Then the same thing again. Then one closer to the car. Vietnamese troops in full battle gear and holding their rifles in both hands were passing on either side of us, ignoring us but obviously involved in some very serious work. I did a U-turn and headed straight back to the office — and never saw my Vietnamese friend again.

Social life was so limited that reporters generally worked together and spent their time off together. The Continental was a lovely old French hotel which in some ways resembled a boarding house. But its main feature was the sweeping staircase that was so impressive when you walked in; this was where the Vietnamese hotelier often stood in his white Western-style suit. The corridors were always crowded with reporters and contractors. Lots of German, Danish and Swedish journalists wandered around, but I mainly mixed with those journalists we saw the most — the four reporters from the *New York Times*, four from *Time* magazine, two from the *Los Angeles Times*, and the *Washington Post* bloke. There were also reporters from the London *Times*, *Mirror* and *Daily Express*, when they were there. We knew them all because they all filed (sent their stories) through our system, except *Time*, which was a couple of doors away.

We Reuter people probably spent more time together than most of the other correspondents there, who were intent on making a quick name for themselves in the United States, and were working at it full time. Others were trying to make enough money to retire and were working in Saigon for several different papers, magazines, and radio stations. Because we were in direct competition with the other agencies, this tended to keep us closer together and at the same time generally pushed us away from their journalists who were our age and might otherwise have been closer friends.

The best feature of the Continental was that there was only a stone carved fence between the restaurant and the main street. Reporters, soldiers, and women passers-by would stop and lean on the fence to talk, so it was a great spot to keep an eye on what was happening. I had lunch there every day, not because of the menu, for which you had to make allowances, but because of the international journalists who might join you, and the boulevard atmosphere in this city that took a two-to-three hour siesta at this time of day. The other reason for eating there was that included in the cost of the hotel bed (paid by Reuters) was breakfast and one other meal a day — and, in an expensive city like Saigon, that could not be passed up. This tariff arrangement was just a small Vietnamese way of doing things, like renting an apartment where the rent for the flat (which was taxed) was about one-tenth the rent for the furniture (which was untaxed).

Lunch every day consisted of awful buffalo meat, with seldom any other choice: because there was so little food in Vietnam besides rice anything different was very expen-

127

sive. Eating that same old meat once a day would have become intolerable were it not for the variety of eating in Danang or Dong Ha or out in the field, where my favourite American combat ration was turkey: if I was lucky enough to draw the right C-ration pack.

Dinner at Dinh's was another welcome break away from the Continental. It was always something to look forward to, particularly if our Chinese communications manager Seah Chiang Nee, who was a Singapore Reuter journalist, was coming along too. The three of us all had the same sense of humour about our plight in being involved in a war, and our various difficulties with Blackman, our boss, whom we all felt worked us too hard. Seah came up with the idea that since each month in the Vietnam War seemed to take a year the last day of each month should be celebrated like New Year's Eve. And this we did no matter what, even if it meant flying back from Danang.

Dinh had a very tiny house in the closely packed suburbs about five kilometres from the office. Houses in these suburbs were all part of long buildings, and they looked more like holes in a wall. The rooms were also very small. But nothing detracted from the enjoyment of being in a home. Dinh's wife would cook us what looked like small chiko rolls which we dipped in "nuoc mam", fish sauce the Vietnamese ate so much of that the Americans called the Air Vietnam airline "Air Nuoc Mam". Dinh's wife and children were always part of the scene, perhaps because there were few other rooms, but Dinh would dominate the conversation with his intelligent perception of events and his willingness to laugh. The house had electric light, telephone, stereo record player, and TV: for Dinh earned good money in a foreign currency.

While Dinh's best friends were Westerners — and Jo Triester of the *New York Times* also made it to his dinners — he never had much respect for the American war effort. He was disappointed that they approached the war in a stupid way, causing the breakdown of the society they were

128

there to save. He believed that the Americans were in Vietnam to cause conflict between China and Russia, and that in that sense the Americans were doing well. As he saw it, in a way we never could, the Russians were sending more equipment than China could into Vietnam and this was upsetting the Chinese. Dinh said the Vietnamese felt the Americans were not fighting for them, but rather for American policy "to sell Coca (Coca Cola) to the Peking".

"Only the money, only financial, that's all they fight. China has almost one billion population — one man one Coca how much American win in there and how much American win in Vietnam? One man only one bullet. They fight in Vietnam to get China and Russia far away and have diplomatic relations with China and sell to the Peking. That all," Dinh said, showing the Vietnamese's historic distrust of the Chinese.

Dinh was unhappy at reports in American papers that the Americans were spending billions of dollars on the Vietnamese because he saw the people were getting nothing. "Who got money? Only leadership, only general, only corruption man. But the people really living in the countryside even one cent didn't got. That reason Vietnamese people angry with American people." As he saw it, it was very difficult to send foreign troops to Vietnam and still keep the people on side. "The Vietnamese don't want any foreigners in their country no matter if Chinese, Cambodian, or American," he said.

These discussions about the war could have gone on into the night were it not for the midnight curfew in Saigon. And the gatherings, while enjoyable, would have been more so were it not that the future was so uncertain. It made Pringle one night at dinner make a pact that after the war we would all come back for dinner at Dinh's. We didn't know then that Dinh would not be there to go back to.

After my first few months in Vietnam I always looked forward to seeing Dinh when I returned to Saigon from the field. Not only was he interested in what I had seen, but he would also tell me everything he had heard while I was away and, not least, the office gossip, which he retold in a hilarious way. One example was the day Mr Bien, the office driver, went to Reuters' "squat" toilet and opened the door to find "Cookie", the Vietnamese woman who cleaned the office and upstairs flat, with her pants down. "Cookie say: 'Mr Bien violation woman,' " said Dinh after consulting his dictionary: "And Mr Bien say: 'I'm your grandfather, how can I do that?' "

I enjoyed talking to Dinh and had plenty of opportunity to do so on the long days and evenings when it was my turn to stay in the office. Mostly it was a matter of just waiting, standing on the footpath, and talking to Dinh. Dinh called these "open talks". I enjoyed the way he spoke: it was refreshing to hear expressions such as: "I not propaganda to you, but . . .", meaning he wasn't just praising me. Or to see him turn and say, "This exactly story." And it was often amusing to hear him using jargon words in his own Dinglish. One day after I had several times expressed interest in a Vietnamese woman called Miss Ha (Miss River) who brought copy to be sent from our office to an American paper, Dinh suddenly promised to act on my behalf. "Give her spywar for you," he promised, meaning psywar. I told him it would be embarrassing if she thought I was unable to speak up for myself. "No, only background, Gunsmoke. Off the record spywar," Dinh promised.

At night the most obvious place to go for entertainment was a girlie bar. There were about thirty or forty of them on both sides of Tu Do Street, each adorned with gaudy neon signs and often named after American cities. At about 10 p.m. each evening the area looked like a giant movie set in an occupied Asian country. There were hundreds of soldiers in civilian clothes wandering from bar to bar or taking off a bar girl for the night — the girls just slightly frowsy, a little overdressed, and a bit too loud. Smiling Vietnamese men were offering lifts home on the back of motor scooters for a price, or else offering to take a man to find a girl. There was also the occasional ten-year-old boy on the fringes slapping his flat right palm over the hole made by his half-closed left fist and saying: "Mister, you want bom-bom my sister?"

Inside each bar, about twenty Vietnamese girls waited for their American customers. Very few dressed in the national Ao Dai costume of pantaloons and a tunic reaching to the ankles. They wore slacks or short, colourful, ill-fitting mini-skirts. Unlike most Vietnamese women, nearly all wore lipstick.

The first time I went into one of these bars, a doll-like Vietnamese girl, her black hair flowing down her back, came up and pushed herself against me. Like most Viet-namese women she had long hair and fine features — not the large round face of the Chinese. (The hair seemed to be an important part of a Vietnamese woman's grooming and the way it was cut could reveal what part of the country she was from: those from the north of South Vietnam cut their hair straight across at the waist, while those in the south did not.) Her bra was obviously padded. An Australian com-mented once: "If you are a tit man or an arse man, you've come to the wrong place."

"You buy me Saigon tea," she said in an unexpectedly demanding voice. "How much?" I asked. It was about US$1.00 to US$1.50 for a thimbleful. Usually they didn't demand more than one every fifteen minutes, but if the girl didn't like you she would gulp it straight down and walk away. In my case, five minutes later, the thimbleful was gone. I had already endured: "I luv you too much," "You number one," and "I want your baby," a number of times.

"You buy more tea?" No. She cuddled up and asked again. Same answer. "You number one cheap Charlie," she said and stormed off. I didn't know why she was so angry because there were plenty of other customers. But I found out later that this was the inevitable reaction, particularly when you told a bar girl she should pay *you* to drink with her.

Some bars had worse reputations than others. For those in the know, the naughtiest was supposed to be La Bohème halfway down on the left. Here the girls dressed in see-through dresses and, to keep a customer interested, they would quickly take his hand and place it strategically under their dress. Pringle took me to this bar after much coaxing and beamed across his beer as he saw the surprise on my face when this happened: "Is that you Hugh," he said mischievously, but I had been too surprised for words. A favourite journalists' bar was the Melody where the girls were said to be younger, prettier, and cheaper. For a fairly substantial amount of money bar girls could be taken home.

Despite the war being so close all around, throughout 1967 there was little sign of it in Saigon. La Dolce Vita restaurant served beautiful Pizza Roma. The Blue Diamond was noted for its sweet and sour pork. Givrol served fried rice which melted in the mouth. La Pagoda served draught beer, which was a change from the usual Bar-me-Bar (Thirty-Three) bottled brand. This bar was the only one that had no girls and the fact that it was Bruce Pigott's favourite again sent Dinh to his dictionary: "Venerable," he then called Bruce.

Saigon could have been a small French city except for the American military police in green flak jackets and steel helmets sitting in round white concrete boxes outside all American installations, their loaded rifles hanging lazily, almost unnecessarily, over the front. The light of far-off flares and the occasional rumble of bombs and outgoing artillery late at night were the closest things to war in those early days.

At Joe Marcel's nightclub young Vietnamese girls in white boots and hipster skirts danced with their long-haired, well-off student boyfriends who had dodged the ARVN draft. They moved to the latest French songs. Next to the dance floor in a gold birdcage a well-built blonde American girl in a red bikini gyrated to the booming beat of the band.

It was a surprise to find that the Vietnamese regarded so favourably their recent colonial heritage. Not only was the women's Ao Dai costume introduced by a Frenchman, but also the practice of writing the language in Western alphabet. At a rooftop open-air restaurant I often went to with Seah and Dinh — the Bong Lai (Fairyland) — Vietnamese women sang local versions of French songs. Perhaps it was an over-reaction to the American presence, but the Saigon middle class seemed nostalgic for the French days and disliked the new foreigners who were there to save them from communism. It was probably because memory softens the past: the old-world romantic French lover chatting up a young Vietnamese girl was vastly different from the big, cigar-smoking American buying her in a bar; the attractive French folk dances contrasted with the prosaic, American, bikini-blonde go-goers; the recollections of the elegance of dress and speech of the French colonial class were at a far remove from the rough, tough, American soldiers in town for a night out. The only thing most of the Vietnamese seemed to like about the Americans was their money.

Dinh was as happy as anyone to spend money in a bar, but he pointed out that the way the bar girls dressed made the older men in Vietnam very angry: "Important thing for woman in Vietnam to cover up, like nun," Dinh said. "Families very poor, now see friend in bar make good money, nice clothes, left husband, throw away children, temporary wife-American. Also Vietnamese student girls go bar," Dinh said. He said Viet Cong radio continually reminded Vietnamese of this "sabotage" of Confucian customs. Dinh said many South Vietnamese army officers' wives ended up in bars to make money because the officers often didn't receive their salaries. Many bar girls too, did not like being exploited and therefore were happy to report back to the Viet Cong what they heard, Dinh said.

It seems strange, but there were more ways to spend time off much closer to the war, at Danang. The press centre there was located in a crumbling, old French motel on the picturesque Danang River and we lived at ground level in small, stuffy rooms that had windows at only one end. They could not have been painted for twenty years and there were up to six beds in each, although really only space enough for a couple. Large organizations such as UPI had their own rooms but Reuters shared with *Stars and Stripes*, of all groups, and we also had visiting servicemen snoring in there too, occasionally. Most of the American rooms were airconditioned, but not ours. The narrow beds had no device for holding up a mosquito net, so when they got bad I used my tennis racquet to hold the net away from my face.

None the less, life there was pretty good. I considered it very safe because it was unlikely the Viet Cong would attack the world press. The sunsets and weather were beautiful. During the afternoon you could play the marines at table tennis or volleyball and almost every night colour movies were screened out in the open little cement square between the river and the bar. An evening in Danang gave me something to look forward to when out in the field, especially the marine restaurant with its thick slabs of imported New York steak and then the movie.

But even in the safe press centre the biggest problem was still staying alive. One night we were all sitting watching a movie when an irate Viet Cong who was missing out sitting across the river opened fire. Everybody hit the concrete at once. Michael Caine kept arguing with his wife in front of one hundred bums as the guerrilla put three holes through the roof of the bar. He was shooting high, another novice it seemed. After the movie there was usually more entertainment from the river's edge watching the fighting over near Marble Mountain, or admiring the carved mountains of the Hai Van pass, or just watching the fishing boats or sleek machinegun boats plying back and forth. You could often see bombing and strafing and tracer machinegun bullets and smoke from Marble Mountain — it was like the fireworks at the Brisbane Exhibition from a few kilometres away. If there was nothing much going on there, you might lie on your back in the darkness and watch for an American satellite to cross the sky like a star, spying on North Vietnam.

On the concrete compound next to the river — where the movies were shown — the US marines played their first cricket match, a match organized by me and a new replacement at Reuters, John MacLennan. We'd known each other well in London and I had written and told him not to come. When he arrived he told me he thought I'd been kidding, until he saw me. "You look ten years older," he said. I'd been in Vietnam just six months. MacLennan and I tried to get the marines to talk about "bowling" instead of pitching and to agree to field in slips. The match ended when a burly marine hit what he called a homer into the middle of the Danang River. CBS television correspondent Dave Schoumacher managed to talk a passing gunboat crew into trying to rescue the ball. After fifteen minutes without success and to jeers from the marines, an over-zealous sailor fell into the river while making his final bid to save the reputation of the navy.

Just across the river, among trees and sandhills, was China Beach, a surf beach of brownish water which was very popular with the Vietnamese. American troops were not allowed there except in their own barbed-wired section. On weekends Vietnamese escaped the war in their thousands to this bay where the girls wore bikinis and little girls sold cut pineapple on sticks; where little boys stole journalists' cigarette lighters; where journalists surfed; and where the Viet Cong reputedly came for R and R; although they didn't cause any problem because they too wanted China Beach left in peace.

It was at China Beach that Bob Ohman won his own hearts and minds for America — by buying peanuts (he really didn't want) wrapped in old newspaper from the little girls in their pyjama-suits and making friends with the families who ran the beer stalls nailed to the many trees behind the beach.

Local fishermen set out from China Beach in scores of two-metre-round baskets which they used like boats — twirling them forward a metre at a time with a paddle, a painfully slow but quaint process and a picturesque one to watch. But they had no power to overcome wind or current, and this was to prove fatal for them later in the war.

We used to go to the beach for a swim occasionally, particularly when some of the women correspondents were in Danang. There was a lovely blonde named Denby from Honolulu whose father, it was said, ran a newspaper there. Curiously she couldn't surf, so one day I took my blow-up, green, US-army mattress to the beach and put her on it. I would push her in front of a wave at the right moment so that it would carry her into the beach. It was more fun than anything else I found to do in Vietnam. The contrast was so great that we would get on such a high at the beach that several of us used to sit on the ocean floor together while Denby pretended to pour us an underwater cup of tea. To do this she insisted we expelled all air and then sat on the sandy bottom.

One such day at the beach began when the UPI fellows complained, in Danang, that they hadn't got the allowance they wanted for the increased risks now involved in covering the war. Virgil Kret had been offered an extra US$50 a week, which he'd rejected because he said it didn't cover the danger; he went back to Japan shortly after arriving. I wasn't too happy either with my one-way ticket to a real war and so the AP, UPI and Reuter guys, and some others too, all guiltily decided that we had had enough: we went on unofficial strike for a day and spent it at the beach. The trouble was that we quickly became bored and soon started making up stories as we lay out on the beach.

Slowly it occurred to us that, because almost every TV, radio station, and newspaper in the world received one or more of these three newsagencies, we could create an event in Vietnam and fool the entire world.

With everyone contributing details we built up a story

about North Vietnamese paratroopers landing in Con Thien and spiking the big US guns and turning them for a blitzkrieg on Dong Ha. We knew that a story like that would have put the White House into a frightful panic — things being the way they were in America; and we hypothesized that such a psychological blow could possibly lead to a nuclear artillery counter-attack or a politically premature end to the war.

It would have been no use the White House denying our invented story when it finally learnt the truth after several hours of panic: their denial would merely have been seen as a blatant cover-up, at least until other journalists could arrive and send back their reports, which might take up to twenty-four hours. What we didn't know then was the Viet Cong had a similar plan in mind to end the war several months later with a sudden, and huge, psychological offensive.

It was while at another South Vietnam beach resort — at Vung Tau, east of Saigon — that I learned how dangerous it was to relax in such a war. Australian journalist Pat Burgess and I were having a beer at a hotel table alongside the only outdoor dance floor I've ever seen — presumably dating from colonial days. A particularly attractive Vietnamese girl was sitting nearby — fragile, soft and, I thought, beautiful. I didn't ask her for a dance and had only nodded to her when she and her two women friends prepared to leave. As they did so she turned and invited me to come along. Thinking she couldn't really be serious — but not wanting to appear to Pat to be afraid to follow up an obviously devastating success — I followed several metres behind expecting to be told to leave when they realized I'd taken up the offer.

Vung Tau was the only place I saw in Vietnam where small ponies drawing ancient, wheeled carts were used as taxis — probably because the town had once been Saigon's beach resort. There was only enough room for the three Vietnamese girls in the sulky but the girl who had invited me along made room for me — and sat on my lap. I really couldn't believe my luck. The girls laughed happily and talked in Vietnamese as we trotted along the main road near the beach, through some suburban streets, then along a darkening dirt road with the houses becoming fewer the further we went. Eventually, after about fifteen minutes, I guessed, we stopped at an isolated house.

Inside, there were several people in a main room in the front — older men and women — and a couple of children scampered around in pyjamas. The girl I appeared to be with ushered me past a number of rooms to where there was a double bed with a mosquito net and a thick eider-down, which seemed unnecessary. The bed wasn't really in a separate room and seemed to be part of a hallway. Other people seemed to be going about the business of retiring, all ignoring us, and I began to wonder who they all were and what they thought I was doing there. Increasingly urgently, however, I wondered how far I was from help. For all I knew they may have thought I was a soldier. I guessed they could tell I was an Australian, but what if they thought I was an American? These girls didn't seem to be bar girls and certainly there had been no mention of payment, and yet, even now, she was undressing. It seemed too good to be true.

Maybe I had been in too many dangerous places in Vietnam. Maybe I had heard too many war stories. Maybe Dinh had told me too much about the cunning of the Viet Cong. I remembered his first warning: "Very quick and easy to be killed." Maybe I had seen too many movies . . . but was this a trap? The perfect way to eliminate one foreign enemy, and frighten a thousand others? If, as the unlikely stories went, bar girls were prepared to put up with VD just so they could pass it on to American troops — or to insert razor blades into their vaginas — then what would hardcore commos do? As I made for the nearest door, she stopped undressing to pull me back towards her. Desperate now to escape, in words and actions I indicated that I wanted to go to the toilet. But once through the door I ran back up the dark dirt road, past the suburban streets, back to the hotel. There Pat Burgess was still sitting on the same outdoor seat drinking his beer. That day bar girls had shouted out "Uc Dai Loi di di". "Uc Dai Loi" meaning "Australian", and "di di" meaning "piss off". And when I recounted what had happened, Pat, an old-school journalist not fazed by anything, burst out laughing and said, "A wee wee di di."

But since then I've often wondered whether my overactive imagination caused me to pass up a memorable night in Vietnam.

Australia:
"Land of great interest"

Because the Vietnamese language depended on tones, or inflections, and was so foreign to my ear I had great difficulty picking up any words or phrases.

Eventually, however, I found out that "Uc Dai Loi", the Vietnamese name for "Australian", actually meant something like "those from a land of great interest". The bar girls had learnt over the years of foreign occupation that Australians didn't have as much money, or spent it as freely, as Americans — which is why the expression "Uc Dai Loi di di" was so often heard. If the Australians had made a reputation for themselves as jungle fighters, they had also made a reputation as "cheap Charlies" (so the girls would say) in the bars. From fifty metres away the acute sixth sense of the bar girls told them who were Australians. "Uc Dai Loi number welve," called a bar girl in tight skirt and blouse poking out a pink tongue from between horrible lipstick-red lips. Twelve, or "welve", was about as far as any of the bar girls could count in English and was the worst insult they could inflict, since "number one" is the best or greatest in Vietnam, as in China.

I wondered how the bar girls knew I was an Australian because I had been living in Hong Kong, England and Singapore for two and a half years before coming to Vietnam. I had an un-Australian haircut and clothes and, though I had the accent, they never had to wait until I was close enough to speak. Later they told me they could always tell an Australian man because his hair was longer; he almost invariably wore long sleeves rolled up slightly; even young

Australians had wrinkles around the sides of the eyes; and they had what the Vietnamese girls regarded as a lazy walk. Some of the bar girls said we Australians lacked a sense of humour compared with the Americans, but it was probably just different. Australians tend to find their own difficult plight amusing.

I found that in Vung Tau Australian soldiers often refused to pay the high prices for "Saigon tea". "Ten bob a time might be all right for the Yanks but it's too much for us," was how one poorly paid Australian conscript put it to me. But although the Vietnamese girls didn't like having the Australians in the bars they couldn't stop them from entering, particularly in Vung Tau which was full of Australian soldiers on nights off. Unlike the Americans they seemed to drink in large groups — in the same way as in the public bars back home. One night in a bar I watched about ten young Aussies singing "Waltzing Matilda" in very flat voices and drinking Aussie beer they'd bought from the Vietnamese after it had been through the black market. The few exasperated Americans nearby asked them to keep quiet and the Australians, who were much smaller in build than the Americans, started making statements like: "One Australian is worth ten Yanks." Luckily, the bigger Americans just treated it as a laugh — they were willing to put up with a lot from the only fellow round-eyes (including the New Zealanders) who would help them in Vietnam. Particularly from the countrymen of a white, industrialized Western nation that was a member of the British Commonwealth. For the Americans knew that by getting Australia and New Zealand to send troops they limited criticism from NATO allies such as Britain, and all other Commonwealth countries. The Australians and New Zealanders (everyone in Vietnam saw them as one) also added that slight extra to the "international" or "Free World" image America wanted to promote in Vietnam. And they were the only soldiers there, apart from the Viet Cong, who were not wearing the American almost-edgeless helmets and not using American rifles. The ARVN, the Filipinos, the South Koreans, and the Thais all looked like Asian Americans in their American uniforms and jeeps. The Uc Dai Lois, however, drove around in Land Rovers and used big SLR rifles with much bigger bullets than the American M-16s, and they wore British webbing and traditional slouch hats with the side turned up.

This made them fascinating to the Vietnamese and it was one of the reasons they were so well known: this distinctive, small army of men who appeared to march everywhere, dressed differently, polished brass, and saluted their superiors on almost every occasion. The average educated Vietnamese in Saigon seemed to like these fellows better than the large body of Americans, perhaps because they were too few in number to threaten the structure of their society. The Australians were limited mainly to two small areas of Vietnam, Nui Dat and the Vung Tau peninsula, so their presence was not overwhelming, as was the Americans'.

Australia also took a high profile by sending its national soccer team to an eight-nation Southeast Asian tournament in 1967 at the Cholon sports stadium in Saigon. When I went to cover the final I thought the Australian team would be the object of some abuse by the crowd of twenty-five thousand, but the Uc Dai Lois were the favourites. Perhaps this was because they beat South Korea who had beaten South Vietnam in a semifinal. The crowd also seemed to enjoy the rough, aggressive way the Uc Dai Lois played what was supposed to be a non-contact sport. It seemed strange to have a soccer tournament in the middle of a war, but Saigon had been without competition sport for many years and no doubt the army, the South Vietnamese government, and the Americans felt it would be good international public relations to show that things were going along fairly normally. Saigon was so starved of sport that Vietnamese told me that among the crowd there were many Viet Cong.

The Vietnamese were interested in Australia because it

was a nation that had been started by the settlement of criminals from another land — they had been taught that all Australians evolved from the imported convicts. For example, one of the things Dinh enjoyed most was to ask provocative questions of newly arrived Australians when there were Englishmen present in the Reuter office. Dinh would say things such as: "What happened to Australian people? English people tell me you are coming jail people?" He received many strange reactions, but none more pleasing than the Australian journalist who finally jumped up and said, "I don't want to fucking talk about English colonialists anymore" — to which the Englishman then objected to the term colonialist. Dinh would also say to Australians, "What your grandfather do? Jail?" and always he kept a straight face for longer than anybody watching could, as the puzzled Australian tried to work out if he was serious.

"Australian people jail people — Australian people 'victim' " was how the Vietnamese really saw us, according to Dinh. It was perhaps because the Vietnamese interpreted our strange heritage in this way — a heritage almost impossible to comprehend for a people who had lived in the same land for thousands of years — that Australians got closer to them than any other foreigners in that ancient land. The Vietnamese have always seen themselves as a nation of wronged people — their land having been ruled by China for almost a thousand years. Theirs was "a society of victims, of people punished for crimes and sins they did not commit," as Vietnamese writer Huynh Sanh Thong once described it. Among themselves the Vietnamese jokingly called the Uc Dai Lois "Con Son people", Con Son being an island used as Vietnam's biggest prison.

Perhaps a nation of black marketeers found it easier to accept a nation of criminals than a nation of bosses. As well, the Australians, it always seemed to me, treated people more equitably than most. They may have been racists in Australia, but in the Asian countries they generally quickly made close friends with the locals. Dinh used to say the Americans tried to be too friendly; the English didn't try at all; and the Australians were "open-hearted". "I like really Australia people very much."

But the Australian who got the closest to Gungadinh was, of all people, the enigmatic Bruce Pigott. This came as a surprise to me because not only did they seem radically different types, but Bruce did not seem to be the sort of person you could get close to. At first, Dinh would often say of him: "this Uc Dai Loi not laughing, just little open mouth." He also complained soon after Bruce's arrival that Bruce had sent some of his bar-girl friends away. "Many bar girl coming to Reuter office my friend. They say: 'Who that man? I ask where you are he never say.' I tell them this man Bruce like Buddhist monk, don't worry." What I didn't know was that Dinh — though he complained — was impressed that Bruce did this and that Bruce himself did not go to the girlie bars.

"Dinh, you family man, you take care your children very important life," Dinh later quoted Bruce Pigott as saying. "Bruce loved me very much," Dinh told me, adding that in Vietnam love included advising someone to do the right thing, "not sabotage you". Dinh was particularly impressed when Bruce noted that the Reuter driver, Mr Bien, was sad. Dinh explained to him that Mr Bien's son had been drafted and Mr Bien had no money to pay corruption "to get back his son". Bruce gave Mr Bien the two thousand piasters, asking Dinh to explain to him that Bruce was very sad.

Like myself, Bruce spent a lot of idle time in the Reuter office talking to Dinh while waiting to take copy from the field or for callouts from MACV. Eventually the two started going to the Vietnamese movies together particularly if there was an old Charlie Chaplin movie on — they were Dinh's favourites. Bruce was so interested in Vietnam (rather than just the war) that I imagined it was this that had brought him and Dinh together so quickly. However, there was another factor at work: the young Australian had made life very complicated by falling in love, and he needed Dinh's help.

Watching Dinh and Bruce I could see the easy rapport Australians could have with Vietnamese. But I had no way of knowing how the Australians went when they were fighting because I was working for a large international newsagency which sent to the world only the biggest news. And the biggest battles were being fought by the US marines in the north of South Vietnam, and by the US army in the Central Highlands. The Australians, however, were fighting essentially a guerrilla war against local Vietnamese labelled "hard core communists", although many Viet Cong probably just thought they were defending their paddies from foreign invaders.

The Australians found their tiny bits of war frustrating. Various officers told me they wished they could send a battalion up to the northern provinces with the US marines to fight some North Vietnamese regulars in a major set-to. But, presumably because the Australian government could not have withstood the political reaction to an Australian battalion suffering some of the huge losses marine battalions were taking, they were never allowed to go. I could just imagine the political uproar that would have ensued in Australia had an Uc Dai Loi company lost seventy-six dead in one fight — more than one-third of their number — as had happened to the US marines. In fact the Americans lost more dead (five hundred) in one week of that war when I was there than Australia did in the entire war which, for them, lasted a decade.

The Australians were in Vietnam for international political reasons, such as giving credence to the term Free World forces, rather than for military reasons; which made being an Australian soldier there even more difficult. They fought local guerrillas in a war in which the dangers were quite different. And, unlike the Americans, they fought the war the way the Viet Cong did — with the disadvantage that the Viet Cong guerrillas were fighting in their homeland.

Dinh learned after the war that the Viet Cong had held the Australians in high regard. And Dinh was not the type to hide criticism or to give false praise. He said a Viet Cong colonel told him that he was very anti-Australian because he was born in Phuoc Thui province where the Australians operated. The colonel told Dinh the Viet Cong feared the Australian night ambushes because they had been used to having the nights to themselves, even during French times. "They never to defend inside, only outside," the Viet Cong colonel told Dinh, explaining the difficulty of fighting the Uc Dai Lois. The Viet Cong considered the Uc Dai Loi soldier was "clever", or, in Dinh's words, "a camping soldier, a caravan man".

The colonel was impressed that the Australian troops slept outside their camps and he said their preparation for a possible fight was very good. Dinh then made his hand move backwards and forwards, right and left, and said, "How you say this?" I suggested, "Like a snake." "That so, that what he tell me. Something like that. He say the Australians very difficult because they all the time move like that." Dinh said the Viet Cong didn't like fighting the Uc Dai Lois, "Because they say the Australians always move out [I think this meant they took the war to the Viet Cong] and that is difficult for them. Of the allied forces they care only about the Australians."

Dinh said the Viet Cong described the Australian–New Zealand forces fighting in South Vietnam as "tactic soldiers" while they saw those from other Asian nations as "PX soldiers".

"The Viet Cong said Filipino 'black market soldiers', Thailand they say 'PX soldiers' and Koreans too," Dinh said. After the UC Dai Lois and the New Zealanders they rated the Koreans; and Dinh himself believed the Koreans fought very well in Nha Trang province.

Dinh denied my belief at the time in Vietnam that the Australians had the easiest place in the country in which to fight. They were about fifty kilometres east of Saigon at Nui Dat and it seemed to me that there were definite advantages in being on the other side of the heavily defended capital from the Ho Chi Minh supply trail down through Laos and Cambodia. It was just about as far from North Vietnam and the DMZ and the flooded Mekong Delta as you could get. But Dinh said the Australians operated in a "very strong hard-core communist area", from what he had learned after the communists won the war. At this time the South Koreans had about 70,000 troops in Vietnam, the Americans had about 550,000, excluding the US Seventh Fleet in the Gulf of Tonkin and their huge airforce bases in Thailand and Guam operating into Vietnam, and the Australians had about 8,000. Just enough to say we had some there — because 8,000 were not going to make any difference at all in that war.

As well as the jungle base at Nui Dat, the Australians had a big logistics base on the Vung Tau peninsular, on the beach just out of the town of that name. Both bases were surrounded by their own protected and mined barbed-wire perimeters. Nui Dat had an airstrip and both bases were serviced by Australian planes. After flying everywhere in American C-130 or C-123 planes, it was a treat to fly to the Australian bases in totally different aircraft — Caribous.

At Vung Tau the Australians, naturally, built a surf club, which, like a lifesavers' clubhouse back home, was full of surfboards and skis. The only difference from Australia was that the surf was dirtier, and warmer. Vung Tau was remote from the war — so remote that it was one of only two or three places that were to be untouched by the Tet Offensive in early 1968 in which the Viet Cong were to devastate South Vietnam. In fact, Vung Tau was said to be a Viet Cong R and R centre.

It was a lovely little beach resort which the French had called Cap Saint Jacques, and getting around in the little horse-drawn carts added to its charm. The lovely old-style hotel with its huge outdoor dining and dancing area was in the French tradition. Vung Tau had more than its share of girlie bars — a couple of dozen — and they were much cleaner and less gaudy than elsewhere in Vietnam.

One of the main differences I noticed was that the American forces were much more conscious of equality and the Australian troops, unlike Australians generally, were much more officer-conscious in the British tradition. While an American colonel was treated by the press, and even privates, as at about corporal status, an Australian captain would march around like a general. An Australian colonel was treated — and acted — like royalty, whereas in the American forces a colonel was treated the same way as everyone else. American reporters often called generals by their nicknames and argued vehemently with them, it seemed, all the time — and always as equals; but even the lowliest-ranked Australian officers treated the press as privates. While every American would give an interview without question, the Australians were all reluctant to talk to the press. No doubt this difference developed because the American Constitution guarantees freedom of the press. Australia is not so lucky.

This distinction was brought home to me very clearly one night in the Australian officers club at Vung Tau camp. A tall, thin, crew-cut American reporter, Bob Kaiser, was talking in a group to a high-ranking Australian colonel, dressed up to the hilt, as was customary for the Australian officers to do each and every evening. The colonel made a remark about the war which annoyed the American. "Don't bug me, man," he said to the colonel. Australian officers standing around looked on in disbelief — their mouths open but not saying anything. Before the colonel could take action, an army public-relations officer had led him aside and was trying to explain that this was not only the way American reporters spoke to their colonels, but also to their generals.

Personally, I liked the American way. There was a great openness about the Americans, an openness which eventually ensured that the world found out what was happening in Vietnam.

This Uc Dai Loi formality also showed even in the way

the Australians walked (rather, marched) around Vietnam. They had their shoes shined, their brass gleaming, and they exchanged salutes, whereas the Americans just about ignored formality and, even in the field, argued with superiors about what tactics to adopt. The Americans were like an army of university students, while the Australians were like an army of well-drilled schoolboys.

There was also an obvious cultural difference between the troops of the two nations. The Australians were not entirely innocent of the arrogance of the average American in Vietnam, though, as with most things, they could turn a racist insult into humour — and from there it was less of a step to friendliness. For example, the Americans called the Vietnamese gooks, and meant it, whereas the Australians picked up the phrase and made a joke of it. A tough Aussie sergeant got a laugh from American correspondents one day at Vung Tau as he stamped up and down in front of his superbly drilled troops waiting for President Thieu to arrive for an inspection. He stopped, glanced at his watch, looked up, and said, "I wonder what's happened to the king of the gooks?"

I did not see the Uc Dai Lois in action. But I did go to Vung Tau to cover a murder trial of an Australian conscript private who allegedly did what American soldiers did often enough in Vietnam for it to develop a name. It was called "fragging", which meant throwing a hand grenade at a hated officer. This particular explosion happened during what the Australians call "stand to", which was right at dusk when the Australian military, unlike the American, always prepared for an attack with the troops in shallow bunkers inside their tents. The company involved was out at a base on a hill in the bush and had been there for a few days. The grenade went off one early evening and the incident told me a lot about how my country's troops behaved.

The defence for the accused established that there were pieces of canvas tied to the barbed-wire perimeter of the isolated camp and, under questioning, army witnesses reluctantly said these were small, covered, beer "shops" where Vietnamese sold beer to the Australian soldiers in the camp. The defence barrister, flown up from Sydney for the trial, asked the witnesses how the Aussie troops got out of the camp to get at the beer. The witnesses, also reluctantly, said they "just sort-of walked out" there. This raised the question of how someone could so easily walk out of a heavily defended position protected by mines and barbed wire. Then it was admitted that the Aussie troops had cut a pathway through their own perimeter so that they could walk out in safety to buy a beer. The defence wanted to establish this so that they could say that it could have been a Viet Cong who walked in on the same path and blew up the officer who, it was alleged, had had an argument with the accused. The defence also established that hand grenades were kept in unlocked boxes and could have easily been taken by a guerrilla.

However, the prosecution did have one key witness who claimed to have seen the accused pass his tent just after the hand grenade went off. So they got him in the witness box and asked him all the right questions: Do you remember an event on such-and-such a date? Yes, he heard a hand grenade go off. How did he knew it was a grenade? Because he had heard them before. And could he tell the court what happened immediately after that hand grenade went off? He was, of course, supposed to say he saw the accused, but instead he said, "When that hand grenade went off," eyes widening, "chaos and confusion reigned supreme."

Effectively, that was the end of the case and the accused private eventually got off. It seemed a just verdict, for it had been established that his best friend had been killed by a Viet Cong when they had been in that exact location (under a different position name) several months before. The Viet Cong had crept inside, turned a defending claymore mine around, and set it off.

Apart from the Australian regular forces in Nui Dat and

Vung Tau there were also some "training advisers" who had been in Vietnam since 1962, three years before Australia announced it was sending troops to the war. There were about one hundred of them from the Australian Army Training Team, to be known later simply as "The Team", among whom there were no troops below the rank of warrant officer. This elite group of Australians called themselves the "Lost 100" because their presence in Vietnam had been ignored by the Australian media, even though their unheralded departure from Australia ultimately involved the whole nation in the war. Most taught South Vietnamese government forces and civilian irregulars how to fight the Viet Cong in the rugged mountains in northern South Vietnam. Members were attached individually to ARVN battalions and local civil defence forces as advisers instructing the Vietnamese in tactics they had learnt in jungle training in Australia and had practised in Malaysia and Borneo.

The first group of training-team members — 30 volunteer warrant officers — arrived in Vietnam in 1962. Their role was to advise regular ARVN units and, in some cases, lead them into battle. By 1972 when prime minister Gough Whitlam pulled Australia out of the conflict, 984 members of The Team had seen action in Vietnam. Their record was impressive and their roll of honour is believed to be unmatched in any other theatre of war. They returned to Australia with four Victoria Crosses, twenty-one Distinguished Conduct Medals, six Military Crosses, seventeen Military Medals, two Distinguished Service Orders, four British Empire Medals, six MBEs, three OBEs, forty-eight mentions in dispatches — leaving aside the many American and Vietnamese decorations.

In 1967 I found out at Uc Dai Loi House in Danang that at a nearby outpost twenty Australian officers from The Team were developing a surprise attack force called "Mike Force"; so I went out to take a look. When I first saw Captain Karl Baudistel, of Bondi, Sydney, at the base near

Marble Mountain, he was strutting across sand dunes telling two American sergeants to smarten themselves up. Despite the heat he looked like he was standing under his own private palm tree. There were no sweat marks on his well-pressed shirt and trousers; and his brown slouch hat with the wide brim was turned down all the way around. As if to add force to his observations he dexterously waved a carved stick in the air with a thick, freckled arm the size of Rod Laver's. Baudistel's lean, straight back disappeared as he turned round and a stern freckled face with thin lips confronted me. "What can I do for you?" he asked, in a way which seemed unnecessarily aggressive towards a fellow Aussie in a strange part of the world.

In a very businesslike manner, he took me to his private tent and explained how it was he was able to order Americans around. He said there were about a hundred Aussie army "warrant officers and higher" in the northern area advising Vietnamese and Americans on guerrilla tactics. Captain Baudistel wasn't modest about the Australian soldiers. The Americans, he said, looked on them as "authorities on tropical warfare", and they used the basic organization and minor tactics born of the Malaysian insurgency. He himself had been in Malaysia for two-and-a-half years and was now in charge of developing a surprise attack force made up of Nung (part Vietnamese-part Chinese) mercenaries, Montagnard mountain tribesmen, US sergeants, and Australian officers. The force did not wear military uniform but rather the Viet Cong garb of black pyjamas. This "Mike Force" of about eight hundred was being kept ready to go to the aid of American "green beret" special forces camps isolated in the mountainous regions of the north. Others of the "Lost 100" lived at the special forces camps with the green berets helping train irregulars. These jungle garrisons were defended by local irregulars headed by about ten Americans. Their job was to look after the people in the area and gather intelligence on the Viet Cong.

The special forces camps had "special" security problems — both from within and without. They were not only alone out in the jungle backblocks but Captain Baudistel also estimated that an amazing 15 to 35 per cent of the Vietnamese troops in any one camp were Viet Cong infiltrators: gates were left open and guns inexplicably set to explode when fired. When the Viet Cong felt a post had been weakened sufficiently, they would attack. That was where "Mike Force" came in — at least in theory.

All or part of "Mike Force" would be immediately airlifted into the area under attack. The tactics used were purely Australian. They did not talk, did not break wood, and buried their waste before moving on. The motto of the Australian training team was "Persevere", and the captain seemed very proud of this ideal. He didn't say so, but I got the impression he didn't think these tactics were at all like the way the Americans were fighting the war.

An American captain commanded the Montagnard tribesmen with Australian warrant officers as platoon leaders. Aussie warrant officers commanded the Nung companies with American lieutenants and sergeants in the same unit.

Captain Baudistel leant back in his small chair behind the makeshift wooden desk as if his tent were on the top floor of a Sydney high-rise. He recalled how he had been in one special forces camp for a few weeks when one night, on checking the camp, he found rocks in the mortars, firing pins out of machineguns, and the pin removed from a grenade in the ammunition store so that when the grenades were pulled from the box the pin would fall out and the grenade explode. Baudistel, who was only twenty-eight, was in overall control of the reaction unit which had built to strength slowly. They had sent talent scouts all over South Vietnam to beg, borrow or steal good men. Basically they got everyone no one else could get or wanted and paid them money and gave them equipment to fight with. (I forgot to ask where the money came from.) The Montagnards lived remote from administrators, and the Nungs were unpopular with the Vietnamese who regarded them disapprovingly as half-castes. Though "Mike Force" recruited plenty of men they didn't always get the right ones; there was a large turnover because those mercenaries who did not come up to standard under fire were sacked, and there were about twelve of those a week. The Australians preferred Montagnards and Nungs because where they fought was where they lived. They knew the mountains and, as Baudistel put it, "how to walk them".

We went for a walk around the camp. A young Nung in black pyjamas who looked about thirteen walked past, holding a big sharp knife. "He looks young," I said. "Yes, but he's big enough to slit *your* throat," said Baudistel, almost seeking a reaction. There was a captured Viet Cong next to a tent in a barbed-wire cage about fifty centimetres high, a metre wide, and two metres long. He had his hands tied behind his back. The cage was in the sun and he looked very hot in his black pyjamas. Captain Baudistel said they had just captured him, and told me how they had once picked up the bodies of three Australians who had their penises stuffed in their mouths, their faces bashed in, their heads scalped, and their tags gone. They had apparently been captured when their mercenary force deserted them under pressure. It was a problem everyone — including Baudistel — faced. "If these fellows want to go, they just go," he said.

Training courses for the mercenaries in that camp had been developed in Malaysia and Australia and included a "confidence course" in which they were put in trenches and live grenades were thrown in front of them and small mortars fired to land behind. This was designed to give the mercenaries the confidence to avoid fire but no doubt it also sorted out which ones they wanted and which they didn't. "Naturally there are some casualties, but it saves lives in the field," Captain Baudistel commented. At the time, in the midst of war, this astonishing practice did not seem at all important.

There was also an ambush course, where the men moved towards a certain point knowing that before they got there they would be ambushed with live ammunition. This was to add suspense and keep the troops on the alert, since they could not predict when the ambush would occur. One of the main developments since the Malaysian campaign was in reaction tactics. If ambushed the Australians now automatically turned their force into the face of the ambush and charged. For they had found that the enemy were probably only ten metres away in the jungle and "through them" lay the nearest point to safety. But they still used complicated special defensive perimeters developed in Malaysia for overnight stops in the jungle.

The developing "Mike Force" had one big advantage, the Australians believed: the Viet Cong never knew where it was or when it would be back — which amounted to pinching the Viet Cong's strong point. "One of the biggest frights we gave them was in a recent battle when we fought all one day, stayed in the jungle, then hit them again the next morning. They were not used to that," said Captain Baudistel, though this success was not to last.

Three months later, in August 1967, Captain Baudistel and his force went to the aid of a besieged American unit. I was told later that he had been shot just above the leg in the lower part of the stomach. He crawled across to the nearest machinegun and, firing from a lying-down position, told the others to continue fighting, that he would be OK. Later they found him still at his gun. He had bled to death.

Sitting ducks

It was one thing for the Viet Cong to dominate the rice paddies and the mountains. But to win the war they needed something more: they needed to be able to pressure the Americans in their safe camps. I wrongly believed that they had found a way of doing this as early as April 1967 when a three-line announcement at the Follies said that the base at Gio Linh was being hit by artillery fire from North Vietnam across the DMZ.

To me that was headline news because the American effort seemed to have relied on making sure their troops were at least safe within their bases. Most of the fighting soldiers were going out on search and destroy missions in the daytime — like going off to work — and then coming home to rest at night, and often on weekends, in complete safety. This kept the morale of the marines high. And all of their back-up people spent most of the war inside these fortified bases: it made things much more agreeable than they would otherwise have been in a war with no front line.

The marine base at Gio Linh was on a tiny, flattish hilltop a kilometre or two south of the DMZ. I got there on a C-130 plane (called a Hercules by the British) to Danang, where I waited for another one to Phu Bai and Dong Ha, and then got a lift the remaining twelve kilometres to the hilltop. From there you could see into North Vietnam across the DMZ and to some mountains almost lost in the mist of distance. This was where the artillery shells were coming from.

Because this seemed so ominous a development I was surprised to find a cheery base headed by an enthusiastic young Colonel Rice. The North Vietnamese began shelling shortly after I arrived, and Colonel Rice explained that they fired in the daytime because at night their location could quickly be picked up by the flashes. In that case this base, filled with guns capable of firing to a distance of thirty-two kilometres, would fire huge volleys of shells back. And the North Vietnamese obviously didn't want that.

From deep inside the lounge room-sized command-post bunker in the middle of the camp, troops yelled instructions to the perimeter on what action to take, and to gunners on where to aim the return fire from the enormous guns that stuck out of bunkers like giant steel drinking straws. Every time a shell went off the bunker shook, but it was so heavily fortified with sandbags that it was fairly safe inside. "How-many-rounds officer!" called Colonel Rice, and a young man ran across. "This is my 'how-many-rounds-officer'," said the colonel, introducing us. The young man was busy ticking off every explosion for the record. This was his job in an armed force that was obsessed with statistics. One North Vietnamese shell buried itself next to the command-post bunker and the blast slightly hurt the radio operator in the corner. Then there was the loudest explosion of all. "What was that?" called the colonel and an old sergeant looked out of the back entrance. "Fuck," he said loudly and with great alarm, "the volleyball court."

Outside the bunker, high on the top of wooden observation towers, brave marines waited out the artillery attack while they watched for any sign of a ground assault — which Colonel Rice expected at any time. Resigned, the marines sat in their perches on floors of sandbags to stop the shrapnel from shells exploding on the ground below. As one optimist said when I climbed up for a look through the telescope, "It will have to be a direct hit to get us. That would be some bullseye." Meanwhile, Colonel Rice called for tanks to be moved to strengthen the southeast corner of the plateau. Their barrels were loaded with rounds filled with small nails, called beehive rounds because of the swarm of material that flies out.

"They can't afford to leave us sitting up here watching them," he said. But even this did not take his mind away from the small things of life on that tiny hill. Dong Ha relied on Gio Linh and Con Thien as early-warning bases. "First thing Dong Ha will do in the morning will be to ring up and ask how many rounds hit us the previous day. Were we ever happy the other day when they got *their* first artillery attack! First thing I did was to get on the blower and ask how many rounds," said the colonel.

I didn't say anything but, being a worrier, this seemed headline news to me. Now even the mighty sprawling base of Dong Ha was getting hit by artillery from up to thirty-two kilometres away. Where next? But no one else seemed too concerned — either in Dong Ha, Gio Linh, or Saigon.

Gio Linh and Con Thien, two hilltops overlooking the imaginary lines of the DMZ, were said to be there to stop infiltration, watch enemy troop movements, and blast any infiltrators with their elongated artillery pieces. But, once at these bases, you could see that truckloads of guerrillas could pass close by without being spotted. These were just two hills overlooking jungle on a seventy-kilometre front — not to mention the limitlessness of neighbouring Laos which was separated from the Vietnamese jungle only on maps.

"What are you going to do now that the North Vietnamese are hitting you with artillery and you are confined to this one small spot?" I asked Colonel Rice. "That's all right," said the colonel, showing me a type of radar instrument with a green screen in the command bunker. "You see this. Well we just work out their position using this and blast them right off the map." If the North Vietnamese were aiming to put pressure on the Americans, it seemed they weren't succeeding.

The strategy sounded simple and I was impressed at the time. But, in the end, it didn't work. The North Vietnamese beat the radar locator and the patrolling fighter-bombers in the air above by never firing the same gun twice in a row, so preventing the Americans from fixing a position. (I learned later the Viet Minh had adopted exactly the same tactic to defeat the French at Dien Bien Phu thirteen years earlier.)

By May the marines were so sick of North Vietnamese artillery landing in the midst of their forward bases and so frustrated at being unable to stop it with their own artillery, that they decided to forget the Geneva Accords, take the initiative — and send troops into the supposedly neutral DMZ to push the North Vietnamese back. No doubt at the back of the officers' minds, too, was the media attention now being focused on these battered bases, and the morale of the troops. As I had found out first-hand in the Hiep Duc Valley, sitting and waiting was not the marines' kind of war.

The events that led to this headline-making marine invasion of the DMZ could best be understood by looking at a map at forward marine headquarters in Dong Ha. It showed three zones: North Vietnam was labelled "Bad Guys"; South Vietnam "Good Guys"; and across the strip of the DMZ had been added "Smart Guys".

The ten thousand marines who went in to the now un-Demilitarized Zone encountered little resistance in the zone itself, probably because their force was so large, too large for the North Vietnamese. But they also failed to stop the artillery barrages which merely worsened once they had left. It was a different story when the marines went in again eight weeks later: this time it was a reinforced battalion of one thousand men supported by twenty tanks (including two flame-throwers) and six gigantic amphibious tracked vehicles.

The press-centre restaurant in Danang buzzed one night with the news: "The marines are back in". At 5.30 the next morning we set out to catch a C-130 to Dong Ha, known by Danang journalists as "the arsehole of Vietnam". Hot and dusty in summer, it was wet, cold, and muddy in winter — and foggy. The landscape had been cleared for the base and

159

all that was left were tents and dirt for as far as you could see.

In the C-130 the seats had all been removed, and we were packed in back-to-back on the floor with nothing to hold on to. This way it was quicker for racing out if, as expected, artillery came in as we landed.

I really hated flying in those C-130s, painted camouflage-green and brown above, and sky blue underneath. Even when they had seats, they were the paratrooper-harness type which lined the walls or were in rows in the middle so that you sat facing one another. The windows were well above head height so there was no view — other than to watch the rods and levers in the ceiling moving the wing flaps. Because the planes were unlined, of course, they were extremely noisy. As I rarely drank alcohol I wasn't able to down a few vodkas before heading for the airport, as so many reporters and photographers did — especially if the flight was going to Dong Ha.

It was much worse landing in Dong Ha in a C-130 than a helicopter because the helicopter would contour-fly quickly into the base and land in a thrice — whereas the plane would arrive, circle — while North Vietnamese artillery got set — and then fly in over Viet Cong-held territory, often drawing fire. The airstrip was far too short because it had to fit inside the base and pilots said they had to make a steep descent and put the plane down very hard on the first fifty metres of strip or pull out and try again . . . there were mined base perimeters at both ends.

Dong Ha was the most forward big base in Vietnam, almost a city of tents, big tents and little tents, on rolling dirt hillsides along one side of the airstrip. At first it was a reasonably safe place to visit, with a nice press hut next to headquarters on a small hill in the centre near the marquee mess tents.

But, by this stage, the C-130s were aborting landings as shells came in, rear doors were left open for fast exit as the arrival of a plane heralded a new volley of shells in the camp itself, and fist-sized holes had appeared in the walls of brick buildings at the airstrip — such was the power of artillery shrapnel. Artillery had scored direct hits on the command post and press huts. Reporters now stayed out in tents with the troops and, when the shells came in, you rolled out of your stretcher into the gutter-bunkers alongside, and hoped no one in a hurry landed on you. Everyone had been mystified by the accuracy of these shellings and how the North Vietnamese managed to single out the command post for special attention until one day a marine witnessed the deliberate stride of a Vietnamese woman worker in the camp . . . and she seemed to be reciting numbers as she paced.

The 3rd Marine Division's deputy commander, General Metzger, spoke to the press in Dong Ha. American TV journalist Dave Schoumacher asked him why the press had not been invited on the operation into the DMZ. "Are you trying to do my job?" asked the general. Schoumacher replied, "I would like to do someone's job because I'm not being allowed to do mine." Like every American reporter he did not mind mixing it with authority.

"Why have you gone into the zone again?" was the next question. The general later probably regretted his answer. "We have gone in to show the southern half of the Demilitarized Zone is ours . . . to show we can go in any place we want, any time we want."

It was a brilliant plan, I thought. One company advanced up the road led by the tanks towards the Ben Hai River which cut the DMZ in half. Through the jungle on both sides of the road, and slightly in front, moved two other companies. The fourth company was lifted by helicopter in front on to high ground five kilometres in, next to the river. This was the classic pincer move. Any North Vietnamese in there were in trouble. The idea was that the marines would circle to the right and come out the next day. We returned to Danang to file our stories.

Next morning we asked if the marines had got out safely.

We were told that some "elements" were out, but not all . . . which was enough for the by now very cynical press corps. Lean, angular Tom Corpora of UPI, tall former navy officer John Lengal of AP, and I, with two TV crews, headed for Dong Ha once again. In the Vietspeak of the American military, to say "elements" were out meant others were trapped inside.

At Dong Ha, General Metzger called for General Hochmuth, division commander (later to be killed in a helicopter crash), who said he had just come from a briefing on the operation. There had been a small fight. He would not give casualties. No, this was not a new rule, it was longstanding, he said. A correspondent said he had heard just before we left Danang that it had been announced in Saigon that seven marines had been killed and forty-nine wounded. "Then that must be right," said the general.

Although it was not a very big story — because the casualties were so few — the other reporters still wanted to go in and see for themselves, though I lacked their keenness. General Hochmuth said it would be impossible for us to get in to the battalion because the troops were moving in heavy jungle near the DMZ. But he would lend us his helicopter to take us to another battalion. "I can promise you something there," he said, but didn't say what.

The general's helicopter was taking off from Dong Ha when Corpora suddenly ripped off his seat belt and jumped out as we hovered between one and two metres off the ground. I followed without thinking because I knew Corpora understood the war very well. It turned out he had spotted two medivacs flying in to the Dong Ha tent hospital in the distance. Medivacs meant American casualties — and also meant a reporter might be able to get in, and out, quickly. The medivacs were bound to be returning to the DMZ to collect more wounded "elements" who had made it out.

We were soon aboard a returning helicopter and as we arrived the marines were just coming out of the DMZ, with the bodies of their dead piled several deep on their tanks. A couple of heat casualties, delirious from the effects of the stifling atmosphere, lay scattered around, jibbering and shaking uncontrollably with others comforting them. As we landed in a small bush clearing, troops raced wounded to our helicopter like desperadoes, as others eyed the trees suspiciously.

Captain Frank Southard was wounded in the right hand. Unshaven and in a green T-shirt he sat on some water-cans. He drew a map on my notebook, awkwardly with his left hand, as he explained calmly — almost too calmly — what had happened. The classic and elaborate pincer move had failed. "We couldn't get around because the streams were swollen. There appeared to be no one around, so we were told to come back down the road. They were waiting with our own unexploded bombs [from air attacks] and mines lining the roads and in ambush position in the tree-line."

I told Captain Southard that the American command at the Follies always complained when we used the word "ambush". They felt they were on search and destroy missions and so were seeking that contact. "OK don't call it an ambush, call it a trap," said the captain.

By now John Lengal, the journalist we'd left behind when we jumped out of the general's helicopter in Dong Ha, had arrived by overland jeep from Con Thien, which showed how hard it was for newsagency reporters to shake one another. Not that Corpora liked it when I followed him out of the chopper — he just looked at me for a moment too long, although he said nothing.

The marines estimated that between 30 and 50 men were dead and 200 wounded, but no one knew exactly. The official figures eventually announced in Saigon days later were 23 killed and 191 wounded.

I watched the marines carefully unload the heavy dead bodies and lay them neatly in a line on the grass, almost shoulder to shoulder as if on parade, to await their turn for the helicopters after the wounded and the heat casualties were out. There were nineteen bodies in that row. Still others hadn't yet been found.

They were lined up like that so they could be lifted quickly into a helicopter by two soldiers, one holding the feet and the other the shoulders. Some of the dead looked as though nothing had happened to them at all and, while I stood gazing at the row of death, I realized that I knew now what thirty-eight parents, nineteen girlfriends, and untold brothers, sisters and other relatives did not yet know. It was an unhappy thought, as if I could personally fire a shotgun of sadness at a map of America.

One group of three young marines sat around a crater and I approached them hoping for an interview. Although they knew I was there none would look up. "We don't feel like talking," one said, without even looking, after minutes of silence. Just then, over near a tank, there was a commotion as a marine levelled his rifle at UPI photographer Dana Stone for taking photos of the bodies. Small, red-haired Dana, who had arrived after me, was talking as fast as he could; he had stopped taking pictures.

Reporters and American soldiers gathered around. "Don't you want the people at home to know what you guys are going through?" asked Stone. Some of the marines had their shirts off in the sun revealing taut, slender bodies. They were ready for fighting, not argument.

"Yes," said one. "They don't know what we are going through here. You fellas tell them we are winning. You tell them we take light casualties when we take heavy. They don't know the hell."(Light, moderate and heavy were terms the American PR machine used when it did not wish to reveal the exact extent of their casualties when an action was still incomplete.)

Another said, "Look at those men," pointing to the heat casualties. "Four weeks ago in winter coats and now in this heat fighting someone they can't even see. This fellow was cleaning windows in snow in New York a few weeks ago. Does that make a good story? Will you make money with that?" We argued in turn that we couldn't know what was happening because everything was usually over when we arrived. If we stuck with one battalion it might be six months or even two years before we got a story. Slowly the argument became an awkward, but more friendly, discussion as we all realized we were on the same side: trying to tell America how bad it was in Vietnam. The marines were very upset at what had happened, glad to be alive, and strangely proud that they had stayed and fought to rescue most of the bodies, although some of the bodies had been blown to pieces.

The troops said the North Vietnamese let two platoons of their leading company pass as they came back out, thinking that their enemy had gone — but then they shot up the third platoon. Those men were left wounded on the road and the tanks could not keep going without crushing them. The soldiers said they now realized that sending the men on foot in front of the tanks on a narrow road had been a mistake.

The two platoons in front fought their way out, and these were the "elements" we were told about in Danang. The rest of the trapped battalion called in bombs and artillery, but they could not be brought in close enough to get at the North Vietnamese who were fighting the "bear-hug" way. This method, they had learned, effectively negated American airpower because they were fighting too close to the "friendly" troops — as Americans called those on their side — for bombs to be used.

It was later announced in Saigon that a body count had revealed 175 North Vietnamese had been killed. But, according to the troops who were there, no one had stopped to count the North Vietnamese bodies. Captain Southard said his company had killed three or four "for certain".

This was the last time American forces went in strength into the DMZ. Just before getting on a helicopter with Corpora I told a black soldier General Metzger's statement about going in "to show the southern half of the DMZ is ours". "Going in's alright man, it's getting out that's the trouble," he said angrily.

In that July, 1967, the Americans found out that the DMZ

could never be theirs. But, if that was a shock, it was not as big as another surprise they got that same month ... the awareness that soon none of their entrenched bases in South Vietnam would be safe from bombardment.

One night something that was almost two metres long, trailed a blue exhaust, and whispered as it passed overhead rattled the Americans: steel-black Russian rockets. They were soon nicknamed "the whispering death".

When these rockets exploded they sent hundreds of jagged pieces of steel, from finger size to what soldiers called "five-pound razor-blades", on a collision course through the air. For the first time in history, guerrillas found themselves with artillery. Artillery which could be fired electrically from a resting position in a tree fork to batter targets up to eighteen kilometres away.

As late as February 1967, the Viet Cong's most potent weapon was the mortar, which had a maximum range of five kilometres. This enabled, no less encouraged, the Americans to build strong bases dotted around South Vietnam with a five-kilometre wide policed and cleared area around it to prevent them being shelled.

But it was impossible to clear and protect an eighteen-kilometre wide ring around a base and, by the end of 1967 — when even Dong Ha had had to be abandoned — there was no place safe in Vietnam from the portable rocket. This adversely affected American strategy, not to mention morale. By the time they talked peace with Ho Chi Minh in May 1968 the Americans in Vietnam were going to bed scared.

It was a night in February 1967 that some marines still awake at the sprawling Danang airbase had heard that whisper-whisper in the air. They had looked up and seen the blue exhausts. Then they had heard the explosions — the first rocket attack in Vietnam.

Though this was only one small attack far to the north of Saigon it was to mean — eventually — that the hunter had become the hunted.

For the next six months Danang became the practice pitch for these rocketings — undoubtedly because it was from here that air assaults were launched on North Vietnam. After that the rockets started appearing further and further south.

The first rockets to be used were short Russian 140 millimetre models, weighing about forty kilograms. They had a range of ten kilometres and some marines expressed concern in the first half of 1967 that they would be able to patrol such a wide area around their major bases. But they needn't have bothered. By July the Viet Cong had almost two-metre long, 122 millimetre models — both fin and spin stabilized for greater accuracy — and they managed to walk them up a line of parked aircraft at Danang from fourteen kilometres away in their first such raid on 15 July 1967, destroying US$80 million worth of equipment. It took only one rocket to destroy a US$3 million helicopter or fighter bomber. And this came in the same month as the demilitarized zone debacle.

That fifty-rocket attack just after midnight killed twelve previously safe servicemen and wounded forty. Yet these men did not fight in the jungles of Vietnam but backed up the American bombing of North Vietnam from the twin-runway Danang airbase — at that time, with the possible exception of Saigon, the busiest airport in the world. Eight supersonic Phantom jet fighter-bombers, the plane the American Air Force pilots in Danang preferred above all others, and three giant C-130s were destroyed. Ten other Phantoms were damaged by shrapnel. One rocket went through the roof of a barracks block housing 120 airmen who suddenly found they were on the receiving end of the war. Previously they had been the ones sending off the missiles.

These few well-placed rockets began to affect morale: for there is a big difference between being bombed in mountains and being bombed in your bed. The trouble with an enclave, the Americans found, is that it can so easily become a target.

167

To understand the effect these rockets were having, take the night we raced in jeeps from the Danang press centre to the airbase for a routine check of a mere two-rocket Viet Cong attack. As worried reporters called to those driving to turn off their headlights so the guards would not think we were Viet Cong, a black guard screamed at us to go away, "We've been hit. We've been hit," he called continually, with emotion cracking his voice.

But it was only two rockets — just enough for the Viet Cong to get the entire ten thousand men at the base out of bed and diving over each other for bunkers. Although no one was injured by the rockets, sixteen had been injured in their terrified flight for safety, some landing on others in bunkers, some falling over beds and running into posts in desperate, dark flight from the cruel tears of steel shrapnel.

The arrival of the press on such occasions never failed to cause comment. "You people would be the only men in the world who would drive *to* a rocket attack," one airforce colonel said, shaking his head. (After this incident, plans to build bunkers at the Danang press centre were abandoned.) The military were always amazed at the lengths the press would go to just for a story. A marine cartoon which appeared in the *Saigon Post* each day told the story of the war through a battered, unshaven marine called Sergeant Mike. One day Sergeant Mike was defending an outpost against waves of guerrillas. He was in real trouble, with only himself and one other left. In the background a big double-ended helicopter had just touched down and men were pouring out the back: "At last, reinforcements," said Sergeant Mike. "No. It's the press," said his companion.

By the beginning of 1968 rockets would batter Bien Hoa airbase twenty-four kilometres north of Saigon. Rockets would then shake Saigon to herald the start of the Tet Offensive and whisper in to batter Saigon's Tan Son Nhut airbase. My worst fears were to be realized, even before my twelve months were up.

Clearly the rocket was rapidly changing the complexion of

the Vietnam War in 1967. It could strike anywhere in the country. It could be fired electrically so quickly and simply that the chances of being spotted while setting it up were very small. The only disadvantage was its weight: it took two Viet Cong to carry just one rocket. But this did not stop them bringing them down jungle paths 1,500 kilometres long from Hanoi.

Hanoi had continually warned over its radio in propaganda broadcasts that for every escalation of the war by the Americans, North Vietnam too could escalate. With the huge American build-up in numbers to more than half a million in 1967 came a matching North Vietnamese build-up of regulars; and with the intense American air bombardment of North Vietnam in 1967 came rockets on the south.

American troops even became worried that the North Vietnamese would be given Russian ground-to-ground missiles that travelled more than 150 kilometres. But the Viet Cong didn't really need them. To break up a war fought from small bases dotted throughout the country, eighteen kilometres was quite enough.

Up until this time it seemed to me that the Americans might have missed the significance of the advent of this form of artillery. But that September they learned that it was probably their greatest threat. For in September 1967 Gio Linh's twin base, Con Thien, began being hit by an incredible one thousand artillery rounds a day; that is, per day, about one shell for every marine in the base or close to one a minute. For the first time, the Americans began to realize that if they couldn't stop this attack on a battalion or more of their boys sitting on a hilltop alone and almost unaided then they were losing the war.

Although tremendous air raids were mounted on the North Vietnamese guns, they kept firing. Experienced pilots, such as triple ace Colonel Blaisse in Danang, told me that artillery could not be knocked out by aircraft unless the gun fired as the pilot was diving. "Stand in a big dark hall and get someone to flick a flashlight, then go and see if you can put your hand where it flashed. See how close you get," he said. "An error of a few inches and you would miss that gun."

Reporters questioned marine Pacific commander General Krulak on what could be done. "We are firing a thousand rounds for every hundred they fire at us," was the general's answer. But the North Vietnamese were firing at a small target, whereas the marines were firing into the countryside.

That September was about the time when even the least cynical journalists started to think the game was up for the American effort in Vietnam. Con Thien, with its thousand rounds of incoming a day, became such a big story that it made the cover story of *Time* magazine; and it was not even the sort of story *Time* was looking for, since until then that magazine had been pro the war effort. The *Time* journalists in their office next to ours in Saigon complained often about the optimistic outlook of their journal.

The battle for Con Thien was the first major turning point of the war. However it might have been overlooked by the press, on account of the large number of bases and battles in the war, had it not been for the work of one American television journalist, Jack Lawrence.

Jack arrived at the Danang press centre one day and I asked him where he was headed. He said he was going to "that place Con Thien" because he'd heard it was getting more than its fair share of artillery. I had written about places getting hit with artillery — Gio Linh, for instance — but after talking to officers I had come to believe that the shellings were more of a nuisance than a threat to the war effort.

But Lawrence said he thought it was an incredibly significant story and he was trusting his judgment, and not the reports. "I'm going to go up there and I'm going to make that the biggest story in Vietnam," he told me. He did a story for national TV in America and one of the marines he interviewed said something like: "If we don't hurry up and stop 'em here they will be in Saigon in no time." That was shown around America. Obviously all the newspaper news editors saw it, and the direct interviews with colour film of incoming artillery and troops hiding in bunkers brought home to them what straight news reporters could not. Immediately they dispatched their reporters in Vietnam to Con Thien with cables urging on-the-spot descriptions of this "sitting duck approach to war". The announcements at the Five O'Clock Follies could not compete with Lawrence, his idea, his colour film.

This time I decided I had better stop away. I could now see that for a British newsagency at that time selling to a very few rich American newspapers which were probably getting all the wire services, I was risking my neck for a few sentences in "an American spokesman said" story put together in London from several Reuters' Saigon stories. I would be supposedly competing with Cheatham and Corpora (UPI) or Lengal and Ohman (AP) who might get by-lined in a few thousand papers across their home country if they got an on-the-spot exclusive. And, if it was good enough, a possible Pulitzer.

I let everyone else go for a few days until, finally, the questions from fellow correspondents and marines, as well as new bureau chief Pringle in Saigon (who I thought wanted to know what was really happening more for himself than for Reuters), began to tell. Coincidentally a friend, marine Lieutenant Gazaway, offered to go with me. So, although all the stories had already been broadcast and published I headed off, very reluctantly, for my look. Luckily, this just happened to coincide with a big announcement on Con Thien in Saigon.

The five-blade rotor of the big helicopter strained for a final effort as it dived for the low run into Con Thien, a base cut off by land by North Vietnamese troops and under constant artillery pounding. The helicopter hovered inside the tight barbed-wire and mined perimeter surrounding the three

171

steep little peaks, dropped off the load of ammunition tied in a wire sling underneath, and settled for two seconds to let seven men out, four of whom were fresh from the United States and had no idea that their baptism was to be the toughest available.

I rushed down the lowering ramp intent on heading for the first bunker I could find — but stopped where I landed, up to my knees in mud. So were the others. The hurrying helicopter did not wait for us to get out of the way. It swung its blades around in a show of strength and the downrush of wind pushed me over on my hands.

Because an attack was imminent, at least one thousand marines (they wouldn't say how many) had been crammed on to the base to repel it. In crowded, flimsy, bunkers on an ill-prepared site they took heavy casualties just waiting for the all-out ground assault of charging thousands that — as at Gio Linh — was never to come. Food, water, and ammunition had to come in by helicopter because the road had washed away in heavy rain after North Vietnamese soldiers blew a gully in it along a vital stretch — using an un-exploded US bomb. And, anyway, it would have taken a battalion to ensure a convoy could make it through from Dong Ha.

Stuck next to me in the mud and laughing, with his teeth clenched so as not to lose his cigar, Lieutenant Gazaway — "Gaz" — still held his Thompson sub-machinegun under his arm as he removed the cigar with a muddy hand.

"Welcome to Con Thien," he said, as we surveyed the bottom edges of the camp. It looked deserted because no one was leaving their bunker just to greet us. Gaz and I had become friends after a game of tennis on an old Vietnamese court in Danang where we were hindered by the coils of barbed wire down each side, presumably there to prevent the Viet Cong playing tennis (there seemed no other explanation).

We pulled each other on to firmer mud and set off up the mudside. We were searching for the command post, but the

172

only people in view on this hill of foxholes were the five who came in with us. We walked with them (people tend to gather much closer in war), which was a mistake. As it turned out, we were too good a target for North Vietnamese gunners to resist.

We walked into a cut-out section of the hill. It was built to hold an amphibious vehicle to be manned by the five men with us, though there was no vehicle there yet. Gaz was ahead of me by five metres as we moved through the cutting and up the slope at the other end to solid ground. As he neared the top there was a quick whistle and a loud explosion. Gaz rolled backwards down the slope, his Thompson sticking barrel-down into the mud and staying there. I instinctively hit the ground next to the wall in the cut-out, on top of a pile of rubbish.

"Everyone OK?" said the sergeant who was with us and in charge of the new four. I thought Gaz must have been hit but he immediately kneeled up to look over the top of the cut-out to see where we could go next. "It's one-twenty artillery," said the sergeant, showing a disconcerting familiarity with being shelled.

Another whistle and I dug my face into the ground. Another explosion. Two more shells, then nothing for a minute. "OK, we better get on to the command post," said Gaz, his Thompson again tucked under his muddy arm. It was a strange feeling to imagine the Vietnamese gunners out there watching us through binoculars with artillery pieces loaded. I had naturally expected lots of artillery fire when I got to Con Thien but I hadn't expected to be shelled personally.

"Let's wait awhile," I said. I really felt like going back to the helicopter, but that was just as far and, anyway, the helicopter wasn't there now. Three more shells came in around us, and each time I sweated it out waiting for the one that would land in the cut-out.

The four young men with the sergeant huddled close to the pile of goods they had carried with them and to each other. "All I want to do is save my arse," said one. "Yeah," echoed another, looking up from the mud for the first time and revealing a blackened face. The other two said nothing. But the unshaven sergeant continued to talk happily.

"This is my second month here now. I know the sound of all their shells. They don't scare me very much."

Now it was all silent at Con Thien. Nothing stirred. No one came to see if we were hurt. Gazaway jumped to his feet and I pulled myself up from my mud-rubbish bed. Again we walked up the slope, this time listening carefully. I knew better now than to talk at Con Thien — you might miss hearing the shells. We made our way across the hillside, through a porridge of mud, and checked at a flimsy bunker to ask someone the way to the command post. I looked down into the dark depths. There was a bed floating in thirty centimetres of water. There was no one home.

We walked for a time in a knee-deep, ill-dug trench but it soon ended, and Gaz and I were back in the open, heading down the hill to an open flat valley thirty metres across. On the other side ammunition box steps led almost straight up to a monument-sized sandbag complex fitted into the hillside like a parody of an Aztec temple: the command post.

Walking across the little valley I was much happier. I felt protected by the slopes behind and in front of me, and strolled slowly across. Some marines on the other side, when I finally arrived, commented on our coolness. "We call this stretch Death Valley because it gets sprayed with shrapnel every time either hill takes a shell," said one of them.

Above the ammunition boxes an officer explained the lack of trenches and drainage systems. "The trench-digging machine hasn't arrived," he said. I assumed he was joking. But perhaps he wasn't. The Viet Cong built vast mazes of trenches just in case someone one day attacked them but, even when under massive artillery attack, the Americans didn't have enough of them. The difference, of course, was that the Americans saw this as a temporary war. Besides, the marines were extremely proud of their reputation as probably the world's greatest assault troops: they didn't like sitting on little hills getting shelled and waiting for someone to attack — they wanted to take hills. "The marines take land. It's the army's job to slobber over it," they said.

Such was the reputation of the United States marines that at first all the marines in Vietnam were volunteers but, as the war dragged on, draftees crept in. It was another blow to their fighting spirit and, like most things, it showed in the Sergeant Mike cartoon. Mike was making a typical second world war amphibious marine assault on a beach; he was unshaven, with cigarette half-smoked hanging from his lips. He was wading ashore from the assault craft when his friend pointed back out to sea to a lone marine heading for the shore on a surfboard. "Draftee for sure," said Sergeant Mike.

Loud explosions sent me diving for cover, but the marines laughed. "Outgoing," they said, and I looked up to see big marine guns pounding shells out into the sea of land that held the North Vietnamese. I wished they wouldn't do that because it was easy to see we were in the worst position for a shooting match.

Nearby an old sergeant good-naturedly abused the young marines who took off their flak jackets and helmets to take in the sunshine — the first sunny day in weeks. These marines were sick of being weighed down. But there was no way of telling if they wouldn't need their helmets for the next twelve hours, or if they would need them immediately. Incoming mortar fire soon solved that dilemma, the noise of it drowned by the nearby crack and burst of big fifty-calibre machinegun fire from the North Vietnamese.

The camp commander had that day been promoted from major to colonel. He told me that when all the press arrived and wrote about the shellings and the lack of food and ammunition at the base a few days before, he had hated them for it.

175

The press weren't very popular in Vietnam because not only was the military unhappy that the war was not getting good write-ups, but also "bleeding heart reporters", as some critics called them, were also given valuable military space on helicopters.

With Con Thien's plight at its worst, a Jolly Green Giant was being loaded ready to go in with badly needed supplies when a colonel arrived with seventeen press people wanting to go there because of reports that the position was in trouble. When the captain in charge was instructed to unload most of the cargo to let the press on, he refused, and kept on refusing until the colonel threatened to take from him every bit of rank he had. However, since the press stories had been published, the camp commander told me, the base had been inundated with supplies and the troops were even eating ice cream. He had been told that President Johnson had personally intervened.

Back we went down the steps and across the valley, this time running.

Gaz was very cool, except in the valley, and otherwise seemed worried only at having to walk past hundreds of fellow marines with a bloke with long hair. "You know, Hugh, these guys are looking at me in a queer sort of way. Your hair is curling up under the end of your helmet," he said. I had let my hair grow long so everyone would know at first glance I was not in the army. I didn't want the experience of fellow correspondent John MacLennan. On his first operation with the marines, he rushed back to base and, hurrying to get a helicopter, ran up to the colonel in charge and said, "What were the casualties? Colonel! The casualties!" A considerate major grabbed him and gently but firmly hustled him outside. "Now sonny, calm down. What's your unit?" he said, thinking MacLennan was a heat casualty.

The troops were pissed off at having to hide in wet bunkers — some with their rotting feet poking up out of the tops of their muddy holes.

Many complained about suffering all of this when a few nuclear artillery shells which could be fired from the guns at Con Thien would stop everything. "We need a few nukes," they kept saying. "You'll probably only get a few gook nukes back," I said, which seemed to put an end to the idea.

A shell whistled in and I dived with the marines into a lot of water. But the North Vietnamese had had the last laugh: the shell exploded in the air, showering the camp with propaganda leaflets about the treatment of blacks in America, quoting US senators who were opposed to the war.

One of the troops produced his own leaflet on the war, a mud-covered piece of paper on which he had scribbled a poem while under fire. It looked as if he had written the poem with his pen dipped in the mud. Con Thien is Vietnamese for Hill of Angels, an apt description, and he called his poem "The Angel". It described the death of a mate by an artillery round. I will always remember the final stanza. After describing the death of "a mother's first-born", the poem said:

And for what?
Our reason is gone.
But on this hill of angels
Death goes on.

But even as we read his poem moves were under way in Saigon to end the battle . . . at least as far as the public were concerned.

The American command in Saigon had decided they must end this "sitting duck" story once and for all, so they called a background press conference at which American generals announced that the battle for Con Thien was over and the North Vietnamese were pulling away in small groups.

Since Con Thien had been headlines for a week this announcement was a huge story, which could only be believed by anyone who had not been there. Some of the journalists at the press conference knew what it was like in this isolated area and many did not but, because of the system, they all filed the story even though the generals could not be named and only "highly informed military sources" could be quoted. All except one.

Jim Pringle told me later how there was the usual rush for the phones outside the Follies when the announcement was made. Pringle was in a difficult situation. He knew AP, UPI and AFP were sending their stories around the world with bells on and Reuters' subscribers would want our version of the story. But Pringle didn't believe the announcement, particularly as he could not quote the generals by name. So he did what probably no newsagency reporter has ever done — and I commend him for it — he decided *not* to file a story. Instead he chose to wait until I had returned to Danang to dictate the on-the-spot story.

Within ten minutes Pringle was getting call-backs over the wire from London via Tokyo. "Primary and secondary opposition reporting battle for Con Thien over. Need matcher urgentest." This type of language was used in all Reuter memos and dated back to the penny-a-word days when two words could be combined to pass as one to save money. Thus all people at Reuters proceeded Londonwards and all stories were uppicked earlier. When one Reuter correspondent wanted to resign in the late sixties, he merely sent the following message to head office in a language all of them understood: "Upstick job arsewards."

Pringle, bravely, memoed London that he did not believe the announcement, that it was illogical, that the generals would not put their names to it and that he was awaiting my on-the-spot story. The reply from London was swift and, for a Reuter memo, long. Basically it told Pringle what he already knew: that it was not his job to decide what was and was not true; that it was the journalist's job to report what people were saying so the world could make its own judgment (although since no names could be used no one had said anything); and he had better file immediately and Lunn could re-lead the story later. Reluctantly, Pringle sat down at his typewriter in the long narrow office and tapped out a

178

story "in style", meaning written in the manner required. It began something like this:

Pro London exPringle
Saigon, Reuter The battle for Con Thien is over and the North Vietnamese are pulling away in small groups, according to highly informed military sources here

Then he waited for me.

When I got back to Danang I had already written my story on a piece of paper on the plane. It followed the principle I had recently learned of writing what I saw rather than what people told me. I inserted some information Pringle told me of what happened at the press conference — what a newsagency calls backgrounding a story. It went something like this:

Con Thien, South Vietnam, Reuter American marines huddled from North Vietnamese artillery in flooded bunkers here today, slogged through knee-deep mud, and came under 50-calibre machine-gun fire.
Meanwhile in Saigon, 400 miles to the south, American commanders announced, off the record, that the battle for Con Thien was over.

I followed up with a quote from the Con Thien commander: "We are being hugged on three sides." The story finished with a quote from a nineteen-year-old marine who sat sunning his rotting foot out of the bunker and saying: "Sure we got them where we want them . . . shoot in any direction and you'll get a gook."

But that is not how it went out to the world.

Months later I saw my story in several old newspapers and it had been re-led with my by-line in London like this:

by Hugh Lunn
Con Thien, South Vietnam, September, Reuter The battle for Con Thien is over and the North Vietnamese are pulling away in small groups, according to highly informed military sources here. . . .

If it hadn't been so sad it would have been funny — quoting

179

as it did "sources" on a muddy hill near the Demilitarized Zone. However, after several paragraphs of Pringle's enforced press-conference report, it then used my eyewitness account material.

While some will no doubt see this as a media plot, I can see how the American off-the-record plan worked even over and above an eye-witness report. Because, when the subeditor in London came to "blend" my story with Pringle's (and I had done that myself in London often enough), I can understand how he would have considered that the real "news" of the day was that the infamous battle for Con Thien (of *Time* cover and TV fame) was supposed to be over. After all that was the story everyone else had . . . and news organizations hate to be alone on a major story.

Probably I should have been stronger in my intro and said: "The battle for Con Thien is not over", but even this would have been changed because it would have been perceived as news comment.

The strangest thing for me though was that while the journalistic side was complicated, the military position was clear: the American generals were still kidding themselves that they were in command in Vietnam.

Ambushed: Hill 875

In November 1967 Bruce Pigott and I both ended up going to the same hill in the jungle, Hill 875. The Americans named it that, the 875 being merely its height in metres, which gave no indication of just how isolated it was.

It is difficult for people who come from countries where everything is accessible to imagine the isolation of such a hill in a small country in what is wrongly considered in the West to be an over-populated part of the world. A US officer once complained to me that Americans just hadn't got the picture straight about Vietnam. "They look at the small map on a globe or in a paper and think, 'Hell, half a million of our troops there. They must be falling off the side,' " he said. He had a pet theory that the best way to show people back in the States what was happening was to "print bigger maps of Vietnam". The only way to get to Hill 875 was to take a flight to the Central Highlands city of Pleiku and then hop a chopper northwest into the mountains to a small base called Dak To, and from there another one over almost uninhabited mountains and jungle valleys to near where Laos, Cambodia, and Vietnam all meet.

Without a helicopter the only way to reach the hill was to hike for several days through the jungle.

Throughout 1967 the marines had been having the big battles with North Vietnamese regular army units crossing the border, while the US army further south fought smaller hit-and-run fights with Viet Cong guerrillas. They had also trudged over these mountains searching for big North Vietnamese units thought to be planning a major thrust further south from the sanctuary of the mountains, but who seemed to be intent on avoiding any battles. Searching for the Viet Cong was like walking through a muddy field: every time you put your foot down you held that piece of territory, but pick it up and the print disappeared.

On 19 November 1967 a battalion of six hundred army paratroopers stomped single file over yet another hill in the Central Highlands. "They all looked the same to us," a soldier told me later. "We didn't expect to see anything." But this time the North Vietnamese were there, dug in deep in bunkers with small firing holes and bamboo-and-dirt reinforced tops. They didn't open fire until the unwitting paratroopers were next to them.

The rear company took the Vietnam-textbook action and raced to a nearby clearing to cut an L Zee (landing zone) for helicopters to take out the wounded and to land reinforcements. But, as they put down their weapons and began to fell the trees, the North Vietnamese, who had surrounded the clearing earlier in anticipation of this move, opened fire. Realizing they had to link up with the others, the paratroopers counter-attacked and fought their way through to the other two companies, but the battalion remained surrounded in isolated thick jungle a hundred metres short of the peak, with no hope of the helicopters getting in because of the thick jungle. The airborne troops fought desperately and, considering their parlous position, did well not to be overrun. They were proud to be paratroopers and always referred to non-paratrooper soldiers as "legs".

Two days passed and the wounded were crying out for medical treatment. Chain saws were dropped in to try to cut a helicopter landing pad to take out the dead and dying. No one knew how many there were, but there were hundreds.

American bombers battered the North Vietnamese positions on top of the ridge which formed the crest of the hill. In the five-day battle they were to drop 180,000 kilograms of bombs on that small hilltop plus napalm and anti-personnel CBUs. One 250 kilogram bomb went slightly astray and landed among the paratrooper wounded. Army men were quick to blame this on "a marine pilot", but no one really seemed to know what had happened, except that many of the wounded — including a number of the officers — were now dead. Apparently the officers had been discussing strategies when the bomb dropped.

The chain saws sliced through sixty-metre high trees, making a long lift shaft to the sky, down which it was hoped to bring the helicopters. The first three helicopters down, however, were hit by machinegun fire from the top of the hill. It became obvious that the only way to get the men out was for other units to take the hill. Reinforcements were sent to an artillery fire support base three kilometres away and from there began to cut their way through the bamboo and jungle, while from the other side troops of the 4th Infantry Division also battled their way to the isolated hill. Meanwhile a couple of helicopters did eventually make it down the tortuous tunnel from the sky despite the slow descent into heavy fire. One of them carried Bruce Pigott.

Pigott later somehow managed to get out on another chopper to file his story, describing the death, bewilderment, and devastation he had witnessed.

One helicopter that was shot down contained Australian reporter John Cantwell of *Time* magazine who had won a draw in Dak To to be first reporter in. Cantwell limped back to Saigon on crutches without having made it, but his luck was to run out for good later in the war.

Bruce was now on to a big story, and I felt he was finally doing what he had come to do. Therefore I was surprised when Jim Pringle told me Bruce had called him from Pleiku — where he had had to fly to file a story. "And you will have to go up to help him, Hugh," Pringle said. I knew it was no use having two people covering the one battle for a newsagency but I could see I was going to be in on this one and I didn't like it at all — particularly now that I was almost into my second last month. And in the last month, under local rules, I would not have to leave Saigon.

The only conclusion I could draw was that it was much worse at Hill 875 when Bruce went in by helicopter than even his reports could convey — reports which were necessarily brief and centred on the statistics of the battle.

The next morning I flew to Pleiku, which I had never seen before, and thought glumly that a reporter was probably the only person in the world who would leave his apartment in Saigon voluntarily to fly to what was probably the ugliest and deadliest battle of this war.

When I got there Bruce acted strangely. It was obvious the idea that I would be "helping" had been forgotten. He just said abruptly, "Right, I'm going back and you're going in tomorrow." He seemed very quiet and was looking past me, straight ahead, as he sat on the floor of a tent and smoked and drank a can of beer. I knew he couldn't be annoyed with me, but he was acting like a person who was. He seemed uptight — so much so that I didn't let him know how unhappy I was at the prospect of going to that battle. Meekly, I accepted his instruction.

That night Pigott was a different person from the guy I had known in Saigon who every now and then would give a very little smile. He had changed from a person absorbed by the war to someone suddenly sickened by its excesses. He looked like a man who had had enough of life. He seemed so sad that for the first time I began to see him the way Dinh once described him, after checking his dictionary: "Melancholy, Bruce melancholy man." He didn't bother with big greetings, he didn't ask me how Pringle or Dinh were, or, most amazing of all, even about Miss Nga, the girl he loved. He just sat on the floor against the wall of the little press tent and smoked many more than his occasional cigarette. He didn't volunteer to tell me anything about what had happened or even offer any advice on how I might get to the hill. He had the attitude of "your turn", with a touch of "now you'll see what it's like". As, obviously, he didn't want to talk I went looking for a bed for the night, for in war everyone leaves for battle at dawn.

There were so many reporters at Pleiku that there was no room at the press centre for me and I had to go down to a big old double-storey wooden building near the perimeter. It was full of beds, had no internal walls, and no one had arrived to sleep. I climbed into a musty-smelling sleeping bag on a stretcher, feeling lonely and anxious about the next day. I kept trying to think ahead to tomorrow evening when, all being well, I would be back here with my story and able to go back to Saigon and the office and Dinh and Jim and be safe for the week. However, I started thinking about Bruce and wondering if the Vietnamese could really read faces. Dinh, who said Vietnam was always "too short of fortune-tellers", had told me once that he feared for Bruce because his melancholy expression meant "Bruce not long live man". Not that he ever said this to Bruce.

Gungadinh was an easy man to like. But Dinh, then twenty-nine and Bruce had developed a deep friendship which seem-ed unlikely between the ebullient chain-smoking Vietnamese and the quiet Australian who rarely said more than a short sentence. Both times that Bruce left Saigon on R and R, he brought back a present for Dinh. Once it was one of those fancy, formal, white shirts from the Philippines which are accepted as their national dress in that country, something prized.

"Bruce look like girl," Dinh always said aloud in front of his friend, but I could see nothing feminine about him. He was tall and slender with boyish sharp features and short hair combed almost straight back. But Dinh saw him the Vietnamese way. "What can I say. He not drinking, he not smoking, and he very thin man. He very young and also he all the time keep quiet. Bruce Pi'gott (Dinh emphasized the second syllable) is slowly man. He speak very slowly like woman, like lady."

I was glad now that I had asked Dinh what my countenance foretold. He just laughed and said, "You a trouble-maker boy. You all the time move quickly, you clever boy. Even you hit by one artillery shell you not die. That reason I call you Gunsmoke."

185

Now, facing Hill 875, I hoped he was right.

I was awaken by four rifle shots which I knew to be from an old carbine. Seconds later the whole perimeter of the Pleiku camp opened fire and for a few minutes every gun was firing into the dark distance. It was all happening and I was alone in a house on the perimeter. Now, even more nervous and uneasy than before, I decided I would feel better if I had a look at what was happening.

The perimeter machineguns spewed red tracer bullets across the rolling plateau outside. That afternoon I had looked at this brown plain and thought how much it reminded me of Australia. But now it looked like Vietnam again as big orange flares floated down from the sky. I wondered what the Americans were shooting at. There was no return fire.

In T-shirt and army trousers I headed back up to the press tent in the blacked-out camp for another attempt to communicate with Pigott. Halfway there, I heard a voice call out, "Who are you?" "I'm a reporter going up to the press tent." "This is a red alert," the voice said. "We must all put on flak jackets and helmets and man our bunkers." Slowly the troopers came out of the big sandbag room and we started talking, until an officer came and ordered them back in and I walked on up the hill unaffected by the red order. Pigott could not phone his story while the red alert was on, and waited at the bar in the press tent until he eventually got through to Jim at 3 a.m.

Bruce still seemed in a daze. In the last day he had seen a soldier with no legs trying to run to a helicopter. I realized for the first time how much war could change a man. It wasn't so much the death and destruction, but the mutilation of man and his society. Here Bruce was involved on two fronts: he lived and worked with American troops, and he hoped to become a part of Vietnamese society by marrying Miss Nga. Her religious family had fled North Vietnam as refugees after the partition in 1954. She had been educated at the best Saigon French schools and spoke several languages.

She was twenty-one, attractive without being beautiful, open-faced, cheery, and vital. Always trimly and neatly dressed she looked to me like she might end up a business-woman. Of course Bruce never told me he was planning to marry her, but he did confide this to Dinh.

Dinh had become the focal point of this beautiful love affair between two very young people from very different worlds. And, although Miss Nga could speak English well, the relationship was obviously difficult, to put it mildly, on account of the emotional trauma it caused between the girl and her parents: they could not believe that their perfect Confucian daughter could have fallen in love with a foreigner waging war in their land. So Miss Nga went to Dinh and wanted Bruce reassured; and Dinh looked up the words and assured Bruce that Miss Nga loved him "exactly, really, already".

Dinh had told me that when I was out of Saigon Bruce would do the nightleads and then ask Dinh to sit with him outside the hot office and look at the trees in the park op-posite. Bruce would ask him detailed questions on Viet-namese customs and history; and also asked how he would go about marrying a girl like Miss Nga — what he should do for her parents, how to talk to them if he met them, and similar points of etiquette. Dinh was impressed by Bruce's interest in Vietnamese customs, particularly after enduring the lack of American interest for so many years. "He very carefully man, not like American who hurry up to marry and early to forget. He loves her carefully. He think-ing too much because he want he and Miss Nga to live together long time," Dinh said. He liked the fact that Bruce continually asked Miss Nga to wear the Vietnamese Ao Dai rather than the Western clothes she usually wore as a result of her French schooling. Bruce also worried a lot about the war and the effect it was having on the Vietnamese. "Really he love Vietnam country," Dinh said proudly. "He has very social heart."

Next morning Bruce left Pleiku for Saigon while some

187

forty other media people and I boarded helicopters for the remote outpost camp of Dak To, eighty kilometres north of Pleiku and just twenty-two kilometres from Hill 875.

The ambush on Hill 875 resulted from a massive US push in the area around Dak To following an announcement that the Americans had intelligence information that the North Vietnamese were moving to take the camp.

Dak To looked very vulnerable to me. It was an eerie spot surrounded by mountain tops and far removed from the world. There was a brittle feeling about the place. Even the fact that big guns outnumbered people added some sort of subconscious tension. It made it easy to understand how people in a wagon train must have felt moving through the old west in America: too far away for help to come in time in a land where a hundred thousand enemy warriors might be waiting over the next rise.

On all sides were twin 40-millimetre cannon anti-aircraft guns pointing into the jungle hills. Each shell was as slender as a female model's forearm and it would burst into hundreds of deadly pieces on contact even with a twig. If it hit nothing it would shatter after eight seconds. The tank-like guns would fire 250 of these rounds a minute.

Even to look at the cold mountain stream that formed one long boundary of the camp gave me an uneasy feeling. It must have been about fifty metres across but on the other side there was a wall of thick jungle which could have held untold numbers of troops. That was why there were so many anti-aircraft guns facing across the stream — they were the only weapons that could really compete with the speed of an attack from such close cover. According to the troops, there were now thought to be four North Vietnamese divisions — more than fifty thousand men — out there in the jungle hills, but who could even guess in such a place. If there were, though, Dak To would last about as long as Custer.

To back up the rifles and anti-aircraft guns there were also the long-barrelled, 175 millimetre (seven inch diameter) artillery pieces that could fire a projectile over thirty kilometres, and 200 millimetre (eight inch) guns that blasted bomb-sized craters in hillsides. These were all to keep the fifty thousand at bay and to support troops out on patrol whose job was to act like early-warning devices.

As at the other American camps, the Stars and Stripes flag flew over the command post, but the Confederate flag seemed to fly from almost every other stick and radio antenna in the camp, probably because the soldiers here felt closer than ever to their past.

Helicopters came and went in groups like taxis at an airport in rush hour, except they did so in clouds of dust. Reporters and photographers raced from one chopper to the next trying to catch a lift to Hill 875; some, it seemed, were just jumping on board without asking because the noise was such that it was no use even yelling. Although I assume American commanders knew what all their helicopters were up to, I'm sure no one else did. Most of them were obviously involved somehow in the plan to take Hill 875 so, after hesitating for half an hour and convinced I was going to my death, I climbed aboard a heavily loaded helicopter, with no questions asked on either side.

After about ten minutes we landed on a dusty bombed-out hilltop surrounded by jungle. There were several mortars, which seemed hastily dug in, trenches, and a command bunker under sandbags. It wasn't what I was expecting. I had expected to be lowered down through trees in a battle raging around me. But here, once the helicopter had un-loaded and set off again for Dak To, it was deadly quiet . . . until a loud explosion shook the ground like an earthquake. More shakes followed as the mortars opened fire. But this was not Hill 875 after all, I was informed, this was Firebase 16 three kilometres away. Here the mortars were being directed on to the North Vietnamese by another battalion of the 173rd Airborne bent on helping their besieged fellow paratroopers who were still cut off.

I fell into conversation with a lieutenant who had not only

189

stayed on in Vietnam after he had been wounded for the third time but who had also extended his tour. He had been in Vietnam eighteen months and was willing to die "to stop the Chinese from taking over the whole of Asia". This part of the conversation had an effect on me: not only was I not willing to die for Hill 875 but I did not believe the Chinese were remotely interested in taking all of Asia by force, or even Vietnam.

Falteringly, a helicopter made its way down to our hill and I hurried across to the L Zee thinking it might be going on to 875. Instead three journalists got off, and the helicopter left. They had been at Firebase 12 and were still trying to get to the hill. I went back to the friendly lieutenant.

Since he was a company commander of experience I asked him what it was like fighting the Viet Cong. The way he saw it, the Americans were at a tremendous disadvantage because they had to travel through unfamiliar countryside. Guerrillas could be waiting anywhere: they could attack any time they liked, at any place they liked, in whatever strength they liked. This time, he said, they had chosen 875.

What he said reminded me of a prefabricated steel bridge I often watched downriver from Danang. It was guarded by an entire American military police (MP) company because, if a bridge is to be protected in war, it has to be protected twenty-four hours a day seven days a week. The MPs had to shoot at any objects floating down the river in case they contained explosives, thereby setting them off before they hit the bridge. They had frogmen who checked under the water every day, and they threw occasional hand grenades over the side to kill any Viet Cong divers who might happen to be swimming around stockpiling explosives. They also had to check all Vietnamese vehicles before allowing them to cross the bridge. All that to guard one little bridge in Vietnam. I think it was watching that bridge more than anything else that had made me change my mind and decide the Americans would never win the war. There were hundreds of such targets all over Vietnam all being protected each minute of each hour of each day of each year . . . just in case the Viet Cong spent five minutes blowing one up.

Another helicopter had arrived at the firebase empty and was being loaded up. A reporter from *Newsweek* who had only just arrived stood by anxiously making sure room would be made for him: this one *was* going to 875. He was so anxious he jumped in and sat on the load. My lieutenant whistled. This veteran of many battles expressed great admiration for the bravery of the reporter "sitting on all that ammo going in there". I didn't tell him that I, too, was supposed to be going on that helicopter — that I was still trying to get up the guts to get on.

Anyway the chopper looked pretty full . . . and I let it go without me. Instantly I regretted having done so. It wasn't as if I could ask it to come back or order another one. Now I might never get to Hill 875. I might not even get a story. I would sit out the battle just three kilometres away knowing I could get more information if I'd stayed in Saigon. Normally I don't tell others of my fears or worries but, in a war, talking about them comes more easily. I mentioned my misgivings to the lieutenant. "No sweat," he said, staring hard at my eyes. "We'll all listen to it together." And he took me over to the radio set just outside the command-post bunker, told me to get out my pencil, and turned it on.

A Major Scott was already directing the taking of the hill. In the last few days, hundreds of new troops, many on foot, had been moved into the area, on three sides of the besieged battalion. When Major Scott confirmed that 4th Division troops were ready at the base on the other side of the hill the airborne battalion which had cut its way through the jungle started up the hill for the big push into the shattered, torn area where American bodies lay unrecovered.

There was a long interval of silence and then gunfire crackled out over the radio. "There's a sniper up here cracking rounds off over our heads," called a Captain

Leonard. Then explosions. Captain Leonard said hand grenades were bouncing down the slope through the stumps and exploding among the troops. "We're in trouble. They're fucking us up. They're really fucking us up," a black radio operator called. Captain Leonard had already been wounded.

"Calm down. Calm down, soldier," called Major Scott. "Well it ain't doin' us a bit of good," said the radio operator. "There's a sniper in a tree. I can see him! I can see him!" called another. They kept shooting at him, but still he stayed — right up until the Americans reached him and found him filled with holes: he was strapped to the tree.

Our firebase and others fired volley after volley of rounds in support and also to stop the North Vietnamese from withdrawing in the face of the big American push. Radio operators reported a series of deep entrenched bunkers had been taken — but there was no one left inside. One pointed out that every time a grenade was thrown into one of them, smoke poured out of air vents twenty metres away. "No wonder the air strikes didn't help," said my lieutenant.

The wounded Captain Leonard heard an artillery grid called over the radio and hurriedly checked his map. "Get off that grid! It's right on my men!" he yelled. Then US helicopter gunships dived past us and we heard their roar as they fired. But the ground troops had moved faster than planned because of the lack of effective opposition and the gunships were spraying the ground dangerously close to them. "Get those cowboys off of here," called Captain Leonard into his small black radiophone.

There was silence for a few minutes except for sporadic cracks of gunfire and then the radio crackled and a faint, barely audible voice said, "We've got this hill." "What did you say?" called back Major Scott from down the ridge in tones of disbelief.

"We've got this goddamn hill," said Captain Leonard.

Within minutes another helicopter landed at Firebase 16 to take in more supplies and this time I gladly jumped on board. Not only was I alive and well but I knew exactly what had happened in the battle, and I had an angle no other reporter had. The colonel in charge of taking the hill had landed on Firebase 16 earlier in the day. When I interviewed him, he had said, "It's November 23, Thanksgiving Day. We're gonna take that hill today and serve turkey and cranberry sauce on the top." All I had to do now was to get to the hill and wait for the turkey to arrive.

Our UH-1A helicopter, nicknamed "Huey" (it was everyone's favourite), not only looked battered but it seemed to struggle up the narrow jungle valley. The engine groaned and strained as the pilot inched it on to a tiny space on the edge of the long narrow top of 875. The area the pilot had to land on was no bigger than a metered parking space in a city — on the edge of a vertical drop. The rotor blade knocked branches from trees as the pilot struggled to get the landing right and I was very happy to leap out on to the hill I had once feared.

Hill 875 was a long razorback with the top only about 10 metres across — an area full of fallen trees and holes and American troops. It was just one of many similar ridges close together, all running in the same direction. Major Scott said air strikes had been unable to knock out the North Vietnamese because only one manned the machine-gun above the bunker and when he was killed another came up from the tunnels below.

The North Vietnamese, it seemed, had played the battle very well. Perhaps realizing it was Thanksgiving Day or, more likely, knowing how many troops had moved into the area, they had all but withdrawn during the previous night. The Americans, however, had said they had "all avenues of escape" battered by red legs (artillery). The Vietnamese left behind a small number of suicide defenders and the others moved to an adjacent ridge. And when the hill was taken, they bombarded the Americans with mortar fire. When I arrived American gunships, bombs and artillery were hitting surrounding ridge tops. The twelve or so jour-

nalists who had made it to the top with the troops were pulling out on the helicopters, but I waited for the turkey I
knew would be arriving.

Some of the time I spent interviewing the three men who
had stayed on to take the hill after their ambushed battalion
had been relieved. One of them said he had had to come to the
top to show that his battalion wasn't finished — though
about 180 had been killed out of 600. Another, who was
digging-in for the night, said he didn't think 875 was worth
it. "We didn't lose all of them dead, but I think we lost them
all, one way or another," he said, making it obvious he
didn't want to say any more. Why did he come to the top, I
asked. "I came anyway," was the reply.

Later I sat on the edge of a small artillery crater, with my
feet dangling over the edge so as not to make too big a
target of myself; also, sitting here, waiting for my turkey, I
wasn't too far from cover if need be.

The light was fading. The wounded had gone and so had
the dead. Still no turkey. I had made a mistake. I had the
battle, the dead, the interviews — but I couldn't get out with
the story. All the other journalists were long gone. I didn't
really care about my job but I knew Jim and Bruce and Dinh
would be disappointed. As I sat inconspicuously on the edge
of my hole a plane dived on an adjacent hillside and the
napalm ran rapidly down the slope like volcanic lava and set
the whole mountainside alight, briefly. Then bombs exploded and, as I looked at the ground, a large piece of metal the
size of a saucer landed two metres away in the grass. It was
smoking.

An officer gathered a group of men behind me. "Listen,"
he said aggressively, "we've got wall-to-wall generals at Dak
To. They want a bodycount. Go around the men and find out
how many North Vietnamese they shot." I knew only three
North Vietnamese bodies had been found on our part of that
hill, but the figure eventually released in Saigon at the Follies
was 175.

This was possibly close to the truth when other units and

the bombing and massive artillery fire was considered. And the Vietnamese, like the Americans, made a practice of carrying off their dead. This helped ruin the opposition's morale. In any case, American officers had to come up with a good figure. So soon after the tragedy of the ambush, the North Vietnamese just had to lose as many men as the Americans.

Besides, it was Thanksgiving Day. And, just on dusk, the same moustached, middle-aged pilot who had flown the helicopter in and out of Hill 875 all afternoon came back for one last journey — this time he brought huge stainless steel trays of hot turkey and cranberry sauce.

Three more dead Americans had since been found and going with them was my way out. I don't think I had ever been happier than that night in Dak To when, having laboriously phoned through my story, I climbed on to a stretcher.

But I never did hear if anyone used the story. I know they used the announcement in Saigon by General Westmoreland that that battle was "the beginning of the great defeat for the enemy".

Lunar surprise:
Tet 1968

Each year in about late January the Vietnamese celebrate
Tet, the Lunar New Year — exactly when depending on the
cycle of the moon. For the 1968 celebrations, the Viet Cong
were secretly preparing a very special surprise for their
frustrated opponents. Hill 875 had impressed on me the difficulties the Americans faced out in the isolated mountains
of Vietnam, but as 1968 began not even the most
pessimistic reporter could have guessed how vulnerable
the Americans were to be in the provincial cities — and
even in Saigon itself.

One of the things I found strangest about this bitter war
was that every year near the end of January the fighting
would stop while the Vietnamese celebrated their lunar
festival. Tet to the Vietnamese was like Christmas, Easter,
the Queen's Birthday, and Show Week all rolled into one
and including, as well, much worshipping of ancestors.

Both sides were, usually, more than happy to honour the
truce. But this year things began to take a slightly different
form. The truce traditionally lasted a full week, and that
was what the Viet Cong wanted this time, starting on Saturday 27 January. However, because of the worsening
military situation the Americans and the South Vietnamese
didn't think it prudent to give the Viet Cong so long a time
to regroup and reorganize: they offered a truce of forty-
eight hours and, in the end, only thirty-six hours — from 6
p.m. on Monday 29 January until 6 a.m. the following
Wednesday. And the truce was abandoned altogether in the
five northernmost provinces. The Americans believed two

North Vietnamese divisions had entered the area and were planning to swamp their isolated base of Khe Sanh. So they also refused to acknowledge the truce for 175 kilometres above the DMZ to allow the bombing of North Vietnam to continue.

It didn't seem much of a truce to me.

Even so, as the Lunar New Year festivities began there was certainly a holiday atmosphere in Saigon. Nguyen Hue Street, the street of flowers, was a mass of blooms down the centre and a market of canvas awnings had been set up. On Sunday 28 January, my girlfriend from the British Embassy and I wandered lazily through the flowers wondering where they all came from in a country that seemed bereft of everything except bomb craters, rice paddies, and jungle. It was a very pleasant afternoon mixing with people who were all obviously and unusually happy. Tet meant double wages for all workers for the month (by tradition wages were paid monthly), and everyone bought themselves new clothes for the celebration. I was happy too because I had survived my time in Vietnam: with a week's owed leave up my sleeve I had just one week to go. My replacement, twenty-nine-year-old English reporter Ron Laramy, had already arrived in Singapore from London. I just had to sit in Saigon for a week and I was out. And as that was a traditional truce week anyway, I knew I had made it through.

The fact that there was a big war going on now seemed to make Tet even more of a celebration than ever, since depth of sadness equals height of happiness. Tet itself is a four-day affair and, although this year's truce was only for thirty-six hours, it was obvious that everyone was expecting to celebrate the full four days. There was a relaxed feeling about Saigon — even among the Follies briefers.

However, one little incident disturbed me and I could not get it out of my mind as the celebrations began. Since I had been in Saigon I had always found the Vietnamese very friendly. But on the Monday morning I was walking along Tu Do Street with my girlfriend and Jim Pringle, towards

197

the Majestic Hotel down near the river. We weren't going anywhere in particular, just wandering the streets enjoying the carnival atmosphere. I was busy talking to Jim and didn't notice that I was on a collision course with a Vietnamese in his mid twenties. I swerved too late to miss him and, as he didn't deviate from his path, we bumped into each other quite forcefully. I turned to apologize and smile but he turned and gave me the blackest look of hatred I had ever seen. It was such a look that I could see it still that night, exactly, truly, already: hard eyes staring, eyes tight, lips turned and slightly open. Who was this bloke who hated me, or what I represented, so much, I wondered. Who was this Vietnamese who wasn't celebrating his Tet? It made me regard as sinister complaints over the Viet Cong radio that thirty-six hours wasn't long enough for a truce.

But I didn't have too much time to dwell on it all because, while it was an easy time for everyone else, a truce was a very busy time for the press. The first accusation of one side breaking the ceasefire was the big traditional Tet story every year — and every newsagency journalist sweated on this because the media love news they recognize and know. Someone had to remain in the office almost all the time: as soon as anyone was shot or a rocket went off the Americans would announce the Viet Cong had broken the truce, or vice versa. This year there had also been threats to end the truce, and the various changes announced by the Americans.

Things outside were quiet that Monday — unusually so, even for a truce. In fact the lack of action was the only story I could write as I sat in the office with little to do. But I was hardly bored or disappointed. Not with just four days and a wake up to go before I was out of Vietnam on my way to Australia. I was sitting back with my feet up thanking fortune that I'd managed to stay alive. It was a nice feeling thinking I'd never have to go out into the field again, where, I now knew well, it was "very quick and easy to be killed".

That night, however, the Viet Cong and North Vietnamese, without any warning, launched withering attacks in the ancient capital of Hue and in the second city of South Vietnam, Danang. Even though these two cities were in the five northern provinces where the truce had been cancelled by the Americans it was still quite a surprise. There had always been some skirmishes during truces in the past, but there were indications that these were major assaults.

Luckily for Reuters it was the first time we had based two reporters in Danang. Bruce Pigott and John MacLennan were both there because of the perceived threat to the lonely outpost of Khe Sanh. They started filing stories on the northern offensive late on Monday evening, including stories on Khe Sanh which was said by the Americans to be surrounded by North Vietnamese regulars hidden in the hills. Jim and I worked all next day taking stories from them by radiophone and adding quotes from the Follies briefers in Saigon.

I had expected to finish early that Tuesday night, and my girlfriend was waiting in the office, her white Mini-Minor parked outside ready to take us off to join the celebrations. There had been so many attacks in the north, however, that I had to write a nightlead summing everything up. I had just started this when, suddenly, Dinh stood up from his desk at the office entrance and, solemnly, walked over to me. He had been unusually quiet this evening. "Gunsmoke, you tell Miss go home," he said gravely. I was used to bantering conversations with Dinh but this wasn't the time and I asked him, politely, why he thought he could run my social life. He stood unsmiling looking down from too close to my desk. "Tonight the VC attack Saigon. She go home," he said. My girlfriend was a secretary at the British Embassy and she never appreciated my telling her that the Americans were losing the war. This had become a point of some friction. Her attitude was that the British Embassy was in close contact with the Americans and she believed the Americans were close to winning. Therefore, since what Dinh was saying was impossible, she believed we were just trying to get her out of the office. She walked out angrily, got in her Mini, and drove off home to the compound of units where British Embassy staff lived.

With the Hue citadel now under assault I was too busy to argue and knew I could patch things up later. I turned to Dinh and said, jokingly, "The VC to attack Saigon? That's a bloody good story. I'll put that in this nightlead here." Dinh, who was always giving me inside information and saying: "You can say government sources," or: "You can say informed sources," this time missed my three-quarter smile. He still looked very serious and said, "No background. No source. No report. But we must be ready. First with big story."

Jim Pringle reacted in his usual way to serious news when I called him down. He stood, one arm leaning on the desk and the hand of the other opened palm outwards on his hip, and stared straight ahead through his thick glasses, lips pursed. We waited for his decision. Eventually Jim too decided that, although Dinh was almost invariably right, this was hard to believe. Even when the French were in Vietnam the Viet Minh never got within miles of Saigon. And there had been no whisper of this from anyone else — American reporters or officials or other Vietnamese. Dinh alone claimed Saigon would be invaded, *and* during a truce. But, still, Jim decided we would have to act as if Dinh were right and stay in the office, just to cover ourselves.

Dinh would still not reveal his source but he said the attack would come at 1 a.m. Although I wanted to straighten things out with my girlfriend, I stayed on with Jim at the office just to see what would happen, if anything. Dinh went home to his family, saying he'd return after midnight. With a few hours to kill, Jim and I walked down Tu Do Street to the *New York Times* office to tell them we had heard Saigon might be attacked — hardly believing it ourselves. Tom Buckley got us a beer each out of their fridge: I think he thought we needed it. They clearly didn't believe it either — by then it was third-hand hearsay anyway — but they stayed talking to us until after midnight.

Jim and I walked back to the office even though it was after the midnight curfew. Occasionally we ignored it but Americans were never seen after that hour. Everything was as quiet as normal at this time of night in Saigon, with little movement and few lights. As we walked up the street alone in the dark I knew that Dinh was wrong, because otherwise we wouldn't have been able to walk about freely. I knew there were hundreds of thousands of American and ARVN troops in camps in and around Saigon. Surely if the Viet Cong were ever going to enter the capital it would have happened a long time ago when the opposition wasn't as strong.

Anyway if something were going to happen the Americans would have known about it for sure and there would be signs of extra defence. And I remembered Dinh had received a Christmas card from President Thieu: he had good contacts, yes, but they were on the wrong side. Maybe he had succumbed to VC propaganda. A week ago American intelligence had revealed at the Follies that Khe Sanh was under threat. Surely they would know if Saigon were similarly threatened.

Back at the office we rang Dinh and told him not to bother coming in unless something happened. When he agreed, any last nagging doubts I had left disappeared. Nothing was going to happen. Still, Jim and I waited until well after one o'clock, just to be sure.

There wasn't a sound in Saigon. About 2 a.m. Jim offered to drive me the two blocks home to the two adjacent flats Bruce Pigott had arranged near the office so we would be within easy reach if something broke. I said I had better go to the British compound. Jim didn't really like the idea but, seeing I was going to find my own way there, he offered to take me. He drove slowly through the dark streets the three kilometres to the unit block of several storeys. The compound was opposite a large US transport depot; and the only people we saw on the journey were a few Americans there who were smoking behind the sandbag bunkers which for many years had guarded it — although never a shot had been fired.

Jim dropped me off and I stood facing the huge solid-steel gates with spikes on the top which barred the way into the compound. The entry was seldom locked, however, and I pushed the gate open and went through. To my regret, I didn't even bother shutting it. Casually I made my way through the parked cars inside and up the few flights of stairs.

My girlfriend was lying on the bed in her flat, apparently asleep. As I'd been working for most of the last eighteen hours, my clothes felt stuck to my body and I decided to have a shower. This would wake my friend up, I hoped, so we could resolve our differences there and then. I got out of the shower and was getting dressed when I heard some explosions and gunfire, and then a louder explosion just outside. A window in the flat went white as I looked out the bathroom door, and it fell in as if someone had thrown a bottle of milk at it.

Immediately my girlfriend rolled over and said coolly, as if she had believed Dinh all along, "It's started, hasn't it?" Only then I realized Dinh had been right.

I rushed out to the balcony and looked down over the side at the spike gates I had come through. Men in old clothes with guns were coming out of a manhole in the ground on the other side. They were firing and US troops were firing back. There was a large block of apartments on a triangular block nearby and a European girl over there who had also rushed out on her balcony was hit by a bullet and, I found out later, died. As soon as I glimpsed what was happening I headed back inside, where my friend's flatmate was now awake and crying.

I knew I had to get to the office. For the first time, Saigon was under Viet Cong attack. This was the big one: poor Jim was alone with the biggest story in history and I wasn't there to help him. But at least he was in the office, as his flat was upstairs, and he would immediately start filing stories. How could I get out? Down the stairs and back out through the steel gate? No way. It was like making a decision not to attend your own wedding. Jim would just have to cover this on his own, at least until daylight. Gunfire had hit cars in the grounds of the compound and I soon began to worry whether we were safe where we were. Even if the Viet Cong had no intention of entering this compound, those outside might be forced in, make a rush up the stairs and break into the flats for hostages. So I locked the plywood-and-cardboard front door and the bedroom door and the bathroom door, and the three of us sat on the floor between the bath and the toilet. This was to protect us from rockets or mortar explosions, although I knew the Viet Cong could get straight in if they wanted.

The flatmate was still upset. It wasn't so much the gunfire outside that worried her, she said, but the exploding rockets. I didn't say anything, but the rockets only meant there were Viet Cong as far as fifteen kilometres away. The gunfire meant heavily armed men downstairs who could easily end up in this bathroom with us before the night was over. . . . particularly as I had left the steel gate invitingly ajar.

My girlfriend was probably the least concerned: the main thing troubling her was that I looked like winning the argument about how the war was going, and in a rather convincing way. She sat with elbow on toilet seat and condemned the British Embassy people who had obviously not known what they'd been talking about.

We sat on the floor for the next few hours and talked and worried and tried to cheer each other up, but for most of the time we listened to the sounds of battle all over the city. A claymore mine blew up the Philippine ambassador's house next door, a rocket exploded far away, bursts of gunfire now very close, again further away. The fighting didn't cease for a moment. As there was no way I could make it to the office in the dark, I tried to convince myself that Jim would realize it was impossible and not be cursing me for not coming.

When the fighting seemed to die down a bit at first light, I borrowed the keys to the Mini and crept down the stairs. I was worried that the first thing the Americans opposite would do when I gently pulled open the gate to drive the car out would be to open fire. Nervously I poked my head around the gate, which now had holes in it and, in order to impress upon them that I was not a Viet Cong, I held my long fairish hair out on both sides as far above my head as I could pull it in a part hands-up position, waved, and then gave them the thumbs-up sign. They were only across the road but they made no sign back. They just sat behind their rifles. To the right on my side of the road in the gutter were three dead Vietnamese in old workers' shirts and shorts. They seemed to carry no equipment — something I'd noticed before about killed Viet Cong — not even ammunition. One of them was half out of a manhole.

I had to assume that the lack of fire meant I was OK.

Getting into a civilian car and heading for the city centre in the midst of panic was not a good idea, I learned later, because the Viet Cong had launched their offensive in civilian cars. They'd done this to catch the Americans by surprise because there were always a few people who broke the curfew, particularly during a truce. I started the engine and headed for the office. The first thing I noticed was that I was the only one out driving on the normally crowded roads; but most worrying of all was that the guards who always sat in the little guard-boxes outside important buildings on the way were all absent.

It seemed everyone had melted away, and I began to realize the magnitude of what was happening. My imagination started up quickly. Would I drive around a corner and run into a battalion of Viet Cong — me with only a few days to go in Vietnam? As I approached the Presidential Palace, which I had to pass to reach the office from this direction, I came upon barbed-wire road blocks, Americans behind them with flak jackets and rifles pointed upwards from the waist, a sure sign that the safety catches were off.

Immediately I jumped out of the car so they could see

who I was. "The VC are in town," they told me. "Get out." I tried a sidestreet and was amazed to find they hadn't blocked that one too. Arriving outside the Reuter office, I knew I had now to face the most difficult task so far that day: to explain to Jim why I'd left him, on this of all nights, with no help. He was bound to go crook — and I couldn't blame him.

He didn't see me at first as I opened the grenade door which, for once, was closed: he was sitting well back in the office typing furiously. He looked up without a hint of recognition, as if I weren't a colleague. I was hoping he would say "Is that you Hugh?" but he just looked. "Listen Jim," I said, "there was just no way I could get here. I was pinned down all night at the compound."

"It's been terrible Hugh," Jim said at last, and I realized more than ever what was upon us. Pringle was tired, exhilarated by the story, and also, if it were possible, scared. He had seen the Viet Cong running past the office as they launched their attacks on the palace and the American Embassy, both one short block either side of our office. He had seen the bullets bouncing off the footpath outside. He had had to telex the stories himself because the Vietnamese telex-operator in the office that night wouldn't come out from under the stairs. And, to top it all, I had not been there during this night of need. "Get down to the American Embassy Hugh. The Viet Cong have got it," he said, and I headed for the door, pleased to be escaping but half scared at what might happen next. Pringle relented as I reached the grenade door, "Watch the sniper across the road Hugh." "This is a good way to start work on a Wednesday morning," I muttered, and set off out of the office the short distance to the besieged embassy.

I cut through the park opposite Reuters to get to the right side of the road. I could have been off for a stroll on a warm sunny morning under a clear blue sky, except for the echoing explosions and bursts of gunfire. When I rounded the old red-brick cathedral the street outside the embassy looked like a movie set. There was an outdated black Citroen parked right outside with rows of bullet holes running in short bursts diagonally up the sides like in an Eliot Ness production; a Vietnamese was slumped at the wheel, dead. There was another shot-up car further down the road and also an American military police jeep, its glass shattered by bullets. In the side of the high white masonry wall that surrounded the six-storey embassy building a small hole had been blown as an easy entry into the fortress, hitherto believed impregnable. There was no sign of the Vietnamese guards — their small sentry-boxes outside were deserted. Opposite the embassy the street was lined with large trees — behind every one of which there was an American. Many were in pyjamas, sometimes blue flannelette pyjamas, which stuck out untidily from under flak jackets. Their wearers were aiming M-16s at their own embassy. The white front of the building was chopped up in three places where it had been hit by some sort of projectile.

Except for the sniper who was thought to be in a partially built building away to my right, being on the embassy side of the road was the safest place to be: all the buildings either had high brick walls or were built right on the footpath so anyone in the embassy couldn't hit this position. And the American troops lining the road on the other side, including those lying under shot-up cars, would presumably stop anyone from coming out of the grounds to fire.

I crept down along the fence past MPs on the pavement reloading their rifles from tins of bullets. Nearby two of them lay dead, face down on the road. They had been shot when stopped by a Vietnamese who turned out to be a Viet Cong.

Despite all the soldiers and guns it was now very quiet in this street, as if the movie projectionist had turned off the sound. I wasn't sure how far to go but I had to get as close as possible, absorb what was going on, and race back to the office and write a story. Against my wall right next to the embassy driveway a cluster of Americans were peeping around the corner, rifles raised from the elbow and held ready to fire. One of them turned to me and told me to get out of the area because there were Viet Cong everywhere, and snipers, and mines. A couple of officers I spoke to told me the Viet Cong were in the embassy building itself, though they didn't know how many.

The Viet Cong had surprised the guards by arriving in civilian cars. A soldier told me that a Viet Cong had got the two MPs by stopping them after the curfew and asking for a smoke. I was up against the wall staring straight ahead at the bullet-riddled Citroen as sporadic firing again started from both sides. One of the group of US soldiers I was with near the entrance, the biggest of them, picked up an M-60 thirty-calibre machinegun and, firing from the hip, dashed through the entrance saying, "I'm going in to get those mother-fuckers." But he made it only two metres into the embassy grounds. After he'd fallen I could still see his boots on my side of the entrance — but I didn't look around the post. Concentrated firing did not break out because the Americans had no targets to shoot at. Ironically, their embassy was too well set up as a fortress to be easily recaptured. No one knew where the four Vietnamese national policemen were who were supposed to be guarding the building, but two of the three marine guards had been wounded and they had retreated to the top floor, fighting as they went. More US soldiers fought their way in and soon dragged the dead fellow out by the ankles. For an hour he lay on the pavement while fighting went on around him.

The Viet Cong were fighting on American soil, at the embassy, for the first time in the war. MPs told the reporters near the gate to clear out. "There are mines all around here," one said. The soldier said the Viet Cong were holding the first five floors of the building.

I crept back to the office, keeping close to the wall, to start helping Pringle compete with the other news organizations: the Viet Cong were in the American embassy; the Americans were behind every tree fighting to get their fortress back; there were still some Americans alive inside;

a soldier tried to storm his own embassy with a machinegun. And it wasn't even breakfast time.

By now Dinh had managed to make it to the office — a very hazardous thing for a Vietnamese to do with fighting going on all over the city and the Americans ready to shoot any Vietnamese not in ARVN uniform. This was lucky for me because Pringle was still upset that I had not arrived during the night. Dinh smiled at Jim and shook his head and said: "No. No, Jim, he cannot to do." Dinh had had to pass the British compound to get to the office, so he was able to tell Jim about the dead bodies outside the units.

After writing my story Dinh and I both returned to the embassy battle. But when we reached the edge of it an American soldier yelled at Dinh, "OK Charlie," and swung his rifle round at him. I'd been expecting danger from the Viet Cong, and I was speechless. It was left to the quick thinking Dinh to shout, "I not Viet Cong, I number one anti-communist." The American put his gun down, but Dinh said later he could see the perplexed look on his face. "For how he really know? Cannot."

We crept back tree by tree and then along the wall and, just as we got to the embassy, some of the brave American soldiers who had fought their way into the grounds were bringing out a captured guerrilla. Four desperate Americans had their rifles pointed into his back. As he walked right past me, his hands in the air, I saw his look of defiance, and then the contorted looks on the faces of the four Americans. An officer yelled at them not to shoot, to keep him a prisoner. I too was worried one of them would pull a trigger. Their angry faces showed how they felt at seeing not only their first Viet Cong, but also the first of the Viet Cong to capture part of America.

Shortly after that a helicopter landed on the roof of the embassy and troops began to fight their way down through the building to others who were now fighting their way through the front door. The helicopter was driven off by rifle fire at first but at the second attempt there appeared to be little Viet Cong resistance — they were probably low on ammunition by now, and demoralized by the fact that the three marines had managed to hold the top floor.

Dinh and I rushed back to the office where I typed everything we had seen for a world we imagined was hungry for news of the shock attack. When we got back to the embassy the nineteen Viet Cong in the suicide squad inside had been killed or captured.

It was now mid morning. Dinh pulled me aside and pointed to two dead Viet Cong lying near us. He remarked that beneath their black clothes were ordinary white shirts, and they both wore jewellery. "Not Viet Cong peasants. Saigon underground man," said Dinh, who believed these two were local people who had awaited the call to fight for the Viet Cong in the offensive. "Not communist Viet Cong man, communist underground man show way," said Dinh. Everyone else in Saigon at that time believed that all of these Viet Cong had come in from the jungle, but Dinh didn't think so. And I believed Dinh now — as I should have done the night before.

Many journalists had come and gone during the battle but now there were quite a few near the embassy. The emblematic seal of the embassy had been shot up by the Viet Cong and lay at the foot of the entrance. The ten-centimetre thick timber doors had holes in them from anti-tank rocket fire and, inside, the floor was covered in blood and debris. The reporters stood around, more cynical than ever, wondering what the American military brass would say now. Clearly the light had gone out at the end of the tunnel.

Around the country, in almost all the cities and towns in South Vietnam, numerous other battles were being fought. Elsewhere in Saigon, the Viet Cong were in a factory, in a graveyard, in a central city building, in Cholon, and at the racetrack. But the battle for the embassy was *the* damaging blow to the already wilting American war effort. Even Dinh said, almost in disbelief, "The VC capture Pentagon East."

It was, in fact, such a psychological defeat that the American PR machine immediately went into action. They rang our office to deny our story that the Viet Cong had been in their embassy. I said I had been there myself. I described to the spokesman how the Viet Cong were firing from within the building and that the embassy had been fired upon by the Americans themselves because they could not get in the front gate. He seemed taken aback. Later they changed their story to say that the Viet Cong had got into the building "but not into the precincts which were the actual embassy", their stance degenerating into semantic niceties. But people around the world, and particularly the Americans, saw the pictures, and read the stories about how the Viet Cong were in the fortified US embassy and they were shocked, appalled: for years they had been hearing that the military situation was getting better and better every month. The world was at last learning that the Americans were losing their first war.

The Viet Cong had also assaulted the Presidential Palace that night, calling: "Open the gates, we have come to liberate the palace." However, they failed to break through and were driven back into a partially built hotel where they held on for three days against tanks and hundreds of troops.

Arms had been stored in places such as the big brewery in suburban Cholon, the Saigon racetrack down Plantation Road, and a new factory complex near the airport that had been held up as an example of the scale of industrialization that would in time be achieved in South Vietnam. This complex, a Viet Cong hideout, was to be bombed in the next few days by government planes.

The Saigon street fighting was worse than covering the war in the jungle because of the echoes: you couldn't work out if someone was shooting at you in the street or if it was just distant gunfire. And my satisfaction that the world would now know that things were not going as well as the announcers at the Follies would have it was tempered by the fact that my last days in Saigon would not be as safe as I had thought.

Despite all the other fighting in Hue and Danang and throughout the country, the embassy story and the size of the offensive itself was enough to clog the news wires and by afternoon Jim and I, along with almost every other reporter in Vietnam, were looking forward to the Five O'Clock Follies to see the military briefers under the sort of pressure they had eluded until now. The question on everyone's lips, now that the Viet Cong had hit more than thirty province capitals, was not: Why did the Viet Cong break the truce? (a truce which had been severely limited by the Americans), but: How is it that all the people except a few Viet Cong are supposed to be on the American side and yet all these Viet Cong can enter all these towns and cities and no one at all bothered to warn you?

The answer, it seemed to me, was that the average Vietnamese wouldn't tell on the Viet Cong.

The American military command obviously realized the significance of this question. Both General Westmoreland and President Johnson said that they had been aware something was on and had been given certain information. This was a blow to those journalists who were hoping the American military would admit they had no idea so that they could write unequivocably that the Americans were not wanted by the vast majority in Vietnam and might as well leave. But, incredibly, the military command's attitude was that the Viet Cong had, at last, been brave enough to come out in the open.

Before Tet probably 50 per cent of journalists believed the Americans were losing the war — but 80 per cent of those who went into the field. After Tet it seemed every journalist was now anti the war. All had been demanding to talk to the United States command director of combat operations in Vietnam, and he was eventually brought along. He was a marine brigadier, General John Chaisson, and I expected he too would have been well briefed to say the Americans knew the Viet Cong were up to something. To the surprise of every journalist in the theatrette, he said,

"I must confess the VC surprised us with the sheer panorama of their attack. It was surprisingly well co-ordinated, surprisingly impressive, and launched with a surprising amount of audacity." He then described it as a very successful Viet Cong operation, while in Washington President Johnson was saying the Viet Cong had "failed to attain their objective".

The reporters were non-plussed at this straight admission by the director of combat operations in Vietnam. One stood up and said that President Johnson, General Westmoreland and the head of intelligence all said they knew something was on, and what did he have to say to that. The crew-cut marine general merely replied, "Well, gentlemen, if they knew they certainly didn't tell me." Everyone ran for the telephones. That was it. The Americans didn't know what was really happening in Vietnam. At least everyone now knew that the Viet Cong were fighting in thirty-five cities and towns and that they had smuggled twelve to fifteen battalions into Saigon — some 4,500 men.

It seemed strange to me that I had been warned about the Tet offensive and the Americans, with all their paid servants, hadn't. Perhaps another thing they didn't know was that Vietnam's most famous warrior, Nguyen Hue, had routed the invading Chinese two centuries before by launching an unexpected Tet offensive.

Viet Cong prisoners were quoted as having said that they had walked about fifty kilometres into Saigon and that some had begun arriving more than a week before. But what the Americans still weren't prepared to acknowledge, or announce, was that some were local cadres who were fighting their first fight for the Viet Cong, having waited years for the chance. Some of the nineteen who captured the American embassy carried forged South Vietnamese government passes, which meant there were Viet Cong at official levels in Saigon.

The press confidently expected that the Americans would now move enough troops into Saigon to put a quick end to the fighting. However, battles continued all week at the racetrack, where the Viet Cong had set up a hospital in the grandstand, at Go Vap Chinese cemetery, where they had a command post, and in various buildings where they were proving difficult to move. The drawn-out fighting did not engender confidence in the American military. They said that the Viet Cong had been told to hold out for only forty-eight hours, and that there would be no more big attacks in Saigon, but in the atmosphere that pervaded in those first tense days it seemed likely that a disaster could happen at any time . . . even that the city could fall.

The night before Tet Dinh had also told me that a company of what were called Vietnamese combat police who dressed in special camouflage uniforms had surrounded Radio Saigon, a Vietnamese language station. This did not indicate that someone knew something was going on: it was a precaution against any military coup attempt during Tet in a country accustomed to such moves. The first thing coup leaders went for was Radio Saigon. Therefore I was amazed to hear the next day that five Viet Cong had attacked Radio Saigon and five got inside. We went there and I asked Dinh to ask a question of the commander of these two hundred combat police. "How is it that two hundred police are designated to protect a building and five Viet Cong attack and five get inside?" Dinh asked, and then turned around laughing at the reply. "He says, the Viet Cong, they not afraid they die." Which probably summed up the whole war. They were unable to operate the equipment, however, and in any case mortar bombardments were called in on the building to make sure they never would.

Pringle, Dinh and I worked non-stop for the first forty-eight hours. All shops were shut, we had little food, and on the first full night of the offensive our incoming telex failed. This meant we were not receiving any messages. In the dark of that night Jim set off in the office car across town to the cable building where our incoming service arrived from overseas. He had only gone a few hundred metres when a US machinegun-mounted jeep, its barrels pointed through the driver's side window, pulled him over. Jim was warned and returned to the office. At first light Dinh and I set out across the city for the cable building.

When we got there the seven- or eight-storey building was surrounded by troops and barbed wire: it was a key installation and the Vietnamese soldiers were not letting anyone past. Dinh yelled out to the technicians on the top floor and one eventually saw us. He put our paper roll of incoming telex messages in a large plastic bag, leant out the window, swung it around and around, then let go. It just cleared the barbed wire. While the bemused soldiers watched, I picked it up and started to uncurl what looked like a big roll of toilet paper and read: "Urgent Saigon unheard you 11 hours. Hope you OK. Trying all avenues to reach you and reinforce you. Keep your heads down." There were many other similar messages. It was the worst news possible. All of our efforts since the previous evening had been wasted.

Earlier messages on the roll said how well we had been doing for the first sixteen hours or so; but now that impetus had been lost and any papers relying on Reuters were not doing very well in the fight to be first with the latest news. But at least all the most important stories from the first day had reached London, and that was something. But it re-emphasized that the only good story was the one that reached its destination.

The only way to check what was wrong was to go down to Cholon about five kilometres away, where fighting was probably the worst. Pringle set off with Dinh to see what he could do about restoring the service while I prepared stories including the main parts of all those that had gone into the cosmos.

When Jim and Dinh arrived at the PTT (Post, Telegraph and Telephone) headquarters they had the problem corrected immediately: there were often problems there and these were usually overcome upon the gift of a bottle of scotch. As they were leaving, the office Volkswagen came under fire from Viet Cong on top of a nearby building and they were forced to abandon it. They jumped out while the car was moving and eventually it rolled into a tree.

It was several hours since they had left the office and, although we now had an incoming and an outgoing service, I began to get an uneasy feeling that I was on my own. Eventually they made it to a phone hoping to dictate their story. I was at a hurriedly called press conference but fortunately John Cantwell from *Time* magazine popped into the office, took the story down, and sent it off. The likeable Australian spent a lot of time chatting to us when there was nothing much happening — not about cricket or football but rather life and guns, particularly his revolvers and pistols.

That afternoon Jim and Dinh staggered back into the office, covered in dirt and without the car. While Jim stood and stared down the long corridor wondering what to do next, Dinh cried out, "I think I die. I think I die Gunsmoke," laughing and crying at the same time with relief. "I think I never to see my children again." Apparently the pair had been caught in crossfire between government and Viet Cong troops. "Gunsmoke, I cry and cry. The bullets go over my head. I crawl behind a big tank but Jim says no they have rockets. I look at Jim. He crawls in one direction then another one, but each way there bullets. One policeman waves us [across], but bullet goes through his hand. I am trying tell Jim something, but nothing comes. I want to tell him look after my wife and my sons, and that when they grow big not be journalists."

Dinh said he and Jim were pinned down near where lots of refugees were passing until Jim saw a child wandering alone in the middle of the road and, under fire, ran and picked her up and carried her to safety. Dinh followed and they made it to the door of an International Control Commission (ICC) house where some Polish people lived. They knocked desperately on the door. "Go away," said a Chinese woman in Vietnamese. "This is a communist

215

house." She thought it was the Viet Cong coming to raid the place. Dinh laughed as he told this, saying, "In Saigon no communist house. Cannot say that."

That evening about 10 p.m. there was a phonecall from MACV saying that John MacLennan had been trying to ring us from Hue with a big story and could not get through. The only way to get it from him, they said, was via a military phone. This meant that one of us had to make it to JUSPAO, three blocks away in the dark. The temptation, of course, was not to go, but Jim and I both knew that MacLennan must have risked his neck for this story because the Hue citadel — the emperor's castle with its ten-metre thick walls — had fallen to North Vietnamese battalions amid much death. MacLennan deserved to be able to get his story out to the world. The MACV source told us MacLennan said the citadel had been bombed by the Americans after the Viet Cong flag had been raised. To me this was huge news, though to the world it was probably meaningless. But it was like being in San Francisco and hearing that the White House had been bombed because there were demonstrators or criminals inside, or hearing in Manchester that Buckingham Palace had been levelled by Britain's NATO allies, or that the Americans had bombed the Sydney Opera House. For Hue, the ancient Vietnamese imperial capital, contained a red-walled city of a few square kilometres surrounded by a moat and full of ancient palaces, trees and narrow roads. For hundreds of years it was the seat of government.

It was my turn to go this time: somehow I had to get to JUSPAO. It was slightly shorter by the back streets but I decided it would be safer to walk down Tu Do Street which sloped gently downhill to the centre of town.

The orange light from American parachute flares now being dropped constantly on the city made the streets an awful colour and, as the wind blew them in gusts, all the shadows of trees and buildings moved suddenly backwards and forwards in orange and black, like a surreal movie. I made my way tentatively to the main street, stepped around a dead Vietnamese, and began to walk in tiny slow steps down the centre of the road, with my press pass held in both hands high above my head. Each sidestreet was blocked off with rolls of concertina barbed wire. All I could see of the ARVN soldiers crouching behind it was the top of the barrels of their guns reflecting the light of the flares.

The colourful stretch of neon-lit bars along Tu Do Street was dark, the bars all shuttered. The bar girls were hiding in their homes, probably now calling the Viet Cong "Number Welve". Joe Marcel's bar was locked and barred: it would be a long time before the blonde American girl again gyrated in her red bikini inside the gold birdcage. Perhaps never.

I thought that if I walked down the middle of the road with my hands in the air I couldn't be mistaken for a Viet Cong. As flares swung violently overhead I caught a glimpse of some faces which were not amused by my presence. I wasn't the only journalist who had had to do this: earlier in the evening some Americans had had to bring their copy to our office along this street of guns. They handed packets of cigarettes to soldiers on the way up so they would watch out for them on the way back. But I didn't smoke.

At last I reached JUSPAO, where I was taken aback to see the panic that prevailed. The foyer table, usually neat like a receptionist's desk, was strewn with all sorts of rifles and guns as well as large round clear-glass bottles half filled with black liquid — gas bottles, I presumed. There were gas masks, too.

As I walked through, people kept saying: "We're gonna be hit. We're gonna be hit." I saw men picking up shotguns and putting them down again in different places. Presumably American intelligence reports were that more Viet Cong raids could be expected. Certainly the Follies briefers had said that the Viet Cong had the power to launch a second wave, although I had felt this was said to save face: the US military command did not want a repeat of the embarrassment of not knowing what was going on.

They showed me to a phone and I rang MacLennan in Hue and took his story on the US bombing of the citadel. Slowly, I walked back the way I came. I felt I was using up my luck.

The Follies briefers in Saigon had said the North Vietnamese were holding only "two corners" of the citadel. But MacLennan reported how the North Vietnamese were occupying most of Hue and that he had watched American and South Vietnamese aircraft bomb the ancient palaces. This had been denied in Saigon. Several hours later an American spokesman rang our office to deny they had bombed the citadel. When I told him MacLennan had actually watched it he said not to worry about the denial.

In fact, Hue had been almost exclusively held by the North Vietnamese. My friend Francois Mazure, an AFP correspondent, had borrowed my jeans to go in dressed as a civilian with photographer Cathy Leroy. As he told me the story later, he was surprised to find no American troops about and they spent the night in a Catholic cathedral with hundreds of refugees. "Next morning," he said, "we walked out to look for MACV and in the square, out of the corner of my eye, I saw the North Vietnamese with their rifles watching us from behind fences. I knew we were caught. They took our cameras and bound our hands behind our backs. But luckily a French-speaking officer came and let us free."

The North Vietnamese troops then posed lazily for pictures on tanks for Cathy and Francois and said they held the entire city except for the American and government posts. Francois wrote this and was expelled by "the South Vietnamese government" within twenty-four hours of returning to Saigon for "mis-reporting". For most of those twenty-four hours he was questioned about the North Vietnamese by American intelligence officers.

After my walk I wrote an atmosphere story of what it was like in Saigon that night.

SAIGON It is quiet enough to hear a bullet drop in the
darkness of Saigon's usually gay Tu Do (Freedom) Street
tonight. President Nguyen Van Thieu and Commanding US
General Westmoreland have said that the back of the Viet
Cong thrust into the South Vietnamese capital has been
broken — but the atmosphere in the darkened streets of
Saigon is more tense than ever. Occasionally the light from a
parachute flare glints off the helmets and gun barrels poking
out behind barbed-wire barricades. The floating flare paints
the locked doors of the bars that line the street a liquid pink,
and then fades. A Vietnamese — no one knows whether Viet
Cong, civilian, or plain-clothes policeman — lies dead at the
corner. The only people moving through Tu Do are foreign
journalists trying to reach the telegraph office at the top of the
street without being shot by either side. They enter the office
cautiously with their arms raised above their heads in the
"Don't shoot" position. American military police and South
Vietnamese government troops are firing at any unidentified
shadows. Still in Tu Do Street, too, are the small boys with no
homes who sit in doorways and try to talk foreigners into
parting with a few coins. But only the journalists are there
now . . .

Dinh and I slept on the floor upstairs in Pringle's single
room. Occasionally rockets came in on the city while we
slept — and I kept hoping none would come through our
roof. I slept between two posts, thinking it might be the
safest place.

Because the Viet Cong had been seen creeping past our
office at night, Dinh was worried that they might break in
while we were sleeping and he hung a big sign on the door
outside: "Bao Chi Anh Quoc", which meant British journalists. Not that he thought it would help much.

On the third day one of our Vietnamese telex operators
made it to the office despite martial law and said ten Viet
Cong had been in his house. They told him to be quiet and
he would not be harmed. He said they looked stern and
brave and not worried or tired. He was more worried that
American air strikes would be called in on his house, he
said.

Three kilometres from the Reuter office heavy fighting

and bombing started near the An Quang pagoda, home of the militant anti-government Buddhist monks headed by venerable Thich Tri Quang. Dinh and I drove off towards the fighting. As we rounded a corner off Pasteur Street, firing broke out around us. "Fastly, fastly Gunsmoke," Dinh urged, waving his hand forward. I slammed down the accelerator. "Round corner," shouted Dinh, pointing left. I swung the wheel and drove straight into a street battle between troops and guerrillas.

"Out, out," called Dinh. But for once I did not need any advice, and all in the one action I pulled the door open and rolled from the moving car into the gutter. As I hit the concrete I was surprised to find I felt no pain, no jolt. Dinh rolled near me and we held our heads to the ground waiting for the firing to stop, as the troops advanced around the corner after some guerrillas. Small bands of guerrillas roamed the streets, and the only safe place to be was indoors.

Later that day *New York Times* reporter Charlie Mohr and I headed down Tu Do Street, but we were forced to retreat when a line of government police came up the road firing their carbines in the air.

That night the office building shook to the sound of explosions which continued for half an hour. We rang the US spokesman. He couldn't hear a thing, he said, although obviously he could. Finally a *New York Times* reporter in the office telephoned a general and was told off the record: "Six city blocks are being shelled. The Viet Cong are holding the area."

At the Follies the next day the US Embassy spokesman told the press that from now on they must not walk on the streets at night or they would be likely to be shot. What was called a "shotgun" curfew now applied after 7 p.m., but those of us who had to file copy after that hour could ring JUSPAO for an escort of five jeeps mounted with machine-guns, no less.

All sorts of announcements about battles and movements were being made twice a day and both Jim and I had to attend each so that one could leave immediately while the other hung about for other stories and questions. Occasionally one of us would be covering something else, and once I found myself writing three urgent stories at once — first paragraph of each, then second of each, and so on — and I found the easiest way to do it was to use three desks and typewriters. They were all such big stories that I didn't know which to write first: there were the casualty figures in South Vietnam — the Americans had already lost more than five hundred US troops dead, and the first week wasn't over; the air war over Hanoi that was hotting up and the Russian fighter-bombers that had been spotted on an airfield in North Vietnam — a worrying prospect for the enclaves of South Vietnam; and the American claims that thousands of Viet Cong had been killed.

The Follies started to run for an hour and a half. It was imperative that we be reinforced by more journalists because we could not keep working and writing twenty-four hours a day. But no planes could get into Saigon airport, which was under siege: this cut us off from our Singapore office and stopped either Bruce Pigott or John MacLennan from returning from the north to help us. Although they were phoning back on-the-spot stories from the battles in Hue and Khe Sanh — it was a tedious task taking down the copy at such a time — much of the news was being lost in the spill of words from Saigon announcements, press conferences, and battles.

The devastating effect of the Tet Offensive on America's allies, let alone America, could be judged by an editorial that appeared a few days after the start in the national newspaper the *Australian*, owned and started by Rupert Murdoch. In part, it said: "These events have torn to shreds the officially propagated myth of security being extended steadily from the growing network of secure base areas. . . . If the American Embassy, the Presidential Palace, the Danang air base, and all the rest of the Viet Cong target areas are not secure then nothing was."

221

However, the Australian government was so committed to the Vietnam War that a government spokesman called the offensive "a hit and run raid". Well, they had hit, but they weren't running.

And the US military command had another amazing view of it all. They persisted in describing the Tet Offensive throughout South Vietnam as "diversionary efforts to distract attention from Khe Sanh". There was a reluctance to realize that the Tet Offensive was the real war and Khe Sanh the phoney. To the American military, Khe Sanh — though only a tiny base in isolated mountains — was vital because they must never allow their men to be overrun. But, to the public, the American military could do nothing if it could not defend the main street of the capital.

I had seen the military obsession with not being overrun before. In April 1967 I had believed Gio Linh was about to be overrun; and that September the military men convinced me Con Thien was about to be overrun. But all that happened in both cases was that troops were crammed into these bases to be shelled unpityingly. Now exactly the same thing was happening with Khe Sanh.

A few days before the Tet Offensive started journalists were surprised when an announcer at the Follies declared that Khe Sanh was surrounded by two North Vietnamese divisions, about sixteen thousand men.

Khe Sanh, as everyone was suddenly to learn, was an American marine base up in the northwest corner of South Vietnam, an L-shaped base said to "cover" North Vietnamese infiltration routes from Laos, just eight kilometres west. The first thought that struck me was why should the American command announce to the world that suddenly the enemy had surrounded them: the announcers were there to make the war sound successful. As we wrote the story back in the office, I mentioned to Jim Pringle that the only reason for the announcement that I could think of was that massive air strikes would be brought in around Khe Sanh so that in a month or two it could be announced that eight thousand of the sixteen thousand North Vietnamese (whom no one had ever seen) were dead, and that the planned attack against Khe Sanh had been defeated. I asked a Follies briefer how the Americans knew the North Vietnamese were there, and he said two prisoners had told them this under interrogation. Could not the prisoners be lying, I wondered. As a marine officer had commented: "Why should the North Vietnamese take these positions? They can't hold them, but they can kill half a dozen marines a day by shelling them."

The other question was whether the North Vietnamese would indeed want to overrun one of these bases and kill more than a thousand marines. Such an action would probably cost them the support of those in the United States who were against the war.

For the next week all the B-52 bomber raids normally used to break up guerrilla concentrations throughout South Vietnam were centred around Khe Sanh. Just before the Tet Offensive had started, more than three thousand marines were moved to reinforce the base, as well as a battalion of government rangers who were usually kept to react to any Viet Cong attacks on a city. Three US brigades, some twelve thousand men of crack air cavalry and airborne paratroopers, were moved to within sixty-five kilometres of Khe Sanh.

The shrewd Pringle disagreed with me on the reason for the Follies announcement about the siege. He felt the American commanders really believed the sixteen thousand North Vietnamese were there. Pringle had his own theory and on 27 January, two days before the Tet Offensive started, he wrote in a nightlead: "Some military observers feel the North Vietnamese move around Khe Sanh could be a ruse to draw air strikes and troops away from other areas." Events were to prove he could not have been more accurate. In the ensuing Tet Offensive the only place that remained free of action was the area actually not covered by the truce — the northern area of South Vietnam around Khe Sanh, except for Khe Sanh itself.

"Does the US command still believe the North Vietnamese plan to overrun Khe Sanh?" a journalist asked at a
Follies press conference after Tet began. I was staggered at
the answer. "Yes," said the briefer, "These [Tet Offensive]
attacks are considered to be diversionary to take the mind
away from the real threat which is Khe Sanh." General
Westmoreland — despite all that had happened — also said
the "main effort" would be an attempt to wipe out Khe Sanh.

I must admit that within the next two weeks I began to
feel that I had been wrong to doubt that any ground attack
would be made on Khe Sanh. Heavy shelling of the base
began, but it did not stop there. The North Vietnamese dug
trenches to within three hundred metres of the base and the
marines were pinned to their bunkers for twenty-four hours
a day; all aircraft ran a gauntlet of fire. Then, for the first
time in the war, the North Vietnamese used tanks to overrun the tiny Lang Vei special forces camp just west of the
base.

But Khe Sanh was never to see the sixteen thousand
North Vietnamese troops said to be ready to descend upon
it. It did seem that the Americans had been fooled by yet
another Vietnamese trick and I congratulated Jim on his
foresight. My theory, I believed, had been wrong.

By the Thursday both the telex machines in our office
started to break down because they had been in constant
use for three days, as millions of words poured out over the
wire. We were not just responsible for reporting, for
Reuters was also providing a communications service for
many other organizations such as the *New York Times*,
Sydney Morning Herald, the Australian Broadcasting Commission, *Baltimore Sun*, *LA Times*, and London *Times*. The
Reuter office was their channel to the world, they were all
depending on us. This arrangement usually worked well but
on the first day of the offensive an enormous problem
developed.

For twelve hours Jim and I were so busy writing stories
we had not a thought for the telex room, which was being

looked after by Alan Lee, a Chinese trainee-journalist from the Singapore office. At least not until Alan came out late that night and, with tears in his eyes and fingers curled up, said, "I can't type any more." He was the only telex operator we had because our three Vietnamese operators were unable to get to the office. I went out to the telex room and Alan showed me a basketful of stories ten centimetres high which he hadn't had time to send. There was no way he was going to be able to telex them now. This was serious because correspondents always complained to us if their stories were delayed. At this time everyone who was allowed was trying to send through us as they were unsure about the reliability of the PTT. To make matters worse, they were all writing the longest stories of their lives, and several each.

Our stories, of course, went first, so we were not affected. Pringle, being in the position of ultimate responsibility, could not take the drastic step I could, particularly as I was not planning a career at Reuters. I had the advantage, too, that non-Reuter correspondents were not allowed into our telex room, and they were too busy now to ask for the telex copy of their stories, which few rarely requested anyway. The decision I took would have made executives do backward flips at Reuters' head office. Jim would have been appalled had he known, and Johnny Apple, Jnr of the *New York Times*, who was always complaining anyway, would have gone berserk: though most of their stories had gone.

I took every unsent story and threw away everything except the first page of each and wrote at the bottom of each first page, "Pick up agencies." That way they all got something out, at least two hundred words. Correspondents often put "Pick up agencies" at the end of their stories: it is an instruction to news editors to take in anything the newsagencies had which they didn't. Donald Wise of the *London Daily Mirror* made a good joke of it when he finally arrived by sending off this message to head office to let them know he had arrived: "Pro London Mirror Ex Wise Saigon   I stood aghast as . . . Pick up agencies."

My action fixed the backlog, until the machines broke down the next day. There were no shops or offices open so we had to find our mechanic, Anh. It was my turn again, so Dinh and I went looking for him at the compound of houses where the communications people lived.

When we got there this compound, like the cable building where we'd collected our telex roll, was also surrounded by Vietnamese troops: it was near heavy fighting around the Vietnamese military police headquarters. They were not interested in our plight and told us to go away. But we could not carry on without Anh. Dinh's way of getting past people was to smile and keep talking and walking, and he told me that he was going to bluff his way through by saying he worked for the PTT. So he walked past the gate and had started walking up the path when the soldier in charge levelled his rifle at him. Dinh still smiled and inched on. I stepped in and told him to come back for I was sure the soldier was going to shoot, although Dinh was confident he wouldn't. So I said, "Look, I'm ordering you back out." Finally he gave in, but he wasn't to be defeated. We drove around the back of the complex and Dinh yelled out for Anh and told him we needed him. Anh disappeared back into his unit and I thought he wouldn't come: why should he risk his life for us. Then I saw an athletic Vietnamese figure with toolbag in hand leaping over balconies and running along high walls. He landed on the ground in front of us: Anh, smiling and ready for work.

On the Saturday — the day of my wake-up before Tet interfered — I was typing away when I looked out the door to see our office surrounded by Vietnamese with guns. These were the infamous red berets who had been brought in to clean up central Saigon. Obviously they had decided to do it block by block. On the street outside, one leant on the office VW (which had been retrieved) with an M-79 grenade launcher aimed through the top window of the office. He wrote casually in the dust on the car. The red berets were considered to be the best fighters in Vietnam — better even than the Viet Cong, the Vietnamese thought. Many were said to be criminals who had been released to fight. They had just been through the *Time* office and dragged out an innocent Vietnamese telex operator because a rifle had been found near him.

When the red berets had set themselves along the footpath outside, three Vietnamese policemen walked straight in our front door, grim faced and with revolvers drawn, cocked and pointed at the floor about three metres in front of them. The office was so narrow it was only possible to walk single file between the two rows of desks and as the three moved in, Jim popped up from his desk which was at the back of the office and stepped suddenly in front of them. With his right hand on his hip, he said liltingly, "And where do you think you are going?" I immediately told him to get out of the way and wake up to himself, and Dinh started laughing — which he always seemed to do when. things were desperate. Having halted them in their purposeful stride, Jim looked up the office at me and said, "But Hugh it might be censorship or something." The police then explained to Pringle through Dinh that they were doing a house by house search for weapons and identity cards, and Jim allowed them through. As always, he enjoyed a laugh about it a few minutes later, and the three of us agreed that this was a story that would make even Bruce Pigott laugh.

Bruce was so interested in the war that it must have disappointed him that while he was up covering Khe Sanh, which everyone had thought was going to be the biggest story of the war, he should miss out almost completely on seeing and writing about the Tet Offensive. Throughout Tet he was desperate to get back to Saigon, although he had written excellent stories on what was happening in Khe Sanh and Hue. But I knew he was also anxious to see Miss Nga who had been out of contact in these anxious days. Bruce asked about her at the end of every sentence he dictated.

Although he had been seeing a lot of Miss Nga — and she

was often in the office either to see him or to find out if he had phoned in — they did not live together, but rather conducted a traditional courtship, which was very unusual in Saigon. I had noticed the way they looked at each other, and knew they couldn't resist holding hands, but only if they thought no one was looking.

Miss Nga had started asking Dinh questions about Uc Dai Lois. As Dinh put it, "She wants to know how digger people. She not know about victims. I told her I very unhappy to see one Vietnamese girl with foreigner in the street, but I very happy to see Miss Nga with Bruce Pigott because Bruce love Vietnam." And Bruce had asked Dinh why Miss Nga was so evasive when pushed on love and marriage. So Dinh took the role of cupid.

Dinh told him, "Love cannot to make quick," saying that Vietnamese women "sometimes love very much, but never to say". Dinh encouraged Bruce, saying, "I very strongly think Miss Nga on the way love you. Why you not go ahead?" But Dinh said Bruce was very careful. "He want more and more information before he decide," he said. Bruce had started meeting Miss Nga after she finished work at about 6 p.m. and Dinh would watch them walk off through the trees "very very nice love of lady and man, true by true, in dark neon light". No wonder Bruce wanted to leave Hue and get back to Saigon.

During Tet it was impossible for civilians to get into the city, even during the day, because of martial law, the twenty-four hour curfew, and the night shotgun curfew. The inner area, after being cleaned out by the Red Berets, was completely closed off, so Miss Nga was unable to get in to see us and maintain contact with Bruce. It was only at the end of the first week that she somehow made it in to the office for an emotional phonecall to Bruce, while we stood outside. But the noise of battle in Saigon was still so loud that earlier I had been unable to hear Bruce or John MacLennan for the sound of tanks firing.

During this time Bruce had been going into surrounded

Khe Sanh, where planes were shot at on the way in and out, and into Hue where he described the destruction of the ancient palaces, so he wasn't exactly the best man to be pinning your hopes for life on. And I think Miss Nga realized this because she seemed very sad, and described herself as an unlucky type of person. And Dinh told me the English translation of a poem by Vietnam's Shakespeare, Nguyen Du, which began:

> One watches things that make one sick at heart.
> This is the law: no gain without a loss,
> And Heaven hurts fair women for sheer spite.

Strangely enough, both Dinh and Miss Nga felt journalism was not the right job for Bruce. They believed Bruce should be — of all things — a banker, or perhaps an administrator, and both wanted Bruce to take up a less hazardous occupation. "He should become a good husband," Miss Nga had once told Dinh, as if that were impossible for a reporter. Perhaps she knew Dinh too well. "She tell me, 'Not like you Dinh, too much girlfriend, too much smoke, too much drinking,' " Dinh recalled. Miss Nga said she believed a man should have only one girl: and she wanted to be the one for Bruce.

Dinh's reason for wanting Bruce to give up reporting was different. Dinh really believed he could see tragedy coming. Not only did he think Miss Nga's face showed she should marry "at high age" but also that it would be unlucky for her to marry young. But there was more: "In Vietnam custom say people like Bruce not living too long. Die very young. I know myself that, really I know that Bruce not long live man," Dinh told me, illustrating the Vietnamese concept of fate. "All things are fixed by Heaven, first and last," Nguyen Du had written.

Dinh and I made another trip outside the cleared inner city area on the Saturday. The fighting had eased in some parts and there were thousands of people standing around looking for something to see. Life for them was going on, except there wasn't much food and no work to go to.

In the middle of a busy little centre in Nguyen Van Thien Street — and in the midst of a war — we got a flat tyre. Searching the boot I found we had no spare and only one spanner. Of all things to happen — and it was my wakeup too. We got the wheel off and Dinh said he knew a bloke not far away who could fix it. The hundreds of Vietnamese onlookers in the street had their first laughs of the Tet Offensive at the sight of a European man hurriedly wheeling a flat tyre along the road followed by a Vietnamese in a district not yet occupied by anti-Viet Cong forces. The bored bar girls in their American-style slacks and old make-up gathered around giggling and, putting their hands over their mouths, shouted that I was "Number one! number one!" Dinh was laughing as people yelled out comments in Vietnamese.

When the tyre was fixed we headed back to the office as fast as we could go. I hadn't seen my girlfriend since the first night of the offensive, but as we passed the British compound there she was with her flatmate, standing out on the footpath. I had just about pulled up to say hello, when an American soldier at the transport compound across the road blew a whistle and soldiers started levelling their guns. They obviously thought the car might be full of plastic explosives. So I had to put my foot down and keep going with just a wave to the girls.

The Tet week had passed and still we had no help and little food, and fighting was continuing. Reuters were very worried that we had so much to do and they were trying to get people in to help us, including Ron Laramy, my replacement. Bruce was so keen to make it back that in the second week he caught an ammunition-laden plane into beseiged Khe Sanh because from there it was returning empty to Saigon. Having hitched a helicopter lift to the American Embassy from the airport in Saigon, he staggered into the office in his military uniform with a wry grin on his face. It wasn't Bruce to ask how we were or to get us to tell him all about it. He just asked sarcastically if anything much had been happening. We were glad to see him, and particularly when we found he'd brought a whole lot of steaks sent down to us by the marines at the press centre in Danang. We were ecstatic until Bruce got them out to cook: they had gone bad on Bruce's long, hot journey back and we had to throw them out. All we had now were some Korean combat rations.

Later that second week Ron Laramy and an Australian, Rick Paris, got in via Bangkok on a military flight. Because they made it in without official stamps and visas Paris was almost unable to get out of the country again later. It didn't matter for Laramy. The pair made it to Saigon's Tan Shon Nhut airport, but were stuck there for twelve hours and survived a few rocket attacks before getting to the office. Immediately they started doing most of the work.

Since the start of the offensive we had been receiving messages of support from London in their peculiar language. Phrases popped up in messages like: "Warmest thanks superb cover under present difficult circumstances. . . . Hats off from desk colleagues sheer stamina your war reporting. . . . Copy coming through well. Do best cope. Keep your heads down. Trying phone calls. Good luck."

These messages were very important at this time because there was no other way of knowing if what we were doing was worthwhile. The general manager sent a message saying: "You very much in thoughts of all colleagues," and Jimmy Hahn, the Asian manager, sent the following extract from the managing editor's review.

> The courageous reporting of our team added up to a stirring and graphic account. Most of them are no strangers to danger or the sound of gunfire. But war takes on a different dimension when it blazes through your home base, and bullets bounce off the pavement outside the office door. Pringle and his colleagues seemed to be everywhere on the job at all hours writing incisive copy which was often broken far ahead of the opposition.

But perhaps the best message of all said simply:

1726: LD25 ATTN SINGAPORE ONPASS
SAIGON   41646 Prohahn please onpass Pringle. Please
convey to all members of Reuter team in Saigon the congratulations of the Directors of Reuters on their magnificent
performance during past few weeks.
    You have lived up to the finest traditions of our agency.
BURGESS, CHAIRMAN, OS — REUTER LONDON

Within a few days of the start of the offensive the
American command announced that more than thirteen
thousand guerrillas had been killed, while allied casualties
were put at about twelve hundred. Journalists queried why
only 2,300 weapons had been captured and why there were
so few wounded prisoners listed. They estimated that for
every dead guerrilla there would normally be four badly
wounded, and that to carry a badly wounded man any
distance requires four men. Calculations based on the given
figure of thirteen thousand dead meant there were probably
more than fifty thousand badly wounded who had been
carried off by another two hundred thousand: that was more
Viet Cong than the Americans admitted to being in the
country. Even the British Embassy let us know at Reuters
that the figure was "beneath contempt".

To try to show reporters the Viet Cong were losing spec-
tacular numbers of men to achieve their world propaganda
victory, the Americans flew up the new general in charge of
the Mekong Delta. This was the place journalists went to
least, mainly because the American troops, apart from
advisers and a handful of others, had stayed out of it. Yet
six million of South Vietnam's seventeen million people lived there and it was the source of most of the country's food
for Viet Cong and government supporters alike.

The Mekong Delta was probably the unsafest place in
South Vietnam, said to be home for eighty thousand Viet
Cong. It was an area the size of Denmark, almost all under
rice-paddy water. At a time when the Americans and most
outsiders thought America was winning the war, in 1967,

there was some embarrassment that this area still had not been tackled. But there was much optimism. Just about the first press conference I had covered in South Vietnam was held by US Ambassador Cabot-Lodge who was about to go home. He said 1967 would see America's military successes in South Vietnam snowball. And they would enter the Delta in force. "It will be the year of the Mekong Delta," he had said. But by the end of that year only one small American unit had moved in.

At the start of 1968, before Tet, another optimistic forecast for the Mekong Delta was made at a press conference. This time it was General William Deasbry, who had been chief adviser to the ARVN in the Delta for two years; he too was about to go home. He said that although there were eighty thousand Viet Cong in the Delta when he arrived and there were still eighty thousand, they were "like the Germans at the end of World War Two: the VC are better equipped than they were, and just as strong numerically — but they lack the motivation and training now," he said.

Three weeks later the Viet Cong fought through the streets of eleven of the sixteen province capitals in the Delta showing the people that the Americans and the government could not offer any protection in return for loyalty.

At the Follies a journalist questioned a guest general about the "kill ratio" the Americans were claiming. He asked rhetorically, "The normal claimed kill ratio is four to one and this is more than fifteen to one?" "Yes," said the general. "What's up general, can't the Viet Cong fight?" the journalist said, and sat down to a theatrette filled with laughter.

Another American journalist asked how the kill ratio could be better when the fighting was in cities and towns instead of in the countryside where bombs and artillery could be used. It was a good point and the unaware general said, "Oh, we've bombed and used artillery." A Follies announcer jumped up and explained to us that what the

233

general meant was bombs and artillery had been used to bomb around the towns to kill escaping Viet Cong. The general agreed with this but he named one town in the Mekong Delta in which artillery had been used. Bruce Pigott went with the press who demanded to see it.

Bruce's story began by saying that the town of My Tho looked like a giant had walked through and crumpled all the buildings. And it was in this town that an American officer made the famous comment to Bruce and other reporters: "We had to destroy the town to save it."

After Laramy and Paris had arrived I again visited my girlfriend. We decided to have a game of tennis on the court in the British compound with her flatmate, who was a bit of a tennis player. When we got on the bitumen court, which had a high brick wall along one side, we had to remove several spent bullets. We had been hitting a while when the flatmate ran in to the net and missed a shot completely. She looked up and said, "It's no use, I can't play while there's gunfire." So we stopped.

A week or so after the Viet Cong had damaged pacification programmes throughout the country, taken the American Embassy and Radio Saigon, and fought in the streets of thirty-three of the forty-four province capitals and Danang and Saigon, the US briefers announced from the stage at the Follies that a summary of 1967 military activity could be found outside in the rack: "This finely bound volume is entitled '1967: A Year of Success,' " he said.

The room full of reporters broke into spontaneous laughter.

"Could you tell me, was that written before or after January 29?" asked a correspondent.

At last the Follies briefer was stuck for an answer.

234

So long Saigon

I was in such a hurry to get out of Vietnam that, in the end, I didn't take a lot of the mementos I had intended. I was going to go up to Danang to say goodbye to everyone at the press centre but I didn't, which was how I left behind *Seven Centuries of Poetry*, my only book. I was going to take an M-16 rifle I had kept but when the time came I didn't. I was going to take my helmet or flak jacket but I didn't. I was just so happy to be getting out after the worry and delay caused by the Tet Offensive.

Although things were almost back to normal when I left more than two weeks after Tet began, there was still the occasional sign of war in the middle of Saigon. The day before I was leaving we had a cocktail party in the Reuter flats and an American spokesman who had become a friend came along. Although our flats were only two blocks through the city centre from his office, he had his rifle with him. I remember this because he leant it up against a wall and half an hour later the building trembled enough for the rifle to fall over with a clang. It was a B-52 bombing raid, we found out at the briefing later: it showed the Americans were still bombing very close to the city.

The next day at the airport my close friends of one year, Dinh and Jim, were surprised to find I didn't look happy. I explained that it wasn't really because I was leaving them but that I wouldn't be happy until the plane was on its way. I didn't want my luck to run out just now.

The airport was extremely crowded because many people, particularly French plantation owners, had finally decided that Tet showed the game was up in Vietnam, and they were leaving the country with everything they could carry.

Rick Paris, who had come in to help us in the crisis, was going out with me. He was looking forward to the bottle of champagne I was going to buy as soon as the Air Vietnam Caravelle took off. Ron Laramy, of course, stayed on; I had written to him in London telling him not to come, but he said when he arrived that he wanted to help his parents financially. Bruce had to stay and mind the office and I said goodbye to him there and that I might see him in Australia, or Singapore. He hoped to return to Australia to work for the ABC, he said . . . and when he and Miss Nga smiled at each other, I guessed I would be seeing her too. At the airport Dinh, Jim and I made a pact that as soon as the war was over we would meet and celebrate in Saigon. It was the thought of this that brought some happinesss to what was actually a sad parting.

We all said our goodbyes — and how difficult it was saying farewell to the Vietnamese whom I had only known for twelve months, and hadn't even liked for the first of them. Pringle was looking his usual worried self — changing from staring blankly to one side to bursting into a smile and saying, as he often did when a job was finished, "Well that's it Hugh," in heavy Scottish brogue. And, as I walked away, he called, "Is that you Hugh?" Like a good writer, he finished the story as he had started it.

As soon as the flight took off, Rick Paris told me to get that bottle of champagne. I told him to hold on, but he kept badgering me, thinking I was going to back out of our bargain. He didn't know that I was looking out at the rice paddies below using the knowledge I'd gained watching altimeters on all my helicopter flights to decide when we had passed fifteen hundred metres: only then would I feel that the Viet Cong had had their last chance of killing me.

I ordered the champagne, and doubt that I have ever felt happier, heading for what I expected to be the most enjoyable holiday of my life once I reached Australia. After about two hours we landed in Singapore and were surprised that Reuters' manager for Asia, Jimmy Hahn, was there to greet us. He had a message from the managing editor in London saying that I had been given a bonus of £200 for my coverage of the Tet Offensive.

At Brisbane airport my mother said she thought it was Bing Crosby walking across the tarmac, I looked so old and thin.

Instead of feeling happy and excited to be back home after four years away I found I felt something like a pain in the heart. At first I thought it was because no one seemed to understand what was happening in Vietnam.

The significance of Tet was not yet fully understood and I would have to wait until the 1980s to read in an Australian newspaper: "The Tet Offensive of 1968 stood at the very epicentre of the US experience in Indo China. Before Tet, all was build-up and optimism. After Tet, all was withdrawal and recrimination."

Maybe this was because by the time I got home the Tet Offensive was being portrayed by American leaders as an American military victory. No longer was Tet a "diversionary effort" to make Khe Sanh easier to overrun, as we had been told in Saigon when it started. It was now an attempt by the Viet Cong to end the war with one huge offensive "which failed to create a general uprising".

I went to visit a girl I had long been interested in. She invited me in, made me feel very welcome, and asked how I had been overseas: "But please don't say a word about Vietnam. I'm sick of hearing about it all the time," she said. Conversation became stilted, then awkward, and I left minutes later and did not return.

All I could manage to do each day was lie on the lawn and listen to the radio and wait for the next news. Every time I heard an interesting story from Vietnam, like the news that, shortly after Tet finished, the American commander there for four years, General William Westmoreland, had been recalled to a new job, I rushed upstairs to tell someone. There was no response from my mother so I started ringing up reporters, who were equally uninterested. Even when I said, "An F-one-eleven has been shot down," one reporter said, "Oh yes, one of those F-one-one-ones." No one seemed to realize that the F-111 was not supposed to be able to be shot down.

In March, when President Johnson — the builder of the Vietnam War — resigned, I was desperate to talk to someone because I knew this move was a consequence of his disappointment at the Tet Offensive and meant the war was now moving to an end. So I rang a teacher–grazier mate thinking he would listen at least and not immediately change the subject to sport. He said it was very interesting — and wondered what effect it might have on cattle prices.

So I had no one to share my knowledge with and, instead of having a great holiday, I found that I stayed home all the time and moped around the house. I was isolated by my consuming interest in a subject that rarely entered the thoughts of people in Australia. What was even worse was their ignorance of what was happening. Not only did people not know what was going on, but they had a small enough smattering to think they knew. Everyone could tell me where I was wrong. They kept telling me the Viet Cong had invaded Vietnam . . . that the Chinese were fighting the Americans there . . . that the Vietnamese had no chance of defeating the powerful Americans.

I found I was suffering like a man who had been in love, and now wasn't.

On 22 March, a month after my return, I got up one morning, safely, in Brisbane and across the front page of the local *Courier-Mail* was a story that began:

FOUR THOUSAND DIE: KHE SANH THREAT EASE.
Saigon (AAP–Reuter)   American military Intelligence in South Vietnam has reported that U.S. air strikes and artillery have killed about 4,000 North Vietnamese and eased the Communist threat to the surrounding frontier fort of Khe Sanh,

238

held by U.S. marines. The heavy toll among the 16,000 Communists around Khe Sanh has deprived the North Vietnamese of their chance for any immediate victory in the area. . . . They have faded away for no apparent reason, the spokesman said.

The interesting thing to me was that the four thousand dead were attributed to American Intelligence reports. Certainly the marines clinging grimly to Khe Sanh had not been out counting them. To me they were four thousand bodies of an army of sixteen thousand no one had ever seen: a product, if you like, of the Follies imagination, and of the system whereby journalists had to report announcements and figures — no matter how strange. Jim Pringle had been right to believe that the sixteen thousand said by prisoners to have surrounded Khe Sanh was a ruse for attacks elsewhere (Tet, as it turned out) but, in the end, I believe I was also right to think the sixteen thousand were created so a victory over them could be announced at a later date.

I had returned home believing I would almost certainly stay in Australia, but eventually I realized that the real reason I was dispirited was that I was missing the war. In April I returned to Southeast Asia, this time to work in Reuters' Singapore office.

With President Johnson gone and America still reeling from the discovery that the Viet Cong were much stronger than they thought, Ho Chi Minh now agreed to talk peace in Paris as, I believe, another way of wearing down the American will to stay on in Vietnam. This meant the focus of the war would shift to other Follies briefings in Paris after each day's talks and that the war would now scale right down. Never again would the Americans suffer anything like the losses of the previous twelve months. (In the next four years American troop numbers in Vietnam were to fall by 250,000.) This made me think how lucky Ron Laramy was, and I was glad for Dinh, Bruce and Miss Nga — especially as they no longer had Jim Pringle there to advise what should be done. He had finished his extended stint in Vietnam and now the war was winding down.

By now Bruce had told Dinh of his plan to marry Miss Nga and take her to live in Melbourne "and explain her digger customs," as Dinh said to me in a letter. Bruce asked Dinh what sort of ceremony would be required and how he should go about being a popular son-in-law. The couple told Dinh they wanted two children.

Because Dinh knew there would be difficulties he started visiting Miss Nga's family often, at first talking about the war and slowly turning to the benefits of their daughter leaving the war and studying in a country like Australia.

"Bruce he have talk with me confidential," Dinh told me. "He wanted marry Miss Nga and take her to Australia and she agree to. I explain very difficult for Confucian family girl to marry him because of family. It was easy for bar girl but not this girl. The family care too much . . . but Nga say she want to marry, that she love Bruce."

For Dinh this relationship was touching, after all the denigration of his people he had seen in the war. And, for Bruce, Dinh's caring actions reemphasized, if it were ever needed, that here was a culture worth loving. But the consent of the parents, Dinh counselled, was absolutely vital, because in a Confucian society rebellion is the worst sin.

Dinh gave fatherly advice to Bruce, who was only six years younger. He explained how Bruce must act. Despite the careful preparations, the parents reacted angrily to the idea. But, with Miss Nga making good propaganda with her mother by crying, the parents accepted Bruce into the family by April 1968 . . . with only a few months to spare until his tour of duty was up. The pair could marry.

However, the peace moves did not mean immediate peace. The Viet Cong communists adopted their traditional tactic of showing their power immediately before negotiations.

The ARVN draft had finally caught up with the cagey Dinh in April and, after a month in training camp, he returned to Saigon for the weekend on Saturday 4 May, just as Bruce came back from R and R in Manila. It was on this occasion that Bruce gave Dinh the traditional Philippines shirt Dinh was to keep for the next twelve years in Saigon, though often he could have traded it for much needed rice.

That night explosions rocked Saigon and the second — and last — big Viet Cong attack on the city before it fell in 1975 had begun. This offensive was nowhere near as big as Tet because it was limited to Saigon: it was to become known as the Battle for Saigon. Dinh, naturally, forgot his recent army training and went straight to the Reuter office at dawn to help, after first phoning through a story based on information from his police contact who was "no more, head killed by accident rocket". There he saw Bruce and Ron Laramy. An AAP reporter Mike Birch — a cocky, very personable, very young fellow from Sydney who worked out of the Reuter office but reported only on Australians — and John Cantwell of *Time* also were there. With Bruce was his journalist mate from Melbourne, Frank Palmos, who had recently arrived in Vietnam.

Dinh and Bruce were particularly happy to see each other because Dinh's military service had kept him away for a month. They agreed to have lunch together that Sunday but first they had to see what was happening in the battle.

People were to say later that they should not have driven off into the fighting, but if you are covering a war you can't write that "There appears, from the explosions, to be fighting in the city." Besides, it was always a reasonable expectation that if you drove outwards from the centre of Saigon, government or American troops would be between you and the attacking Viet Cong. Dinh went with the bureau chief, Tony Baker, to the north of the city in the office car — and Bruce, Ron, Cantwell, Birch, and Palmos set off in Cantwell's Mini-Moke — with its "Time Magazine" sign — to go to Cholon. Most unusually for a journalist in Saigon, John Cantwell, who was driving, carried one of his favourite revolvers.

As the group drove through refugees fleeing the fighting

Bruce said, "It's the people who always suffer." Those were to be among his last words.

That was at 8 a.m. and when Dinh returned to the office at 10.30 a.m. he heard, he said, "Rumour say no more Bruce". This is what he later told me.

"Saigon police chief my friend, call me and said: 'Any Reuters correspondent go to Cholon this morning?' And I said: 'Yes, two men there.' And he said: 'Sorry, something not good news for you.' That's all he said. I said: 'What happened Colonel?' He said at least two people killed. Five people in mini-jeep.

"We went to police station nearby where they reported shot. And I say I must go to the area to see if Bruce Pigott wounded and not dead yet. Police chief very angry with me because he friend of mine. He say: 'Are you crazy boy? How much do Reuters pay you to do that?' I said: 'Nothing. My heart order to me to do that. But nobody pay me. Because Bruce friend of mine I miss him very much. I love him.'"

Dinh then set off to walk one kilometre into the heavy fighting, unarmed, to see if his friend Bruce was still alive. Vietnamese refugees poured out — only Dinh walked in the opposite direction. Nobody else would have approached that area in less than company strength, and then backed up by tanks and grenades. And, for the moment at least, no army was going in there just for the sake of a few reporters.

After he and Jim Pringle had been pinned down by fire in this area soon after Tet began, Dinh had vowed never to go there again. Now he walked "step by step" into what he described in a letter to me later as "very quiet area". Then, fifty metres away, he saw the Mini-Moke and some bodies. As he moved closer suddenly two men "black pyjama AK arm" pointed their guns at him. " 'Where you going boy?' they say. They were ready to shot [sic], because battlefield going on now. Air strike, bombing, artillery, anything going on, mortar, something like that," said Dinh. He told them he lived there and, because of the danger, wanted to get out.

It was not in the Viet Cong's interest to kill every fellow Vietnamese in sight, and Dinh, being clever, and talking to them in their own peasant lingo, managed to win a brief confidence. The men told Dinh it was all right to clear out, but he had still not found out whether Bruce was alive. So he ignored the Viet Cong instruction to go and moved straight to Bruce, whom he could now see slumped over the other side of the Moke.

"I saw Bruce legs still in car and head lay down on the land, and Laramy sitting back something like that." He realized that if the Viet Cong thought he were a friend or relative (his word) they would shoot him. So he asked, "Is that American GI soldier?" And the Viet Cong leader said, "No, that is the CIA. We must kill them. We must shoot them." Dinh felt obliged to agree. "I said, 'Ooh, CIA, then that is correct you must shoot them.' " But this renunciation of Bruce hurt him. "I looked like crying at that time, but stopped. I quickly stopped. I saw Bruce's body and I want to cry immediately. But I stop myself. I said, 'Stop.' I said to myself, 'Must stop.' If I cry then they already know who am I. So I stopped. And I said, 'That is CIA then you should kill them because CIA do dirty job in Vietnam. Let me see the body of CIA?'

"One said: 'You can look that body quickly boy.' "

Dinh then described the tragic scene. Holding up his left hand with the fingers tightly together and straight, like a priest, he said, "I put my hand in Bruce's heart," and he put the hand over his own chest, inside his shirt. "And Laramy's heart," and he did the same again. "But finished. No, nothing more. And I moved back to the police station and report."

Dinh did not check the bodies of Mike Birch or John Cantwell, though he was sure they too were dead. (The autopsy was to show that the smallest number of bullets in any of the four journalists was ten — the most, twenty-six.)

When he returned to the office from his expedition Dinh wept. "I cry because lose my friend," he wrote in a letter to me in Singapore. He said the Viet Cong did not know they were shooting British and Australian journalists. "Difficult for the VC to know who are Americans who are English, who are journalists who are army, because all look same. And CIA never to wear military uniform." Vietnamese in the market did tell him the journalists tried to call out "bao chi" (journalist) when the gunfire started but Dinh said there was no way the peasant guerrillas would understand an Australian trying to yell out city Vietnamese.

Frank Palmos, the other passenger in the car, miraculously escaped the hail of Viet Cong fire by feigning death and then sprinting clear. He said later the Viet Cong commander had repeated Birch's call of "bao chi" and clearly understood it. Palmos also said claims by a Vietnamese cameraman that eye-witnesses had said one of the reporters pulled a revolver as the Moke reversed from a Viet Cong road block were incorrect. "The only weapon in the car was John Cantwell's and that was a tiny handgun he was taking home to give his wife . . . at no time was it drawn against the VC. . . . the only 'weapon' drawn during the ambush was a piece of plastic-coated card four inches by two: Michael Birch's press card which he waved to the commander who then shot him full-front," said Palmos. He said when he warned them the VC were up ahead, Bruce told Cantwell to keep going. Bruce loved his story too much.

These were only four of the forty-five journalists killed on duty in Vietnam and eighteen still missing, compared with three in Korea and thirty-nine in the second world war. But these statistics forget many things, including Miss Nga.

Dinh could accept Bruce's death. He had told Bruce that the Vietnamese believed that if your friend dies his soul follows you, and helps you. But he had to tell Miss Nga of the events of that Sunday May morning. "She cry. She lay down and make noises. She like died lady," he said.

In Singapore I had been on the overnight shift and was woken up by a phonecall at my hotel room saying "first reports" said some Reuter men had been killed. When I got to the office everyone was standing around the telex machine waiting for confirmation, and hoping that the first reports were wrong. However, we all knew that they were usually right — that the reporter knows the facts but can't yet quote anyone.

Then it came through, one letter at a time. Cantwell, Birch, Ron Laramy, and Bruce Pigott were dead.

Jimmy Hahn asked me if I wanted to return to Saigon with him to help out. It was a very difficult decision to make. I had escaped Vietnam purely through luck. But now my colleague, Bruce, and my replacement, Ron, had been killed and the Reuter office faced a crisis. It was a time to step into the breach, time to save the day. I thought about it for a few seconds, and said no. Jimmy said he understood, and went by himself.

In Singapore I watched the messages on the wire go back and forth telling Jimmy what belongings the parents of the two dead Reuter correspondents wanted: "Laramy's parents want only his silver ring and give the rest to the other boys." The bodies of Bruce and Ron were to be put in caskets and sent to London for Fleet Street to mourn at a ceremony in the Church of St Bride next to Reuters on 14 June 1968. Bruce's parents were flown to London for the ceremony which included hymns, a lesson, an address by British publishing chairman and Reuters' director Hugh Cudlipp and a blessing at the end with all kneeling, which ended:

God be at my end,
And at my departing.

Dinh fights Hanoi

My leaving was the end of Vietnam for me, or so I thought at the time. But, as many soldiers who fought there have found, the Vietnam War never ends.

For a while I had to resist the urge to alter or reject stories coming through the Singapore office from new Reuter correspondents in Saigon who, I felt, had yet to learn what it was all about. Only once, in January 1969, did I give in to the temptation. The Americans announced in Saigon that a pair of US navy patrol craft "firing machine-guns" had destroyed forty-five small, round basket-type boats "found bobbing inside waters restricted as a security measure for US craft". One or two Vietnamese were in each boat. The Americans said they were Viet Cong. Dutifully Reuters reported the story. I sent off the following message to the Saigon office and felt it was so important I kept the copy.

service rtr saigon:
40950 pro . . . exlunn spore tks [thanks] daylead vietnam. Onpassing my experience that each day Danang fishermen set out from China Beach in these six-foot diameter circular basket-type craft with small nets aboard. With the tide they paddle into the distance until they can be seen bobbing in scores on the horizon. Each basket holds two or three fishermen and sometimes small girls will take out a craft alone, standing up spinning it slowly forward like a top. The craft move at about half a knot and would present no menace as an attack craft — escape would be impossible. They could not flee from a navy patrol boat. Note spokesman says challenges made in Vietnamese before machine-guns opened fire — but how could fishermen answer? Presumably challenge made

over loud-speaker from safe distance. Note no captured weapons listed. Thanks, regards. Reuter HL.

But my message was ignored and the report went out to the world including the statement of the obvious that "there were no US casualties".

Dinh had been congratulated for his bravery "in going to the bodies of Mr Laramy and Mr Pigott" by the Reuters board, and, with peace talks still going on, the war stumbled on slowly with no major battles.

With the Americans withdrawing more and more troops each year in order to "Vietnamize" the war, the result was inevitable. At the start of April 1975, with the North Vietnamese moving inexorably further and further south to Saigon, Reuters offered to evacuate their favourite reporter, Pham Ngoc Dinh. Dinh allowed his family to be evacuated but said, "If a journalist see the beginning he must see the end," and elected to stay on, thinking he could always get out at the last moment.

On 30 April, with the Viet Cong and North Vietnamese already on the outskirts of Saigon, Dinh decided, "Time go, war finished." So too did thousands of Vietnamese who were afraid of what would happen now that the last of the Americans were leaving in their helicopters which, as was shown on newsfilm, were unceremoniously tipped off US ships into the ocean to make room for others that were arriving. Anyway, they didn't want to leave them for the communists.

At JUSPAO there were six buses to carry Americans and important Vietnamese to the airport for a last evacuation. Dinh tried to get on the second bus but was kicked off by an American military policeman and put on the fourth. This was very unlucky because at the airport only two buses went inside. Dinh was to find out that the four buses at the back were driven by Viet Cong ... and, along with everyone else on these buses that did not go to the airport, he was returned to central Saigon where there was now no way out.

247

Once he realized that escape was impossible, he ran back to the office and searched upstairs and downstairs. He was worried there might be a gun there; he also burned any old pieces of military uniforms left by Reuter correspondents and hurried to his house. But he didn't think to remove the pictures of his favourite co-reporters from under his desk glass.

The next day, when Dinh went to the office with Saigon now under communist rule, there was a machinegun post outside Reuters' grenade door defending the area around the Presidential Palace. Dinh noticed that there was now a bullet hole in the small British flag outside the door.

Ever the cheeky reporter, Dinh said to the occupying Viet Cong, "This is a Reuter office." But they said, "No, it is a CIA office," and escorted him outside. So Dinh had to report to the new communist foreign ministry, the ministry which registered all foreign newsagencies. The communists had confiscated the scores of pictures from his desk and he was questioned about each one. During a full month of "political re-education" Dinh was asked to analyse each of us in writing, and to give our political point of view. Dinh told them I had come in 1967. "He cover the stories. He never too anti-anybody, he just report," Dinh told them.

Because France had kept relations with Hanoi, Reuters sent in a French correspondent. But he was kicked out after seventeen days. Then they tried an Asian, and then Australian, Neil Davis. But they too were kicked out.

Dinh continued for a while as Reuter correspondent, but each story had to be censored. Accustomed to dealing with the Americans, he was surprised to find the communists would never say how many were killed or wounded during the war. He was also surprised when, inexplicably, he was called before the communist police for writing about an explosion in the newly christened "Allied Forces Memorial Square". Dinh continued to file censored stories until 1976 when a general election was hailed as giving unity to Vietnam and making Hanoi the capital, something even the

Viet Cong did not want. This meant, the regime said, that the Reuter office must go to Hanoi. Reuter immediately assigned Dinh to Hanoi, but he was refused leave to go there by the new government.

So Reuters tried "assigning" him to Singapore and later Bangkok. But those moves too, were refused.

Dinh was now in a twilight zone: he had no job and lived in a land where he was not trusted. He had trouble communicating with the Viet Cong because they had generally spent their lives fighting, and knew little. When they saw the telex machines in the Reuter office they told him that they were "spy machines". Even the top people were difficult for Dinh to talk to because they were almost all from the north, the Viet Cong National Liberation Front having lost 85 per cent of their number during the long war, Dinh was told. Three times they arrested him in the office, which he refused to leave. He lived above the Reuter office and opened it every day, even though there was nothing to do. Luckily for him, Reuter sent him money or he would have starved because food had become so expensive in Saigon, now Ho Chi Minh City. Dinh found it had been a better place to live in during the war. Now there was little food, a much more extensive black market, and more corruption.

Two policemen came to the office one night and said the next day he would get a visa to leave the country. But the following morning at the police station a North Vietnamese official demanded to know why he worked for "a capitalist newsagency". Dinh replied, "where were you so I could work for you at that time?" Confused, the official asked Dinh where he was during the war and Dinh answered shrewdly, "Under control by the former government." There was a South Vietnamese official present too and he said to the northerner, "Well, each man has a situation of his own, how can you ask that?" Dinh began to find that the local Viet Cong were prepared to treat him much better than the northern Vietnamese.

The Viet Cong were now sticking up for the South Vietnamese because the northerners had taken all the powerful positions. A lot of ill-feeling had developed among the Viet Cong, particularly after General Van Tien Dung, commander-in-chief of the North Vietnamese forces, published a book saying how the North Vietnamese troops won the war.

This prompted a book in reply from General Tran Van Tra, who was commander of the Viet Cong forces that attacked Saigon during the Tet Offensive and later military governor in Saigon for two years after the city fell in April 1975. He wrote that what the North Vietnamese general had said was untrue, and that the North Vietnamese troops had fought only "behind the Viet Cong". His book revealed, Dinh said, that the Viet Cong had suffered horrendous casualties during Tet, as the Americans had claimed at the time, though no one believed them. According to the general they lost 50 per cent of their men in those assaults.

But the book was confiscated and the general was placed under house arrest. "He was then called to Hanoi and nobody knows what happened to him," said Dinh.

Dinh soon found that some of the Viet Cong were happy to have a chat with him and ignore his political views. But many had the fault of those who are too committed to anything: they never laugh and find everything serious. Other Viet Cong were only serious at official investigations of Dinh and, because of his winning ways and, especially, his peasant background, a few were helpful and would "talk free". But this did not mean Dinh was safe from arrest at any time.

Reuters, realizing the danger their man could be in now that he was no longer officially their correspondent, and wanting to reunite him with his family, now took more direct action. A tourist was asked to try to see him. Dinh did not think this a good idea, but a meeting was arranged by a friend. The tourist gave him a watch which Dinh, conscious of his dodgy situation, immediately showed to the Viet Cong; they opened it to see it didn't contain any message.

Reuters also sent Dinh cigarettes, toothpaste, medicine, and warm clothes, but clearly there was little else they could do. Dinh knew he was being closely watched.

An Australian journalist arrived as a tourist and went straight to the old Reuter office. Dinh was sitting in the office "very sad, look at trees, raining, raining". The journalist came up to him with a tourist official with him to translate, and Dinh saw two men he recognized as secret police with them as well. "The Australian said, 'Hello Dinh. How are you? What you doing? You all right, you OK?' " Dinh recognized the journalist but surprised himself with his quick answer. He turned to the men he knew to be Viet Cong secret police and said, "Who is he? What he say? What he talking about?" They said in Vietnamese, "This is your journalist friend from Australia. He wants to see you." "No, I don't want to see any journalist," Dinh replied. The Australian was, Dinh related, bemused. "He say, 'Dinh you speak to me. You forgotten English? Can't you speaking English anymore?' "

Dinh turned to the Viet Cong, "What he talking about? Please translate for me." Dinh said this went on for almost half an hour and the secret police were very upset and worried this might be "bad propaganda for them". "Talk to him," they ordered, to which Dinh replied, "If you want me talk to him please sign here. Today, what day, who you are, what your rank, accept and agree I talk with this guy by English language."

The Viet Cong police signed and Dinh explained his difficult position.

Over the next few years Dinh saw many Westerners he knew from the war turn up in Saigon but he did not speak to them. A Reuter man who came in from Hong Kong was one of them. In a bar he gave a letter to a girl working there saying he was from Reuters and paid her money to deliver it to Dinh. "It was a shock letter to me," said Dinh. "It said: 'I am coming here want to see you please come to this bar in Tu Do Street.' I worry about this lady coming. Maybe CIA, maybe Viet Cong. I say: 'According to law I cannot see you. Please understand my situation.' "

But apparently this man did not understand the position he was putting Dinh in. "The next day she coming back and say: 'Believe me, I am not CIA I am Chinese woman who work for bar but I worry too much because he ask me to go to see you many time.' But definitely I not talk to him. And the last night before he leaving he send another girl coming to ask me. I ask my cousin: 'Take me by Honda fastly to the bar.' I see him from here to there [very close] already. I never to see him before but the bar girl she say: 'That's the man. That's the man.' I say: 'Hello' and go straight away." The girl had probably wanted to help Dinh, but he could never have been sure of that. Dinh said he had "two feelings" about the attempt. "I very happy to see they show they care my situation, but also very dangerous."

In 1979 Dinh was placed in an even more difficult situation. Reuters had got word to him enquiring which country he would like to migrate to if their continuing official efforts to get him out were successful. Dinh replied: "Not USA — Australia," because of his liking for the Australian reporters he had met . . . and perhaps because it was the home of Bruce's soul which ought to have been looking after him.

In September 1979 the Australian immigration minister Michael Mackellar wrote a letter to Reuters saying the Australian government had approved the admission of Dinh to Australia as a special case "in view of Mr Dinh's extraordinary services to Australian journalists in Saigon during the 1968 Tet Offensive". (Actually he meant the Battle of Saigon but I knew that Tet applied equally as well.)

When Dinh got that letter the police came to his house and took him to headquarters: "Tell us exactly what you did for the Australian Embassy in Vietnam," they said. Dinh replied that he did nothing except work for Reuters. "They say: 'Why they give you special visa boy?' I say: 'Humanitarian reasons.' They say: 'What you mean?' I say: 'I jobless. No food. No clothes.' "

Dinh was so far down now — more than four years after the war had ended — that, like the Viet Cong before him, he now did not care he die. "Tell me you want I stay or you want I leave. I don't care I stay, I don't care I leave. Let me free. Don't push me like that. Tell me if I have something wrong, put me in jail. Nothing wrong, let me free." But Dinh noted the Viet Cong interrogators were impressed by his strong performance.

After that, every day for three months, the police questioned him. The same questions. Instead of telling them some things, Dinh just kept saying: "I said I don't know, I forgot everything. My head now nothing. Not enough food or clothes, very cold."

Then, in April 1980, Dinh was finally given his exit visa. The man who had clung doggedly to the Reuter office, opening it every day though there was nothing to do, now officially handed over the office and its equipment to the Vietnamese officials. But he demanded they sign for everything, at which the officials became angry and immediately confiscated the telex machines and typewriters.

On 8 May 1980, almost exactly five years after Dinh caught the wrong bus at the end of the war and almost exactly twelve years after Bruce was killed, Dinh left his homeland with his new wife and their children by Air France to Bangkok. He didn't even have one cent in his pocket, having sold everything he owned to pay for food.

At Bangkok airport Dinh's troubles were not yet over. He thought no one was there to meet him, and he panicked because he had no money. Desperate, he tried to borrow two baht for a phonecall. The Thai man he approached at first refused, but two minutes later changed his mind and Dinh rang the old Reuter office number only to be told that Reuter had moved from there several years before. He had used his two baht. "I very upset," he said later. "I very worried."

An Australian Embassy official had been at the airport to meet him but somehow they had missed each other. Finally, the Bangkok Reuter correspondent found him. They had never met before but Dinh was very happy when the correspondent walked up and put his arms around him and said, "Welcome Reuter family."

An Australian Embassy official drove Dinh to a big hotel where he stayed for two weeks. Reuters gave him $3,000 to go shopping for clothes. Dinh also bought a pair of reading glasses, which he had been unable to buy in Vietnam. "Three years I cannot read because no glasses. Only one can buy that at official price [communist] government official, but private people cannot."

Jim Pringle was now stationed in Bangkok for *Newsweek* and, when he discovered Dinh was there too he took him out every night. Dinh was inundated by messages from journalists around the world. Journalists in Reuters' head office took up a collection among themselves that amounted to $1,000. Jim Pringle gave him $1,200 and another correspondent $1,000 to help him restart his life in a foreign country. It showed how much Dinh meant to them.

Reuters' Sydney chief correspondent Len Santorelli met Dinh and family at Sydney airport at the end of May 1980 and put them up at the Northside Garden Hotel. "I never to live in hotel like that before," said Dinh, amazed at the treatment he was getting.

And Reuters arranged a job with Australian Associated Press in its economics service. The only thing Dinh had brought out of Saigon with him was the brass sign "Reuter London" off the wall outside our Saigon office, together with the small British flag now with the bullet hole in it. He handed them to Reuters' Asian manager, with the note: "Dinh and family born again second time by Reuter in Australia."

Dinh told them he would be forever grateful for the money Reuters sent him every week for five years after the fall of Saigon. "They lost money with me in Vietnam during five years," he said, but obviously Reuters felt differently.

When I saw Dinh in Sydney there was one question I was

254

dying to ask him: How did he know the Tet Offensive was going to start that January night in 1968? He replied that his source was a Vietnamese journalist working for one of America's biggest weekly news magazines. He and Dinh often talked on the footpath outside Reuters.

Dinh recalled what he'd found out just hours before the start of the offensive. "He saw me at 7 p.m. in the street and he say: 'Look Dinh, something big news happening tonight. Are you ready?' and I believe him because I know he have good VC source. He say happen after midnight and only the Viet Cong fight in Saigon. I said: 'Terrorist, bomb, rockets?' and he say: 'No, more than that,' and walk away.

After the fall of Saigon Dinh found out how it was that his friend knew so much, and why he had been so right. He had been born in the south and lived there, although his father had elected to go north when the 1954 Geneva Accords divided the country into communist and non-communist — a clue that should have been picked up by the CIA perhaps. At first Dinh's friend worked for the government news organization Vietnam Press, where he was so skilful at gathering information that he was sent to the United States to study journalism at university. In 1960 he returned to join Reuters as a reporter, and soon developed a reputation as a very good one. It was he who taught Dinh journalism, Dinh having started in the office by then as a messenger.

In 1965, with Dinh well on the way to being a good reporter himself, a Reuter bureau chief sacked his friend, saying (significantly) that his stories read too much like Hanoi Radio. However, the reputation of this reporter was such that he did well as a freelance until landing the job with the American magazine.

He became very popular because of his political and military knowledge and good sources, and Dinh used to complain, perhaps a little enviously, that visiting American journalists would come to the Reuter office and ask him if he knew where this reporter was. "I want dinner with him," they would say. "Most big journalists of USA who covered war during 1960s know him very well," said Dinh.

255

This reporter was also very friendly with General Ngo Du, director-general of military operations at Joint General Staff headquarters and a close friend of Doctor Tran Kim Tuyen, chief of the Vietnamese Central Intelligence Service.

"All the generals of the ARVN forces his friend," Dinh said, banging his fist angrily on the table. "All the corps commanders, joint general staffs, he knew everything. Even the US Embassy. He could go there very quickly if he want, anytime. He see generals anytime he want. And some Vietnamese generals, including the high operations commander, could call him for advice: 'Our forces move this way, this map, this one and this one.' And he could go to the joint general staff."

Dinh said ARVN officers wanted to help this reporter because they worked for Americans and wanted "good propaganda" in the United States.

A year or so after the fall of Saigon Dinh ran into his colleague in a Saigon coffee shop. Dinh was surprised to see him because a month before Saigon fell his wife and four children had been evacuated to the United States by his magazine. Yet within six months they were back in Vietnam. He told Dinh he sent his family to the United States because he was "worried about artillery shells in Saigon", but Dinh felt he was playing games with the CIA. They had returned, he said, via Moscow, Peking, and Hanoi. Asked why he had brought his wife and children back when so many people wanted to leave, he had replied: "I don't want my children to be Yankees."

Dinh then asked him straight out if he was a Viet Cong during the war. He did not deny it directly, saying, "Oh well, somebody told me that, what do you think?" and Dinh said, "Of course you are a communist Viet Cong." And his friend laughed.

Later he took Dinh to his Saigon home, and Dinh was surprised to see it was a luxurious former British Embassy house. He now knew he was with a very powerful figure.

"Many rumours said I am a Viet Cong. I never deny or confirm that. Now I show you one magazine," he said to Dinh. He opened a safe with a key and, to Dinh's everlasting surprise, produced a photo of himself in a North Vietnamese magazine — with Ho Chi Minh. The caption read: "Comrade [his name] with Uncle Ho". The date was 1969, the year after the Tet Offensive when he was still working as a reporter in Saigon.

"Thus he confirm he a Viet Cong with rank of colonel," Dinh said. "I surprised. And also surprised that woman who come look for him our office many times VC major, he said his 'liaison officer'."

With his eyes suddenly blazing, Dinh said: "How can American win war? How can ARVN win war? What CIA doing? Something corruption, black market? He very important in the war for VC. Any story he have all information he can give to VC, but, more important, he can give American journalist anti-Vietnam war information."

Dinh said that no doubt he gave the US Embassy information, "and not good information".

The only possible reason why Dinh's friend had agreed that his family be evacuated to America before the fall of Saigon was "to bullshit CIA — why else a Viet Cong want to go USA?"

It perhaps tells much about the complexities of the Vietnam War that, in the end, it was not the Australian government or influential Reuters who got their faithful reporter Dinh out of Vietnam but this Viet Cong colonel, who acted as "guarantor" for his friend and former journalism pupil, and used his influence to get him a visa. Dinh commented, "Because he work with me so long he know I not pro-American, not pro-communist. I only report. I do nothing during the war." Because of this help Dinh prefers that the name of this reporter and his magazine not be disclosed.

Although Reuters did help Dinh in Saigon and arranged a non-reporting job with AAP in Sydney, after four years in

Australia Dinh was sad that Reuters had apparently forgotten him. He felt that with his record of service they would have eventually assigned him to report in some Southeast Asian city where he could gather information to be translated from Dinglish to English by one of Reuters' many rewrite journalists.

And, as for me, I was saddened to see what happened to Reuters. Hundreds of correspondents, believing it to be a *non-profit* news trust, had given or risked their lives, building its reputation for great speed and accuracy. In 1984 it was sold off by its British and Australian newspaper owners on the stock exchange for thousands of millions of dollars. As usual, Dinh found a telling way of putting it: "But Reuter started by news, not by money."

Looking back on the war recently, Dinh, now proudly an Australian citizen, saw the sixteen-year American effort to stop the communists in Vietnam as evidence of stupidity. Of their military tactics, he said: "If they want to occupy this position they call for defoliant chemicals to clear, air strike, artillery, shell, tank, Coca, hamburger, apple, everything — but Viet Cong already move away." And of their political tactics: "All American soldiers want temporary Vietnamese wife — very good reason for communist propaganda."

The hurried withdrawal of the Americans from Vietnam in 1975 showed up their lack of responsibility, he said. "Americans make war in Vietnam, Americans live in Vietnam, they left about half a million veterans [ARVN] there now. What they doing? No food, nobody help them. About half million widows who husband killed, father killed by war and Americans nothing to care. In Vietnamese custom we say it is the same as you bring a baby to the middle of the market and go away and don't care. And this is what the Vietnamese say about American. They say Americans treat Vietnamese like lemon — crush it for use and then throw away. They use the people like that, the people's cooperation like that. That is the American tactic."

The US Embassy building in Saigon is now occupied by

the Vietnamese National Oil Company and a plaque on the wall where Dinh and I stood on the morning of the Tet Offensive says what happened on that day which turned the fortunes in the long war. A Vietnamese at the gate translates the plaque for the tourists.

OTHER COOPER SQUARE PRESS TITLES OF INTEREST

NAM
The Vietnam War in the Words of the Men and Women Who Fought There
Mark Baker
328 pp.
0-8154-1122-7
$17.95

HEROES NEVER DIE
Warriors and Warfare in World War II
Martin Blumenson
432 pp.
0-8154-1152-9
$32.00 cloth

HANGED AT AUSCHWITZ
An Extraordinary Memoir of Survival
Sim Kessel
New introduction by
Walter Laqueur
200 pp.
0-8154-1162-6
$16.95

MENGELE
The Complete Story
Gerald L. Posner & John Ware
New introduction by
Michael Berenbaum
400 pp., 41 b/w photos
0-8154-1006-9
$18.95

THE JEHOVAH'S WITNESSES AND THE NAZIS
Persecution, Deportation, and Murder, 1933–1945
Michel Reynaud &
Sylvie Graffard
Introduction by
Michael Berenbaum
304 pp., 22 b/w photos
0-8154-1076-X
$27.95 cloth

JULIUS STREICHER
Nazi Editor of the Notorious Anti-Semitic Newspaper Der Stürmer
Randall L. Bytwerk
264 pp., 31 b/w photos
0-8154-1156-1
$17.95

CANARIS
Hitler's Master Spy
Heinz Höhne
736 pp., 29 b/w photos, 3 maps
0-8154-1007-7
$19.95

THE MEMOIRS OF FIELD–MARSHAL WILHELM KEITEL
Chief of the German High Command, 1938–1945
Edited by Walter Gorlitz
New introduction by
Earl Ziemke
296 pp., 4 b/w maps
0-8154-1072-7
$18.95

THE MEDICAL CASEBOOK OF ADOLF HITLER

Leonard L. Heston, M.D. &
Renate Heston, R.N.
Introduction by Albert Speer
192 pp., 3 b/w photos, 4 graphs
0-8154-1066-2
$17.95

KASSERINE PASS
Rommel's Bloody, Climactic Battle for Tunisia

Martin Blumenson
358 pp., 18 b/w photos, 5 maps
0-8154-1099-9
$19.95

THE DESERT FOX IN NORMANDY
Rommel's Defense of Fortress Europe

Samuel W. Mitcham, Jr.
248 pp., 8 maps, 9 tables
0-8154-1159-6
$17.95

TRIUMPHANT FOX
Erwin Rommel and the Rise of the Afrika Korps

Samuel W. Mitcham, Jr.
224 pp., 26 b/w photos, 8 maps
0-8154-1055-7
$17.95

THE WEEK FRANCE FELL
June 10–June 16, 1940

Noel Barber
336 pp., 18 b/w photos
0-8154-1091-3
$18.95

SIEGFRIED
The Nazis' Last Stand

Charles Whiting
312 pp., 24 b/w photos, 6 maps
0-8154-1166-9
$17.95

SWING UNDER THE NAZIS
Jazz as a Metaphor for Freedom

Mike Zwerin
With a new preface.
232 pp., 45 b/w photos
0-8154-1075-1
$17.95

THE HITLER YOUTH
Origins and Development, 1922–1945

H. W. Koch
382 pp., 40 b/w photos, 2 maps
0-8154-1084-0
$18.95

ANZIO
The Gamble That Failed

Martin Blumenson
224 pp., 4 maps
0-8154-1129-4
$17.95

WARLORD
Tojo Against the World

Edwin P. Hoyt
With a new preface.
280 pp., 10 b/w photos
0-8154-1171-5
$17.95

DEFEAT INTO VICTORY
Battling Japan in Burma and India, 1942–1945

Field-Marshal Viscount
William Slim
With a new introduction by
David W. Hogan, Jr.
576 pp., 21 b/w maps
0-8154-1022-0
$22.95